Treasure Island
City Hall (duplicate of Capitol in Wash.
St. Mary's Cathedral (Japantown) (Victorians survived earthquake)
Alamo Square (views of old & new)
Golden Gate Park
Japanese Tea Garden   Marin County
Cliff House (Seal Rock)   Palace of Fine Arts
Sea Cliff ($1-$2 million # homes   Pacific Heights
Golden Gate Bridge   Octagon House – Union St.

Sunset Travel Guide to

Northern California

Hyde St.
Cable Cars

ferry at
Hilton
① right
Mason – 5th – Harrison

By the Editors of
Sunset Books and Sunset Magazine

Lane Publishing Co. • Menlo Park, California

Hours, admission fees, prices, telephone numbers, and highway designations in this book are accurate as of the time this edition went to press.

Maps have been provided in each chapter for the special purpose of highlighting significant regions, routes, or attractions in the area. Check automobile clubs, insurance agencies, chambers of commerce, or visitors bureaus in major cities for detailed maps of Northern California.

Book Editors: Barbara J. Braasch
Julie Anne Gold

Design: Cynthia Hanson

Cartography: Ted Martine

Illustrations: Susan Jaekel

Cover: Mendocino's graceful Victorian architecture faces grassy headlands, steep bluffs, and secluded coves at mouth of Big River. Photographed by Ells Marugg.

Thanks . . .
to the many people and organizations who assisted in the preparation of this travel guide. Special appreciation goes to city and county visitors bureaus and chambers of commerce, as well as other visitor service agencies throughout the Northern California area.

Photographers

Craig Aurness: 3. **Barbara J. Braasch:** 94 top left. **Ron Botier:** 34, 63, 67 top, 78, 83 bottom. **William Carter:** 94 top right, 99 bottom. **Glenn Christiansen:** 22 bottom, 42 bottom. **Ed Cooper:** 91 bottom. **Lee Foster:** 39 top, 107. **Gerald R. Fredrick:** 22 top, 30 bottom, 39 bottom, 47 top left, 102 top, 118. **Gerald L. French:** 55 bottom right, 91 top right, back cover (bottom). **Peter Fronk:** 27 bottom. **Bruce Hayes:** 19 top, 70 top left. **René Klein:** 102 bottom left. **Russell Lamb:** 75 bottom left. **Hal Lauritzen:** 6 top right, 19 bottom right. **Luther Linkhart:** 30 top, 115 top left. **Jack McDowell:** 14 bottom right, 47 bottom, 70 top right, 94 bottom, 99 top, 115 top right. **Ells Marugg:** 70 bottom, 75 top. **Chuck O'Rear:** 126 all. **John Reginato:** 115 bottom. **Dick Rowan:** 50, 58 bottom, 102 bottom right. **Carol Simowitz:** 14 bottom left, 67 bottom. **Ted Streshinsky:** 6 bottom, 19 bottom left, 42 top, 55 top and bottom left, 58 top, 83 top, 86, 91 top left, 110, 123, back cover (top right). **Tom Tracy:** 10, 14 top, 27 top, 47 top right, 75 bottom right, back cover (top left). **Phillip Wallick:** 6 top left.

Editor, Sunset Books: David E. Clark

Third printing October 1982

Contents

SHIP SLIPS into San Francisco Bay under fog-draped Golden Gate Bridge.

Introduction   6

San Francisco   10

The Bay Area   34

Monterey Peninsula   50

The North Coast   62

Wine Country   78

The Sierra   86

Northern Wonderland   106

The Central Valley   118

Index   128

Special Features

Festivals & Festivities   9

Golden Gate National Recreation Area   20

Gourmet Tips for City Dining   33

For Family Fun—Pick a Park   49

Fore!   53

Monterey's Path of History   56

Smile, If You Call a Man a Haireem   69

Inns Are In—Up North   77

How to Become a Wine Snob   85

Gold Country Hostelries   100

Apples, Wine & Christmas Trees   101

What Is a Steelhead?   109

Bigfoot—Man or Myth?   116

Historic Sampler   117

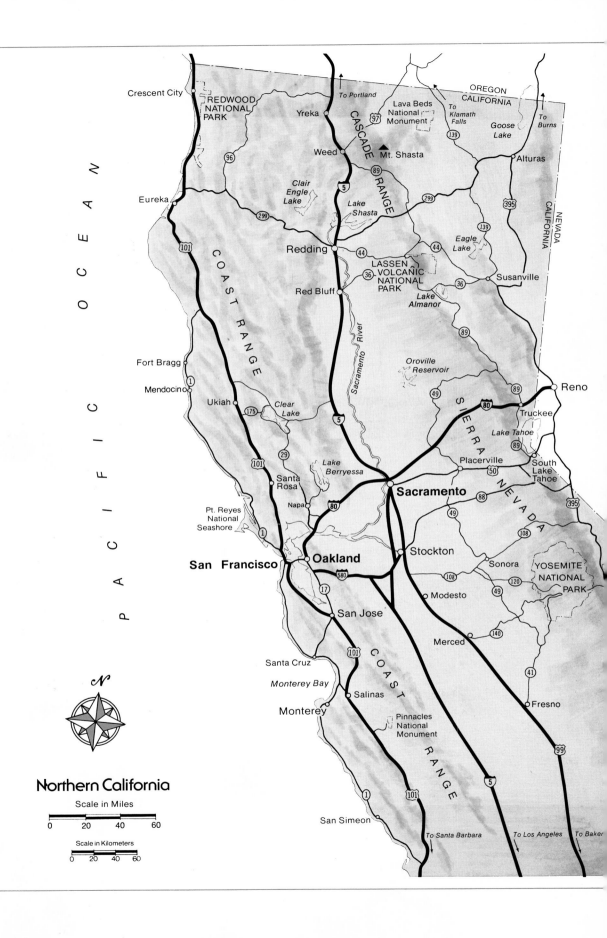

Northern California

Scale in Miles

0　　20　　40　　60

Scale in Kilometers

0　20　40　60

Crescent City

REDWOOD NATIONAL PARK

OREGON
CALIFORNIA

To Portland

Yreka

CASCADE RANGE

Lava Beds National Monument

To Klamath Falls

Goose Lake

To Burns

Weed

▲ Mt. Shasta

Alturas

Clair Engle Lake

Eureka

Lake Shasta

Redding

LASSEN VOLCANIC NATIONAL PARK

Eagle Lake

Susanville

NEVADA
CALIFORNIA

Red Bluff

Sacramento River

Lake Almanor

Fort Bragg

Oroville Reservoir

COAST RANGE

Mendocino

Reno

Ukiah

Clear Lake

Truckee

Lake Tahoe

SIERRA NEVADA

Placerville

South Lake Tahoe

Lake Berryessa

Santa Rosa

Sacramento

Napa

Stockton

San Francisco

Oakland

Sonora

YOSEMITE NATIONAL PARK

San Jose

Modesto

Santa Cruz

Merced

Monterey Bay

Salinas

Monterey

Pinnacles National Monument

COAST RANGE

Fresno

San Simeon

To Santa Barbara

To Los Angeles

To Baker

Pt. Reyes National Seashore

P A C I F I C   O C E A N

Northern California

Areas of Interest

Redwood National Park—Cathedral-like coast redwoods *(Sequoia sempervirens)* blanket 46-mile stretch of Northern California coast. Three state parks fall within the national park boundary, offering camping, recreational facilities.

Mount Shasta—Mountain's sheer size dominates landscape in California's far north. Glaciers, pristine lakes, wide valleys, and vibrant wildflowers lure ambitious climbers.

Lassen Volcanic National Park—Steaming streams, bubbling mudholes, sulphur smells, and hissing vents against the backdrop of forested slopes, clear lakes, and steep peaks make Lassen one of country's showiest thermal areas.

Mendocino—New England architecture characterizes this former lumbering port along the coast north of San Francisco; at grassy headlands, enjoy walking, fishing, wave-watching.

Lake Tahoe—Second highest lake in the world straddles California-Nevada border; area provides year-round playground, with California's finest winter skiing and summer boating.

Sacramento—California's capital city, once known for lusty gold rush life, dominates agriculturally rich valley. Tour State Capitol, Capitol Park, historic Old Sacramento; or leisurely cruise the Delta on a houseboat. Sacramento is a gateway to Sierra Nevada, Lake Tahoe, and Gold Country.

Napa Valley—Best known of wine country valleys north of San Francisco. Tour and taste at wineries dotting State Highway 29 near St. Helena. Picturesque country roads, quaint towns and missions, historic museums, and mineral health spas attract teetotaling travelers as well as wine enthusiasts.

Point Reyes National Seashore—Marin County's long, lonely, windswept beaches contrast with grassy, forested slopes; at the visitor center, explore Morgan horse ranch, blacksmith shop, and earthquake trail.

San Francisco—Sparkling city by the bay fulfills every visitor's fantasy. Ride cable cars, stroll through Fisherman's Wharf and Ghirardelli Square, relax in Golden Gate Park, explore mysterious Chinatown, cruise bay to Alcatraz or Angel Island, or just drink in breathtaking views from city's famous hills and bridges.

Yosemite National Park—Here nature's spectacular magic shows off on a grand scale; park boasts cascading waterfalls, ice-carved granite cliffs, far-reaching meadows, and groves of massive sequoias.

Monterey Peninsula—State Highway 1 dips, twists, climbs, and falls between Santa Lucia Mountains and pounding Pacific Ocean on its way to Big Sur. Explore Monterey's Cannery Row and Fisherman's Wharf; sample 17-Mile Drive's spectacular scenery and golf courses; tour Carmel's delightful shops.

Pinnacles National Monument—Spires and crags stretch 1,200 feet above canyon floors at Pinnacles, southeast of Monterey. Duck, crawl, and squeeze through dark caves when you explore these fascinating remnants of California volcanic activity.

San Simeon—William Randolph Hearst's "castle on the hill" dominates spur of surrounding mountains. La Casa Grande tours lead you through an eclectic collection of mansions and gardens that now form a state historic monument.

HORSE BRAKES SHARPLY *as roper settles lasso over calf's head (below). Summer rodeo at Taylorsville is one of Northern California's western events, culminating in prestigious Grand National in San Francisco Bay Area.*

BRIGHTLY COLORED SAIL *(right) catches bay breeze. In background, San Francisco's distinctive skyline rises dramatically from waterfront Golden Gate National Recreation Area to cone-shaped Transamerica Pyramid Building.*

BIKERS TOUR *valley floor (left) at Yosemite National Park. Half Dome, in background, is one of park's glacier-carved pinnacles.*

"Kaleidoscopic" is the best word to describe Northern California. Vacationers can choose from a wide range of activities: hiking, camping, and fishing in the high mountains or recapturing the past at a ghost town in the Sierra foothills; beachcombing along the coast or strolling through stately redwood groves; savoring San Francisco's big-city pleasures.

This *Travel Guide to Northern California* contains information on exploring both the well-established, well-known attractions and the lesser-known but equally appealing spots.

San Francisco—famous for its bay, bridges, hills, views, waterfront, and fine food—is Northern California's biggest tourist attraction. Along with the surrounding Bay Area, this is also Northern California's largest cultural, business, and industrial center.

The state capital, Sacramento, is the main city in the agriculturally important Central Valley. Sacramento has recently renovated its downtown area, including a stellar re-creation of the Gold Rush era in Old Sacramento. To the east of the valley rises the mighty Sierra Nevada, whose western foothills hold remnants of days when gold ruled the lives of Californians.

Other popular destinations in Northern California are Sonoma, with its Spanish landmarks; the Napa Valley, with its vineyards and wineries; Monterey, with its historical buildings and waterfront; Carmel, with its quaint shops; and Mendocino, with its dramatic coast and arts and crafts atmosphere. Those who prefer to get away head for the Northern Wonderland, above Redding, where lonesome roads lead to small villages in which time seems to have stood still. The most visited spots for outdoor recreation are Lake Tahoe, Yosemite National Park, Lake Shasta, and Redwood National Park.

Land of contrast

The area covered in this book differs from the southern part of the state in climate, history, topography, and temperament. For this reason, separate books are devoted to exploring Northern California and Southern California.

The boundary line that we have used to divide the state begins at the ocean near San Simeon, continues across the Coast Range and the southern tip of the Central Valley, and then turns northward across the Sierra Nevada south of Yosemite National Park. The area south of this arbitrary dividing line is described in the *Sunset* book *Travel Guide to Southern California*.

Climate & terrain

Northern California has three distinct climate zones. Coastal temperatures are mild the year around; rarely will there be extremes in temperature. Fog frequently blankets the coast during the summer, especially in the morning and evening, and in winter it rains.

As you move inland, the seasons become more pro-

Discover in these pages the diverse attractions and experiences that are uniquely Northern California. From high mountains to ghost towns, redwoods to big city life, this area offers something for everyone, any time of year. The area map on pages 4 and 5 points out boundaries and special interests of this northern part of the Golden State.

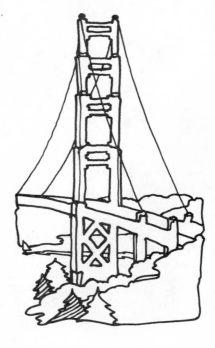

Introduction

nounced. Summers become hotter (with relatively little humidity), winters colder (with an occasional snow). The Sierra Nevada has the most dramatic seasonal changes. Summer days are warm, ideal for outdoor recreation; autumn brings a crispness to the air and dramatic fall colors; heavy snowfalls during winter make the mountains a mecca for skiers.

Getting around

Major highways carry a heavy flow of traffic, especially near large cities and especially during the morning and evening commute hours. California's roads are exceptionally well maintained and well signed—most thoroughfares are divided, four-lane express highways.

For scenic beauty, the best north-south route through Northern California is State Highway 1. It's a winding coastal route, overlooking the ocean most of the way; plan to drive it leisurely. If you're in a hurry, take the inland routes. U.S. Highway 101, Interstate Highway 5, and State Highway 99 are the faster routes. The most heavily traveled east-west routes are Interstate highways 580 (U.S. 50) and 80, which connect San Francisco and Lake Tahoe.

Public transportation. Greyhound offers efficient and convenient bus service throughout Northern California from major western cities.

Greyhound's affiliate company, California Parlor Car Tours, includes bus tours to some of Northern California's most scenic highlights. Especially popular are 3 to 5-day trips to Yosemite, Monterey, Hearst Castle, and Lake Tahoe. There are also excursions (new in 1980) to Mendocino, Eureka, the redwood country, and coastal Oregon. Tours include transportation, accommodations, and meals. For more information contact California Parlor Car Tours, 1101 Van Ness Avenue, San Francisco, CA 94109.

Amtrak runs daily trains from San Diego and Los Angeles, through Northern California, then on to Oregon, Washington, and British Columbia. The San Francisco Zephyr still traces the original transcontinental rail line from Reno to Sacramento. Once aboard you cross the scenic Sierra Nevada above Donner Lake with a stop at Truckee. West Coast trains offer lounge cars with beverages, snacks, and card tables; some cars have sleeping accommodations. Amtrak also offers tour packages to major Northern California attractions. For information on schedules and prices, contact Amtrak Public Affairs, 425 Mission Street, San Francisco, CA 94105.

Where to get information

The San Francisco Visitor Information Center, Hallidie Plaza, Powell and Market streets (lower level), should be a city visitor's first stop. Here you can get city maps and information on hotels, restaurants, and attractions. For information in advance, write to the San Francisco Convention & Visitor Bureau, 1390 Market Street, San Francisco, CA 94102. In the city, dial 391-2000 for a 2-minute summary of daily events, as well as numbers to dial for foreign language summaries.

The Redwood Empire Association publishes a free Visitors Guide for San Francisco, Marin, Sonoma, Napa, Lake, Mendocino, Humboldt, and Del Norte counties. For the booklet, write the Redwood Empire Association, 360 Post Street, San Francisco, CA 94102; send $1 for postage.

The Wine Institute, 165 Post Street, San Francisco, CA 94108, lists the Northern California wineries, describes tasting rooms and picnic facilities, and includes the hours they are open.

For travel information on the Monterey Peninsula, stop by the Chamber of Commerce and Visitors and Convention Bureau at 380 Alvarado Street, Monterey. Or write in advance to P.O. Box 1770, Monterey, CA 93940.

Accommodations

Major cities and resort areas usually have plenty of hotel and motel space. If you want to stay at a particular place or if you are traveling during the summer or on a weekend, it's best to make reservations.

If you're uncertain where to stay, write to local chambers of commerce. They offer listings of accommodations.

Camping

In some state parks, there is a 7 to 15-day camping limit during the heavy-use period (usually June 1 through September). Extended limits apply to most state parks the rest of the year. Camping fees are based on the type of campsite. For a pamphlet listing California's state parks, write to the Department of Parks and Recreation, P.O. Box 2390, Sacramento, CA 95811.

Though reservations are not required for camping in most state parks, they are advised for the summer months, holidays, and weekends. Reservations may be made at any of the 150 Ticketron offices around the state (they're closed Sundays). To locate the nearest Ticketron office, in San Francisco call (415) 788-2828 and in Sacramento call (916) 445-8828. Information number for Ticketron in Los Angeles is (213) 670-2311; in San Diego call (714) 565-9947. You will pay the campsite fee and a small reservation fee.

National park and forest campsites are available on a first come, first served basis except during the summer months when many national forest campgrounds (and Yosemite National Park; see page 88) are available on a reservation-only basis through Ticketron outlets. Reservations can be made in person or by mail only to Ticketron offices. For a list of campgrounds requiring reservations, write to the U.S. Forest Service, 630 Sansome Street, San Francisco, CA 94111. For information on national park campgrounds, write to the National Park Service, 450 Golden Gate Avenue, San Francisco, CA 94102.

Hunting & fishing

Rules change yearly governing the hunting season and the animals you may hunt. The Department of Fish and

Game, 1416 9th Street, Sacramento, CA 95814, publishes a pamphlet every May that lists the current hunting regulations.

A pamphlet distributed in the spring by the department outlines both fresh-water and salt-water fishing regulations.

Vacation headquarters

Though this book is aimed primarily at the visitor and new resident, it includes information on possible discoveries for "back yard" vacations for those who call Northern California home.

New to Northern California or not, you'll be energized by its variety of offerings—San Francisco, the North-land's charismatic city; burgeoning Bay Area attractions; historic Monterey and charming Carmel; towering redwoods and the scenic north coast seashore; wine touring and tasting; majestic mountains; foothill villages founded by gold.

Outdoor activities are as varied as the area. The athletically inclined have choices from parcourse or golf course. Tennis buffs can get in a few sets at public parks or private resorts. Water enthusiasts are in their element, as boats dot San Francisco Bay, ply the Delta, or tow water-skiers on large lakes; others trailer their craft to remote bodies of water.

In the Sierra Nevada—the main winter sports area in Northern California—most major ski resorts cluster around Lake Tahoe. Other skiing centers are in the Donner Summit area, along State Highway 88, U.S. 50, and Interstate 80, and at Yosemite National Park.

FESTIVALS & FESTIVITIES

Here is a sampling of annual events and festivities of interest to Northern California visitors. Dates often change—so check with the chambers of commerce of individual cities and counties, or contact the San Francisco Convention and Visitors Bureau, 1390 Market Street, San Francisco, CA 94102; or the Redwood Empire Association, 360 Post Street, San Francisco, CA 94108.

January
Año Nuevo Beach—Elephant Seal Watching (San Mateo Coast State Beaches)

Stanford—East-West Shrine All-Star Football Game

Pebble Beach—Bing Crosby Pro-Am Golf Championship

February
San Francisco—Chinese New Year (Chinatown)

March
Bodega Bay—Bodega Bay Fisherman's Festival

Pebble Beach—Victorian House Tour

April
Monterey—Adobe House Tour

San Francisco—Daffodil Festival (Maiden Lane)

San Francisco—Cherry Blossom Festival (Japantown and Golden Gate Park)

May
Mendocino—Spring Art Fair

Angels Camp—Jumping Frog Contest

Sacramento—Dixieland Jazz Jubilee

June
Boonville—Buck-A-Roo Days and Rodeo

Gold Country—Melodrama at Coloma, Drytown, Columbia, and Oakhurst

Klamath—Klamath Salmon Festival

July
Bear Valley—Music From Bear Valley

Carmel—Carmel Bach Festival

Ferndale—Humboldt County Fair

Pebble Beach—Feast of the Lanterns

August
Marin County—Renaissance Pleasure Faire

Santa Rosa—Scottish Gathering and Games

September
Monterey—Monterey Jazz Festival

Sonoma—Vintage Festival

Weaverville—Bigfoot Daze

October
Half Moon Bay—Half Moon Bay Art and Pumpkin Festival

San Francisco—Grand National Livestock Exposition, Rodeo, and Horse Show

November
Mendocino—Thanksgiving Art Fair

December
San Juan Bautista—Las Posadas Fiesta

San Raphael—Festival of the Trees

San Francisco

The West's most enchanting city, San Francisco, is a cornucopia of sights, sounds, and excitement. Climb on a cable car to dizzying heights atop the city's famous hills; stroll or skate through Golden Gate Park; splurge in Union Square shops; take in one of the country's finest operas; enjoy impromptu performances of street artists; and drink in the awesome meeting of land and sea at the Golden Gate.

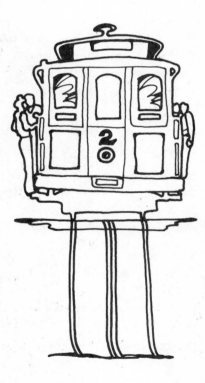

What makes San Francisco so compelling? This is a question often asked by people who have never visited "The City," and it's hard for even a native to answer. Much of its charm lies in its location, its climate, its topography—and its people.

Surrounded on three sides by water, San Francisco still harbors the flavor of its early day remoteness. And because of its setting, the weather is tempered to perpetual spring.

It's a city of hills. Someone once said that if you get tired of climbing them, you can always lean against them. But it's from the tops of these hills that you get the well-touted views—watching the fog roll in from the ocean across the Golden Gate Bridge, gazing east along the meandering span of the San Francisco-Oakland Bay Bridge, or peering north across the bay, past the islands anchored in the channel, to the bluffs of Marin County.

San Francisco was a city from the first cry of "Gold!" Few miners found anything here worth shouting about, but the Gold Rush transformed the town into a booming metropolis where literally anything went, provided you could pay for it. The wide assortment of nationalities who settled here gave the city its aura of cosmopolitan sophistication—an urban world center quite out of proportion to its actual size.

San Francisco is a big city without being big. Even with a total geographical area of only 47 square miles and a population of less than 700,000, it has the qualities common to all of the world's great cities—a rich historical background, a diversity of activities, cultural depth, hustle and bustle, pervasive charm—and more.

"The City" (as it is called by aficionados; *never* call it "Frisco") is noted for its many and various-size hills and spectacular sweeping views. Its skyline is jagged with skyscrapers dwarfing once-tall buildings; a closer look shows crowded row houses and apartments marching endlessly up and down the hills, roof-to-roof.

One of the world's most visited cities, San Francisco welcomes its guests. Whether the visit is your first or your fifth, you will enjoy seeing old landmarks as well as discovering the new ones.

Maps in this section include the downtown area, a scenic drive, Golden Gate Park, and the Golden Gate National Recreation Area.

Tales of the city

Though founded in 1776 by the Spanish as a mission post, San Francisco hardly existed until the discovery of gold in 1849. The peninsula village was transformed from a drowsy Spanish pueblo to an instant city as "49ers" came rushing to California from every point of the compass. These immigrants—a unique blend of

GOLDEN GATE BRIDGE veils view of "The City" from Marin Headlands across bay. Historic Fort Point huddles beneath bridge's southern tip.

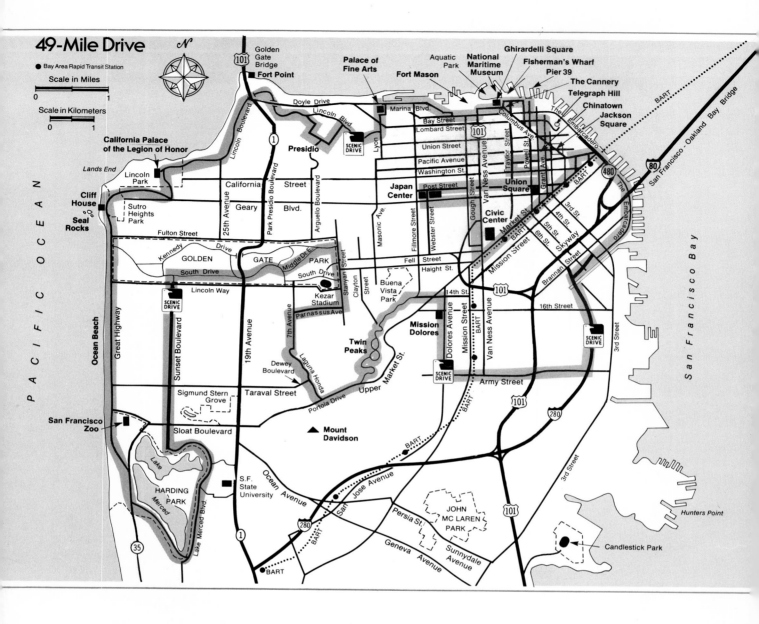

49-Mile Drive

● Bay Area Rapid Transit Station

Scale in Miles
0   1

Scale in Kilometers
0   1

N

Golden Gate Bridge
Fort Point
Palace of Fine Arts
Aquatic Park
National Maritime Museum
Fort Mason
Ghirardelli Square
Fisherman's Wharf
Pier 39
The Cannery
Telegraph Hill
Chinatown
Jackson Square
BART
San Francisco - Oakland Bay Bridge

Doyle Drive
Lincoln Blvd.
Marina Blvd.
Bay Street
Lombard Street
Union Street
Pacific Avenue
Washington St.
Post Street

California Palace of the Legion of Honor

Lands End
Lincoln Park
Cliff House
Sutro Heights Park
Seal Rocks

Presidio
SCENIC DRIVE
Lyon
Columbus Ave.
Van Ness Avenue
Taylor Street
Powell St.
Grant Ave.
The Embarcadero

Japan Center
Union Square
Civic Center

California Street
Geary Blvd.
25th Avenue
Park Presidio Boulevard
Arguello Boulevard
Masonic Ave.
Fillmore Street
Webster Street
Gough Street
Market St.
Mission Street
3rd St.
4th St.
5th St.
6th St.
Skyway
Brannan Street

Fulton Street
Kennedy Drive
GOLDEN GATE PARK
South Drive
Middle Dr. E.
South Drive
Lincoln Way
Stanyan Street
Fell Street
Haight St.
14th St.
16th Street

SCENIC DRIVE
Kezar Stadium
Clayton Street
Buena Vista Park

Parnassus Ave.
7th Avenue
19th Avenue
Dewey Boulevard
Laguna Honda
Twin Peaks
Upper Market St.
Mission Dolores
Dolores Street
Mission Street
BART
SCENIC DRIVE
Army Street
Van Ness Avenue
SCENIC DRIVE
3rd Street

Sunset Boulevard
Great Highway
Ocean Beach

Sigmund Stern Grove
Taraval Street
Portola Drive
Mount Davidson
BART

San Francisco Zoo
Sloat Boulevard
Lake Merced Blvd.
HARDING PARK
Lake Merced

S.F. State University
Ocean Avenue
San Jose Avenue
Persia St.
Sunnydale Avenue
Geneva Avenue
JOHN MC LAREN PARK
BART
BART

Hunters Point
Candlestick Park

PACIFIC OCEAN
San Francisco Bay

---

races, customs, and nationalities—set the pattern for the city's future personality. An adage of the era was, "The weak never made it to California and the timid never tried."

Growth accelerated with the discovery of Nevada's Comstock silver lode and the completion of the first transcontinental railroad to San Francisco in 1869.

In the earthquake of April 18, 1906, and the 3-day fire that followed, 28,000 buildings were destroyed and about 500 people died. But San Franciscans rebuilt, showing off their "new" city at the Panama-Pacific International Exposition in 1915. Later, Treasure Island, dredged up in the mid-bay, became a stage for the Golden Gate International Exposition in 1939 and 1940.

Today, the city is still changing: ultramodern skyscrapers jostle venerable Victorians; old factories become unique shopping areas; fountains splash where warehouses once stood; and part of the formerly raucous Barbary Coast (Jackson Street) is now a tamed, handsome showcase of interior design.

The city's culture has been enriched by the traditions and life styles of countless ethnic groups. Three distinct "cities" exist within San Francisco: Chinatown, the largest Asian settlement outside of the Far East; North Beach, magnet for nearly 150,000 San Franciscans of Italian descent; and Japantown, landmarked by the $15 million Japan Center. You'll find some 22 foreign language publications throughout the city, and its lauded cuisine offers choices of food from all parts of the globe.

The connecting links

Whether you drive on the bridges or merely glimpse the spans across the water from one of many observation spots, you'll notice the dramatic relationship between San Francisco and the water.

The bridges link the city to the rest of the world, to the east and to the north.

Most glamorous of San Francisco's bridges is the Golden Gate, designated the country's most popular man-made attraction. One of the best things about this suspended structure is that you can walk and bike across it. As a pedestrian or bicyclist, you can enjoy gull's-eye views (220 feet down) denied the automobile traveler. Park your car at the toll plaza and walk out to the middle and back for some magnificent views of the San Francisco skyline. The Marin County lookout at the north end of the bridge gives an exceptional wide-angle view of the city. You pay to cross the Golden Gate Bridge only when coming south into San Francisco; northbound you don't stop. Golden Gate Transit provides bus service to the toll plaza. For schedule information, call (415) 332-6600.

San Francisco's main bridge connection to the east is across the San Francisco-Oakland Bay Bridge. From San Francisco, two spans are joined at a central anchorage. The roadway follows a tunnel through Yerba Buena Island, coming out on a 1,400-foot cantilever span followed by a series of truss bridges. The bridge has two levels (east bound traffic uses the lower deck; westbound, the upper deck) and altogether extends 8¼ miles.

Two bridges connect East Bay towns and cities to the peninsula communities that stretch from San Francisco to San Jose. They are the San Mateo Bridge, from San Mateo to Hayward, and the Dumbarton Bridge, from Menlo Park to Fremont; another crosses north of San Francisco between Richmond and San Rafael. One-way toll collections (westbound) help the flow of traffic.

The water around San Francisco keeps the city air-conditioned all year. The average high is 65°F/18°C, the low 45°F/7°C. Fog is frequent in early morning and evening, especially during the summer. Usually the rains begin in November and last into April. September is normally San Francisco's warmest month.

The city's continual mild temperatures call for light-weight wools at any time of the year, and it's a good idea to bring a coat. Residents tend to shy away from casual clothes, preferring to dress conservatively and elegantly, especially downtown.

CABLE CAR CLIMBS California Street (left) on its way up Nob Hill. At top, riders catch glimpse of Bay Bridge.

TREES FORM shady nave (below), secluding young couple from skyscrapered and shopper-thronged Market Street. Attractive benches, lights, and brick-paved mall provide refreshing oases in bustling downtown area.

A FINE HOW-DO-YOU-DO greets visitor to Maiden Lane's Daffodil Festival (below). Each spring the 2-block alley closes to traffic as mimes, musicians, and minstrels revel among blossoms.

How to see San Francisco

San Francisco is a compact city. Part of its charm lies in the ease with which a visitor can move from attraction to attraction. You can park your car if you wish and get around on foot, by cable car, streetcar, bus, and BART (the modern transbay subway). If you're a first-time visitor, we suggest following the 49-Mile Drive (see page 12), a marked route leading throughout the city.

The first stop for any newcomer to San Francisco should be the San Francisco Visitor Information Center at Hallidie Plaza (Powell and Market streets). Here you'll find information on transportation, lodging, and what's happening where. By dialing 391-2000 you'll get an around-the-clock daily rundown of special events, cultural happenings, sports news, and sightseeing trips. From outside the Bay Area, phone area code 415 first, to take advantage of San Francisco's tele-itinerary.

Ever ride a national landmark?

A cable car ride is a must for every visitor. An excellent means of transportation in the most heavily congested part of the city, the cable cars also provide thrills and good views.

You'll find three cable car lines—two that run on Powell Street and one on California Street. Cars from the line on Powell leave the turntable at Powell and Market (Hallidie Plaza) and are spectacular hill climbers. They take you up steep Powell Street, then down and around several sharp turns to arrive in 15 or 20 minutes at their respective turntables at the north waterfront. Cars marked "Powell and Market/Bay and Taylor" clang through the edge of Chinatown and along a section of North Beach, coming to the end of their line at Bay and Taylor at Fisherman's Wharf. The cars marked "Powell and Market/Hyde and Beach" bypass most of Chinatown and North Beach. But they take you down Hyde for a magnificent view of the bay and a hang-on-tight ride to your destination below Hyde and Beach at Aquatic Park.

The red-painted cars of the California Street line leave from California and Market and take you through the financial district and Chinatown, up steep Nob Hill, and finally down a gentler grade to the end of the line at Van Ness Avenue.

San Francisco's "municipal rollercoaster" costs $1.00 to ride, and a bus or streetcar transfer is given upon request.

There's no easy way to get on or off a cable car. Usually there are more people waiting to ride than there is room. When the car stops, step right up to find a place. If you're on the outside, hang on tight. Don't ring the bell when you want off—just tell the conductor.

In October, 1982, the cable car system will be closed for two years for restoration. During that time, buses will cover approximately the same routes as the cable cars.

The museum, exhibits, cars, and gift shop will be moved from the Cable Car Barn to Embarcadero Center #4, Podium level. Visit the center (open daily, except Sundays) to get a close look at how a cable car works; phone 474-1887 for further information.

Other ways to get around

Wherever you are in the Bay Area, public transportation departs frequently for San Francisco's downtown Transbay, Southern Pacific, or Greyhound terminals. There is also ferry service from Sausalito and from Tiburon to the city.

Whether you ride above ground or below, take a cab, or join a tour, San Francisco is one of the easiest big cities in which to get around.

Buses and streetcars run frequently on an efficient schedule from morning through early evening. You will find a route map and a description of routes at the front of the classified section of the San Francisco telephone directory.

The city's municipal railway system (buses, cable cars, streetcars) operates an information service. By mailing a stamped, self-addressed envelope to San Francisco Municipal Railway, 949 Presidio Avenue, San Francisco, CA 94155, you'll receive a copy of MUNI route descriptions. If you call 673-MUNI, information center personnel will tell you which line reaches your destination. Take note: Express buses, making limited stops, may not stop at your destination. Local buses and streetcars charge 60 cents a ride. Since drivers do not carry change, you must have the exact fare ready.

Special price Tour Tickets Sunday/Holiday offer unlimited daily rides over the entire system. You may buy the ticket at the end of the cable car lines.

Bus service is available between San Francisco International Airport and the Downtown Air Terminal at Taylor and Ellis Streets. Buses run every few minutes during the day; less frequently after 10:00 P.M.

Taxicabs are more numerous than in most western cities. Because distances are short between most of San Francisco's main points of interest, taxis are popular.

BART (Bay Area Rapid Transit), a modern, direct, and comfortable subway system, operates in the East Bay and in San Francisco, connecting the two areas by a tube under the bay. In downtown San Francisco, you'll find four stations (see map on page 13). Phone BART's Information Center—(415) 465-BART—toll free from San Francisco for schedule information.

Guided sightseeing tours are popular—particularly with first-time visitors. Gray Line offers several different ones. You can make arrangements to be picked up at major hotels, or you can board a shuttle bus at Union Square (opposite the St. Francis Hotel) which will take you to the depot. Buses leave from First and Mission streets at the East Bay Bus Terminal.

Several sightseeing companies offer limousine tours for small groups. Native Sons Tours (guided by people who grew up in San Francisco) offers a chance to view the city with "insiders." Bilingual tours in Japanese, Chinese, and Korean are given by California Travel Services. Some tour groups specialize in architectural or cultural walking tours through the city.

(Continued on next page)

... *Continued from page 15*

Make arrangements for any tour through your hotel or check the classified section of the telephone directory.

The 49-Mile Drive

San Francisco's excellent public transportation system, convenient touring schedules, and compact size allow you to explore without ever getting into a car.

If you do drive, one way to grasp the city as a whole is to follow the scenic 49-Mile Drive; later you can return to explore on foot the places that interest you most. Well marked by blue, white, and orange seagull signs, the 49-Mile Drive is easy to follow, though it does take you through the most congested streets of the downtown area. You should allow about a half-day to fully enjoy the sights along the route.

You can start anywhere, but here are some highlights, beginning at the Civic Center on Van Ness Avenue and McAllister Street:

Van Ness Avenue. Automobile row. Look for elegant showrooms.

Union Square. Heart of the shopping district downtown; bordered by Geary, Post, Powell, and Stockton streets.

Chinatown. Grant Avenue leads through this exotic, bustling community. (See page 18.)

North Beach. San Francisco's Italian community, its Bohemia—a region of good restaurants and a lively center of night life. Where Columbus Avenue crosses Grant and north to the Wharf. (See page 21.)

Telegraph Hill. Coit Tower crowns this site of spectacular bay and bridge views. (See page 28.)

Marina. Beautiful residences look out to the Yacht Harbor across Marina Green—favorite place for flying kites, walking dogs, jogging, sunbathing. (See page 24.)

Palace of Fine Arts. "Temporary" structure for 1915 Panama-Pacific International Exposition, now restored and housing a museum of science. (See page 24.)

Presidio. Active military post established by the Spanish in 1776. Adobe Officer's Club is one of the city's two oldest buildings. Historic Trail Guide, available at Military Police office, offers hikers a look at terrain, views, and points of interest.

Lincoln Park. Home of the California Palace of the Legion of Honor, a city museum. (See page 28.)

Great Highway. Successor to the original Cliff House Restaurant stands at the north end, with Seal Rocks behind it. Up the hill is Sutro Heights Park, once the grand estate of Adolph Sutro, Comstock Lode millionaire.

San Francisco Zoo. One of the country's leading zoos borders western end of Golden Gate National Recreation Area. (See page 28.)

Golden Gate Park. Probably the finest city park in the country; includes museums and Japanese Tea Garden among its attractions. (See page 25.)

Mission Dolores. Sixth mission in the California chain, it was established in 1776. (See page 31.)

Ferry Building. Living reminder of days when the only traffic on the bay was the ferry. The World Trade Center and geology exhibit are here. Vaillancourt Fountain is across the street.

Major city areas

Once you take an overall look at San Francisco, you will want a closer view of some of the city's areas. Because of its compact size, the major points of interest are easy to reach. Bring comfortable shoes and plan to do some walking; it's the best way to make your own discoveries.

Civic center—dynamic heart of the city

A monumental group of federal, state, and city structures, San Francisco's Civic Center stretches from Franklin Street to the intersection of Market Street at the United Nations Plaza. Ornate City Hall, a model of French Renaissance grandeur, crowned by a lofty dome rising 300 feet above the ground, dominates Civic Center Park. The War Memorial Veterans' Building houses the San Francisco Museum of Modern Art and the 911-seat Herbst Theater, setting for intimate chamber music concerts and other recitals. Its companion building, the War Memorial Opera House, site of the United Nations Charter signing in 1945, is now home to the San Francisco Opera and the San Francisco Ballet.

Breathing new life into the Civic Center is the bold, $36 million Performing Arts Center project. Most of this money was used in the construction of the handsome Louise M. Davies Symphony Hall, home of the San Francisco Symphony.

Situated opposite the Opera House at Grove and Van Ness streets, this $27 million, 3,000-seat concert hall provides a permanent home for the symphony, as well as expanded space for visiting performers. When the Zellerbach Rehearsal Hall is completed, the Performing Arts Center (Opera House, Louise M. Davies Symphony Hall, and Herbst Theater) will offer a combined seating capacity of 7,200, giving San Francisco the country's second largest performing arts center, just behind New York's Lincoln Center—with all the benefits of either the Lincoln or Kennedy centers.

Also part of the Civic Center is the Civic Auditorium. Seating more than 8,000, it is the scene of conventions, as well as sporting and cultural events. Subterranean Brooks Exhibit Hall, underneath the Civic Center Plaza, was added in 1958. The Main Public Library, another handsome neo-Classical building, is open Monday through Thursday from 9 A.M. to 9 P.M., Friday and Saturday until 6. Nearby are the Federal Building, the Federal Office Building, and the State Office Building.

Union Square—for shoppers

For browsing and shopping in the downtown area, Union Square makes an ideal starting point. You can park your car in the cavernous garage beneath the square—it goes down four floors and provides places for over 1,000 automobiles.

Stop first at the square itself. On a nice day, its benches will be lined with people relaxing in the sun or feeding the hundreds of pigeons that swirl about and congregate around the feet of anyone offering a handout. On the sidewalks, street artists will be displaying their wares.

Union Square is a hub of activity, hosting fashion shows, rallies, and concerts. In spring, Rhododendron Days are celebrated—huge tubs of colorful plants are placed throughout the square. A summer highlight is the Cable Car Bell Ringing Contest. In the center of the square stands a 97-foot granite monument commemorating Admiral Dewey's victory at Manila Bay during the Spanish-American War.

The fashionable St. Francis Hotel is on the west side of the square, across Powell Street. Many visiting dignitaries stop here—if you see a foreign flag displayed above the entrance, you can assume it is honoring a very important guest from that country. You'll enjoy browsing through some of the hotel shops. For good skyline views, ride the tower elevators to the top.

Post, Stockton, and Geary streets also border the square. The Children's Fountain in the plaza of the Hyatt on Union Square deserves a stop. Designed by Ruth Asawa, who also designed the fountains in Ghirardelli Square and Buchanan Mall in Japantown, it takes a whimsical look at the city's history.

Around Union Square and spreading south toward Market and east toward Kearny Street are some of San Francisco's fashionable shops.

You can't miss the colorful sidewalk flower stands, a kind of streetside almanac: sprigs of daphne and violets in spring, tiny Pinocchio roses in summer, chrysanthemums in fall, and holly in winter.

On the east side of the square across Stockton is Maiden Lane, a 2-block tree-lined alley transformed from its bawdy past to a street of intriguing shops. Of particular interest is a building designed by Frank Lloyd Wright, with an unusual yellow brick front and an interior circular ramp; it houses a boutique.

In early April, Maiden Lane welcomes spring with the annual Daffodil Festival. The lane is then closed to traffic; local dignitaries, bands, and troubadours celebrate among the blossoms.

More tempting shops and large department stores are located along Grant, Geary, Post, and Stockton. The floral shop of Podesta Baldocchi is especially interesting. The displays in its windows and inside the shop are indeed remarkable, especially at Christmas time; visitors are welcome.

A major attraction in the Union Square area is Gump's on Post near Stockton. It is noted especially for its Jade Room, which contains a unique collection of jade in many shades. Other rooms contain rare imports and unusual locally made items.

The financial district

North of Market Street, impressive office buildings shade the narrow slot that is Montgomery Street, heart of San Francisco's business and financial district. Here, and spreading into the nearby streets, are the banking, brokerage, and insurance firms that are a part of the Wall Street of the West. Here also are the general offices of many of the West's largest business organizations.

The heart of the financial district is the Pacific Coast Stock Exchange (Pine and Sansome streets), where business begins at 6 A.M. to coincide with the hours of the New York Stock Exchange. One block west of the stock exchange is the Bank of America Building, headquarters for the world's largest bank. The 779-foot-high, 52-story structure, with its bronze-tinted, bay-windowed façade, covers most of the California, Pine, Kearny, and Montgomery block. From the Carnelian Room on the 52nd floor, you'll see a magnificent view of the city.

The 853-foot-high Transamerica Pyramid at Montgomery, Washington, and Clay streets projects its unique shape on the ever-changing San Francisco skyline.

Another skyscraper, the Wells Fargo Building at 44 Montgomery Street, rises 43 stories—561 feet. On the 16th floor of this unusual glass and steel structure is Montgomery Lane, where a collection of diverse shops cater to employees. Visitors are welcome during the day. Just below the main lobby level is a restaurant displaying early California artifacts from the Wells Fargo History Room. The History Room, at 420 Montgomery Street, highlights photographs, documents, and mementos from Gold Rush days to the 1906 earthquake. The collection includes a circa-1860 stagecoach that ran from San Francisco to the Santa Cruz Mountains. Visiting hours on banking days are from 10 A.M. to 3 P.M.

The Bank of California's Collection of Money of the American West, finest of its kind in the country, features pioneer gold quartz, gold and silver ingots, privately minted gold coins, and currency from the West. Open during banking hours (10 A.M. to 3 P.M.), it's located on the lower level at 400 California Street.

Along the Embarcadero

How do you change decaying waterfront property into a revitalized urban landscape? Take 51 acres of land, add $150 million, and come up with the Golden Gateway Center. In the late 1950s the San Francisco Redevelopment Agency did just that. Bounded by Clay, Battery, and Jackson streets, this former produce marketplace blossomed into a slick urban center of apartments, townhouses, offices, and parks.

From the heart of the center, the dark-glassed, diagonally braced Alcoa Building rises dramatically. The 2-block-square Maritime Plaza, an elevated park, provides a place to stroll and relax. Here pedestrian bridges serve as elevated passageways to all sections of the center.

South of the Golden Gateway is architect John C. Portman's ambitious Embarcadero Center. Hailed by one critic to be "superbly conceived, fine in taste, and full of life," the center is a stunning success of multi-use urban development.

Truly a "city within a city," Embarcadero Center comprises three major towers (a fourth is under construction) and a grand hotel. Each elegant, wafer-thin tower springs from a common three-level pedestal of plazas, promenades, and shopping arcades. Current buildings include the 45-story Security Pacific Building (One Embarcadero Center), the 35-story Levi Strauss Building with its plaza-level historical room (Two Embarcadero Center), and the 35-story Three Embarcadero building. Four Embarcadero Center, a twin 45-story structure, should be completed in 1981.

The architecturally innovative Hyatt Regency Hotel (Five Embarcadero Center) is fast becoming a favorite San Francisco attraction. Charles Perry's 40-foot sculpture, *Eclipse,* graces the awesome 16-story atrium lobby from which glass elevators speed you up 20 stories to a revolving restaurant offering 360° views of the city.

Elevated pedestrian bridges connect the various parts of Embarcadero Center, separating visitors and shoppers from the traffic below.

Adjacent to and north of the Hyatt Regency is the Justin Herman Plaza, adding a green oasis to this financial district. At noontime, artists and brown baggers congregate around the controversial Vaillancourt Fountain.

Across Market Street, south from the Hyatt Regency, One Market Plaza creates yet another "people place." A soaring skylight connects the old Southern Pacific Building's façade to two new office towers, creating a block-long airy atrium. Sunlight pours in over the tree and flower-lined concourse of shops and restaurants.

Across the street on Mission and Spear, at the Rincon Annex Post Office, the colorful WPA historic murals are worth a look. You'll get speedy mail service here—pick-up every hour on the hour until midnight.

Though the cavernous 2,000-car Embarcadero garage offers plenty of parking space, public transportation efficiently serves all the centers along the Embarcadero. BART's Embarcadero station meets the California Street cable car across from the Hyatt on Market Street. MUNI's streetcars, buses, and cable cars also take you within walking distance of the centers. Ferry service to and from the Marin County towns of Sausalito, Tiburon, and Larkspur leaves from the pier of the Ferry Building across the street from the Hyatt Hotel.

Jackson Square

Once San Francisco's rowdy Barbary Coast, this part of the city became a dismal warehouse area when the city rebuilt in other directions following the 1906 fire. The old buildings were eventually boarded up and deserted and remained so until, in 1951, an enterprising group pioneered the development of the exclusive and unusual design center that is today's Jackson Square. Chic specialty shops and fine restaurants add to its charm.

Though most of Jackson Square's showrooms are closed to the general public (except for once a year, usually in October), anyone with enthusiasm for elegant old buildings or anyone who simply enjoys window shopping will find a stroll through Jackson Square rewarding.

This unique merchandising district supplies Bay Area decorators, architects, and retailers with interior furnishings and accessories. The wholesale houses occupy handsomely restored buildings in the area surrounding Jackson Street—bounded by Pacific Avenue and Montgomery, Washington, and Battery streets.

Restored buildings include such old structures as the A. P. Hotaling Co. liquor warehouse, now the Kneedler-Fauchere Building, housing four wholesale fabric showrooms. Around the corner the McGuire Company has restored the old Hotaling livery stable. Oldest of the area's buildings is 472 Jackson Street; it was the Lucas, Turner & Co. Bank, established in 1853 by General William T. Sherman.

Lawyer Melvin Belli owns the Barbary Coast landmark building at 728 Montgomery which houses a courtyard and his purposely peekaboo office.

Chinatown

The largest Asian community outside the Orient, San Francisco's Chinatown covers about 24 blocks and is roughly bordered by Kearny, Mason, and Bush streets and Broadway. It's best to arrive in Chinatown on foot or by public transportation, for the area is heavily congested with traffic.

Grant Avenue is the main street, where for 8 blocks, between Bush and Columbus, visitors are guaranteed a delightfully unusual walk. You can get there from either the financial district, Union Square, or Nob Hill. Remember that if you are atop a hill, your walk will be down several steep blocks. The California Street cable car will put you in the heart of Chinatown.

One of the most colorful approaches to Chinatown is a walk down Sacramento to Grant. You will see peaked pagoda-style rooftops and bright-colored balconies in the foreground and the bay and bridge beyond. Along Grant Avenue is the tourists' Chinatown—curio shops, import shops, restaurants.

To get a glimpse of the "inside," prowl up and down some of the cross streets and explore the side alleys that parallel Grant. Scattered among gift shops and restaurants are stores and markets with exotic smells and sounds. The langauge here is still mostly Cantonese.

In the early morning, Friday through Sunday, Stockton Street, between Washington and Broadway, becomes a throbbing open-air market. Truck farmers in sidewalk stalls sell anything from live turtles to squawking chickens and ducks. Each weekend over 10,000 Chinese gather to shop and socialize.

Between California and Pine is St. Mary's Square, a quiet little park with Beniamino Bufano's striking marble and stainless steel statue of China's one-time president, Sun Yat-sen. Beneath the park is an underground garage; entrances are on Kearny, Pine, and California.

Old St. Mary's Church, a San Francisco landmark since 1854, stands at Grant and California. The Gothic structure was built of granite from China and brick brought around Cape Horn from New England.

Waverly Place, paralleling Grant Avenue to the west, reveals some of Chinatown's few remaining temples. Of special interest is the Tin How Temple, 125 Waverly (top floor), dating back to Gold Rush days. The main shrine is dedicated to T'ien Hou, protectress of travelers. The temple is open from 10 A.M. to 4 P.M. daily. Also on Waverly is the Chinese Culture and Arts Center. On weekends instructors teach classes in caligraphy, *tai chi chuan,* Chinese violin, and butterfly harp.

(Continued on page 21)

CROWNING TELEGRAPH HILL, Coit Tower (above), offers grand clear-day views of bay, Alcatraz, distant Marin hills.

"IT REALLY IS CROOKED!" squeal motorists (left). Lombard Street, snaking between Hyde and Leavenworth, reveals blossoming hydrangeas and breathtaking views.

UNDULATING LINE of Embarcadero Freeway (below) dramatically sweeps above noontime lunchers enjoying verdant park in Golden Gateway Center.

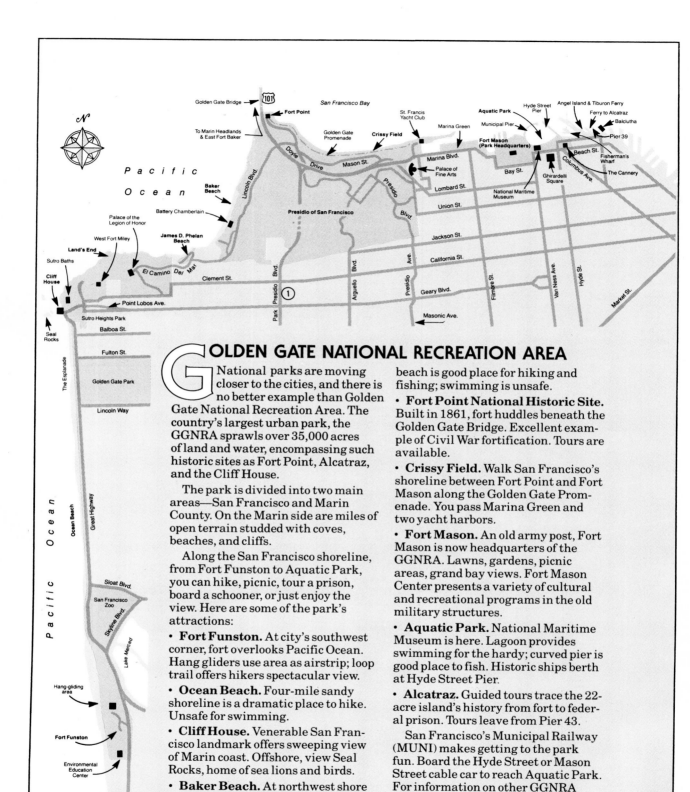

GOLDEN GATE NATIONAL RECREATION AREA

National parks are moving closer to the cities, and there is no better example than Golden Gate National Recreation Area. The country's largest urban park, the GGNRA sprawls over 35,000 acres of land and water, encompassing such historic sites as Fort Point, Alcatraz, and the Cliff House.

The park is divided into two main areas—San Francisco and Marin County. On the Marin side are miles of open terrain studded with coves, beaches, and cliffs.

Along the San Francisco shoreline, from Fort Funston to Aquatic Park, you can hike, picnic, tour a prison, board a schooner, or just enjoy the view. Here are some of the park's attractions:

• **Fort Funston.** At city's southwest corner, fort overlooks Pacific Ocean. Hang gliders use area as airstrip; loop trail offers hikers spectacular view.

• **Ocean Beach.** Four-mile sandy shoreline is a dramatic place to hike. Unsafe for swimming.

• **Cliff House.** Venerable San Francisco landmark offers sweeping view of Marin coast. Offshore, view Seal Rocks, home of sea lions and birds.

• **Baker Beach.** At northwest shore of Presidio facing the Golden Gate, beach is good place for hiking and fishing; swimming is unsafe.

• **Fort Point National Historic Site.** Built in 1861, fort huddles beneath the Golden Gate Bridge. Excellent example of Civil War fortification. Tours are available.

• **Crissy Field.** Walk San Francisco's shoreline between Fort Point and Fort Mason along the Golden Gate Promenade. You pass Marina Green and two yacht harbors.

• **Fort Mason.** An old army post, Fort Mason is now headquarters of the GGNRA. Lawns, gardens, picnic areas, grand bay views. Fort Mason Center presents a variety of cultural and recreational programs in the old military structures.

• **Aquatic Park.** National Maritime Museum is here. Lagoon provides swimming for the hardy; curved pier is good place to fish. Historic ships berth at Hyde Street Pier.

• **Alcatraz.** Guided tours trace the 22-acre island's history from fort to federal prison. Tours leave from Pier 43.

San Francisco's Municipal Railway (MUNI) makes getting to the park fun. Board the Hyde Street or Mason Street cable car to reach Aquatic Park. For information on other GGNRA destinations, call (415) 673-MUNI.

. . . Continued from page 18

Walking tours offer keys to many of Chinatown's mysteries. Since little English is spoken in some of the more intriguing places, you may want to arrange for a guided tour. The Chinese Cultural Center, Ding How Tours, and J. J. Walking Tours offer guided walks covering cultural, culinary, and social aspects of Chinatown. All require reservations; some include dinner.

Portsmouth Square, just east of Grant Avenue, at Kearny and Clay, is where San Francisco began. Here Captain John B. Montgomery raised the American flag in 1846, proclaiming the Mexican village to be a possession of the United States. Portsmouth Square (named for Montgomery's ship, the USS *Portsmouth*) today is a landscaped park atop a parking garage.

Though Portsmouth Square doesn't have a Chinese name, it is Chinatown's village plaza. In the early morning students practice *tai chi chuan,* exercises perfected by Chinese monks centuries ago. By afternoon, elders gather for chess and conversation while youngsters romp in the nearby playground.

From Portsmouth Square you can cross a footbridge east over Kearny Street to the dramatic 27-story Holiday Inn housing the Chinese Cultural Center on the third floor. Open Tuesday through Saturday from 11 A.M. to 5 P.M., the center presents films, exhibits, lectures, and tours.

The Chinese Telephone Exchange at 743 Washington (now the Bank of Canton) is a Chinatown landmark. From 1909 to 1949 the building held the main switchboard for the "China" exchange, when Chinese operators memorized as many as 2,400 names and numbers of Chinatown subscribers. You can see photographs of these exceptional women at the Chinese Historical Museum on Adler Place, an alley one-half block south of Broadway off Grant Avenue. On display are memorabilia covering a century of Chinese life in America. The free museum is open Tuesday through Saturday from 1 to 5 P.M.

North Beach

Not really a beach at all, the area traces its name to the 1850s, when a finger of the bay extended inland and the neighborhood was a sunny shore between Telegraph and Russian hills.

Here, in the center of the Italian community, are Italian bakeries, pastry shops, delicatessens, and kitchen specialty stores. In the pastry shops you'll find rum babas, marzipan, and cylindrical *cannolis* filled with sweetened ricotta cheese and glacéed fruits.

The bakeries, or bread shops, offer long loaves of sweet and sourdough French breads and *panettone,* a round, sweet, Italian bread filled with raisins and fruits.

Kitchen specialty shops sell noodle machines, cheese graters, *caffè espresso* machines, ravioli rolling sticks, baking irons for *pizzele* and *cialdi* cookies, copper *polenta* pots, and round-bottomed pans for *zabaglione.*

Excellent meals are served in the restaurants of North Beach. Beside the well-known establishments, look for modest, unassuming little ones serving savory specialties.

For many years a flourishing colony of painters, writers, and craftsmen has had its headquarters in the North Beach area. Once a year, usually in June, these artists display their crafts in a street bazaar that draws thousands to look or to buy. To inspect this interesting area, walk north on Grant Avenue beyond Columbus. You'll pass small galleries, studios, and shops—some brightly painted outposts of the city's bohemian life. Inside are ceramics, paintings, jewelry, and poster art.

Interspersed along Grant and adjacent streets are meat markets, cafés, and bakeries.

Parking in the district is at a premium at all times, but the Taylor and Bay cable car runs along Mason between Vallejo and Union. From there it's only a 3-block walk east to shops on upper Grant Avenue.

Broadway, San Francisco's Bohemia in the heart of North Beach, comes alive at night. Fanning out from the intersection of Broadway and Columbus, North Beach becomes a lively mosaic of cabarets, small theaters, bistros, and *cappuccino* houses. Here the flavor of Italy mixes with some of the city's wildest nightlife.

Washington Square, at Columbus and Union, is a perfect spot for a picnic lunch in the sun. The Church of Saints Peter and Paul is across Filbert Street from the square. Its two tall towers, illuminated at night, are visible from many sections of the city. The two statues in the square honor San Francisco's firemen and Benjamin Franklin—a typically unusual San Francisco combination.

The north waterfront

Once run-down and neglected, San Francisco's north waterfront is now pulling and pleasing tremendous crowds. Today, this 22-block district facing the water is a mélange of restaurants, unusual museums, art galleries, excellent shops, small theaters, even a national recreation area.

Here are the turn-around points for two of the city's cable car lines and the piers for the bay tour boats.

In the north waterfront district, you'll see items ranging from painted seashells and postcards sold near Fisherman's Wharf to bronze turnbuckles at a ship chandlery, from zebra skins in an import shop to a choice of 200 cheeses on sale at The Cannery.

The biggest and most famous retailer is Cost Plus Imports, a rambling bazaar of housewares, antiques, foods, jewelry, and garden supplies. At the east end of the district is the Northpoint Shopping Center. Its street floor has a candymaker, a market, an ice cream parlor, and several restaurants.

At the west end of the district are Ghirardelli Square and The Cannery. A majority of north waterfront shops are open every day of the week.

Fisherman's Wharf (Jones and Jefferson streets) is a world-famous combination of tourist attractions, sidewalk seafood stalls, steaming cauldrons, and seafood restaurants.

Jefferson Street is one vast open air fish market where you'll see oceans of steaming crabs and mountains of sourdough French bread. Try a "walkaway" seafood

NEON SHROUDS *the night in San Francisco's Chinatown (right). After dark, dragon-laced latterns illuminate a labyrinth of restaurants, shops, and specialty stores along Grant Avenue.*

EAST MEETS WEST *as Taiwan expert teaches American enthusiast the timeless grace of* tai chi chuan *(left). Early morning workouts enliven Chinatown's Portsmouth Square; by afternoon, square becomes gathering place for Chinese of all ages.*

cocktail, sold in a disposable container. Beyond the seafood counters, activity centers around the fishing boats coming in with their catch. At the foot of Jones and Leavenworth, fishermen hoist crates of fish to the pier.

For thousands who come to the city, a San Francisco visit calls for a meal at Fisherman's Wharf. The view is the big reason to go. If you get a window table, below you are the bobbing fishing boats. In the distance loom the tall orange red towers of the Golden Gate Bridge and beyond them the purple Marin hills.

At the seafood restaurants, specialties include fresh crab (during the season, early November to mid-June or July), cracked and served cold with lemon and mayonnaise; crab Louis, the classic wharf salad, served with San Francisco's sourdough bread; abalone; and *cioppino*, the heroic shellfish stew you eat with your fingers.

Restaurants elsewhere along the north waterfront are not easily categorized—however, if you're looking for Italian, Japanese, Mexican, or American food, you can find it here.

About 2 blocks east along the wharf is the berth of the *Balclutha*, a regal old three-masted sailing ship. Refurbished and restored, she looks like what she was: a Scottish-built, square-rigged ship that plied the seas between the 1880s and the 1920s and logged 17 Cape Horn doublings. Though presently berthed at Pier 43, the *Balclutha* is part of the fleet of the National Maritime Museum at the foot of Polk Street in Aquatic Park. She is open from 10 A.M. to 10 P.M.; there is a fee.

Aquatic Park is now part of the Golden Gate National Recreation Area (see page 20). Its ship-shaped National Maritime Museum houses an extensive collection of ship models, nautical artifacts, photographs, and paintings. The most pleasant way to reach the museum is by the Powell and Hyde Street cable car; the turntable is just south of the museum.

Most of the National Maritime Museum's historic ships are located at the Hyde Street Pier. The ships include three-masted schooner *C. A. Thayer*, steam-driven *Wapama*, ferry boat *Eureka*, scow schooner *Alma*, and steam tug *Hercules*. You can board most of the ships; audio earphones are provided for a self-guided tour. Admission to the ships and museum is free; museum facilities are open daily from 10 A.M. to 5 P.M.

Boat tours offer striking views of San Francisco from the water. For a sightseeing tour of the bay, go aboard one of the trim ships of the Red and White Fleet, leaving Pier 43½ near Fisherman's Wharf, or the Blue and Gold Fleet, leaving from Pier 39's west marina. Their routes extend to the Golden Gate Bridge, past "the rock" (Alcatraz) and Treasure Island, under the Bay Bridge, and along the waterfront. From shipboard you'll see the city of San Francisco as a dramatic rim around the bay. North lie the gentle hills of Marin County, and to the east Oakland and Berkeley spread out along the shore and up into the hills. It gets chilly on the bay so take along warm clothing.

Boats for the 1¼-hour excursions leave frequently, beginning at 10 A.M. daily all year (weather permitting). Prices are moderate, and you can get snacks on board.

You can also take guided excursions to Alcatraz, now part of the Golden Gate National Recreation Area. A

federal prison until it was abandoned in 1963, Alcatraz is now visited by more than 400,000 people each year. Tours leave Pier 43 every 45 minutes from 9 A.M. to 3 P.M. (longer hours in summer) and are so popular that the boats are usually filled. Tickets for each day go on sale at 8:30 A.M. at the ticket booth on the pier; reservations are suggested. For information and reservations, call (415) 546-2805.

In summer and on winter weekends, excursion boats take picnickers from Pier 41 to quaint Tiburon and then to a day's outing on Angel Island. For information call (415) 546-2810.

Ghirardelli Square, just south and west of the National Maritime Museum, covers the block bounded by Beach, Larkin, North Point, and Polk streets. First a woolen works and later the Ghirardelli Chocolate Factory, this red-brick building complex has been remodeled and restored to contain an enticing miscellany of shops, art galleries, restaurants, and a theater.

Ghirardelli Square includes a number of buildings (with names such as Mustard, Cocoa, and Chocolate), all of which are situated around an inviting plaza. The brick tower that marks the square was copied from one at the Chateau Blois in France. If you wish to rest, select one of the benches near the splashing fountain or one that affords a view of the bay and boats. In the plaza, entertainment may range from an impromptu concert to a brief ballet.

Shops in the square contain imports from such places as Africa, Holland, Ireland, the Orient, Finland, and Greece. Stores feature wearing apparel, toys, cutlery, flowers, kites, jewelry, and leather goods.

Part of Ghirardelli's charm lies in the outdoor cafés and in the variety of food available here. For instance, you can watch thin crêpes being made, and sample them, as well as Mexican, Chinese, Hungarian, Indian, or Italian food. And you can enjoy a Twin Peaks sundae or a Golden Gate banana split at an old-time ice cream parlor. At the Ghirardelli Chocolate Manufactory you can watch chocolate being made.

The Cannery is similar to Ghirardelli Square in some ways. Bounded by Beach, Leavenworth, and Jefferson streets, it was originally constructed in 1894 to house the Del Monte Fruit and Vegetable Cannery. Today, the old brick building with its concrete walkways and arched windows has been restored and refurbished.

The Cannery contains three levels of shopping and eating pleasures. You can buy an assortment of goods, from contemporary household furnishings to primitive art objects. Other shops feature such items as candles, fine foods and wines, apparel, flowers, linens, books, and pet supplies. If you're not shopping, or just want to rest, stop at an outdoor café to enjoy a puppet or mime show— there's even a human jukebox waiting to entertain you.

Outside escalators and stairs provide access to different floors, or you can take a glass-enclosed elevator from the ground floor to the top. From the third floor, you can see Alcatraz Island, the Bay Bridge, and Coit Tower.

On the west side of The Cannery is a plaza containing a small garden center, outside tables, and an oyster bar. Other restaurants feature Oriental, Mexican, French, and English food.

(Continued on next page)

Across Leavenworth Street from The Cannery is a parking lot that provides an hour of free parking with your validated ticket from The Cannery.

Pier 39, once an abandoned shipping cargo pier, is the newest of the restaurant-shopping meccas along San Francisco's northern waterfront. Just east of Fisherman's Wharf, this pier—the length of three football fields—embraces 22 restaurants, over 100 specialty shops, and two marinas, as well as a bayside park. Adding to the authenticity of the complex is a two-level arcade built from weathered wood salvaged from the demolition of other piers.

One of the nicest features of Pier 39 is its 5-acre waterfront park. Step away from the bustling shopping arcades to enjoy serene views of the surrounding bay. The park stretches along the southwestern edge of Pier 39 to about the middle of Pier 41. When completed, it will extend to Pier 35.

Marinas flank Pier 39, offering 350 berths to fishing boats, pleasure craft, and guest boats. The Blue and Gold Fleet runs bay tour excursions; instructions in windsurfing, sailing, and sportfishing are also offered.

There's no lack of entertainment at Pier 39. Musicians, street artists, jugglers, even a high-dive stunt team perform on the pier's three main stages, adding a carnival dimension to the nautical atmosphere.

A covered pedestrian bridge over Beach Street leads from a parking garage to the second level of the complex. Mini-buses provide free transportation along the pier.

The Marina

This lovely residential area with a Mediterranean flair now offers most of the bayside walking in San Francisco. Though the Marina Green is still a city park, it is now within the boundaries of the Golden Gate National Recreation Area—a preserve encompassing over 35,000 acres of land and water in both San Francisco and Marin counties (see page 20). In the Marina, this urban recreation area opens the shoreline from Aquatic Park and Fort Mason to Fort Point, huddled beneath the Golden Gate Bridge.

The Golden Gate Promenade is a 3½-mile shoreline walk between Aquatic Park and Fort Point. Since its incorporation into the GGNRA, the promenade has changed on its eastern end. From Aquatic Park you walk west to Fort Mason. Once army land, off limits to civilians, Fort Mason now houses the headquarters and visitors center of the GGNRA. You can wander around the historic buildings and enjoy grand bay vistas. The area around Fort Mason will become a grassy park where visitors may rest and picnic.

Along Fort Mason's waterside portion are the piers and buildings of the old Port of Embarcations, now the Fort Mason Center. A unique cultural complex, the center houses performing arts groups, art galleries, and a small restaurant. Classes are offered in anything from ballroom dancing to fitness conditioning. For information and a schedule of events, call (415) 441-5705.

A paved path leads to the Marina Green. A favorite of both residents and visitors, the Marina Green is the perfect spot for flying kites or sunbathing—and it's a jog-

ger's paradise. Try the parcourse exercises on the way to Chrissy Field.

Chrissy Field is a quiet stretch of shoreline skirting about a mile along the water's edge. With its great views, driftwood, and windblown sand, this is a quiet retreat from the urban jostle.

To reach the end of the promenade, head west past a U.S. Coast Guard station to Long Avenue. Long Avenue leads you to Fort Point and the Golden Gate. Walking enthusiasts can retrace their steps to the Marina; the less hardy can climb the hill to the Golden Gate Bridge toll plaza and catch an inbound Golden Gate Transit bus back to the downtown area.

The Palace of Fine Arts (3601 Lyon Street), along the route, was built for the Panama-Pacific International Exposition in 1915 and restored to its original splendor in 1967. It houses the Exploratorium, a changing exhibit focusing on science, technology, and human perception (open 1 to 5 P.M. Wednesday through Sunday, 7 to 9:30 P.M. Wednesday; slight fee for adults except on Wednesday). There is also a theater where the San Francisco International Film Festival is held each October. Other cultural and entertainment events also take place here.

Japantown—Japan without a passport

Today over 12,000 people of Japanese descent live in San Francisco. Though the first Japanese arrived here in the 1860s, it was not until after the 1906 earthquake that many Japanese chose to rebuild their homes in this part of San Francisco. Houses, businesses, churches, shops, and restaurants were often patterned after traditional Japanese architecture. It was not long before the area took on a Japanese character and became known as *Nihonmachi*, or Japantown.

In 1968, the dedication of the multimillion-dollar Japan Center complex supplied the community with a much needed ethnic focal point. Designed by architect Minoru Yamasaki, the 3-square-block center exudes the serenity and dignity characteristic of Japanese architecture. A string of handsome white buildings between Geary Expressway and Post, the center begins on the east at Laguna Street, boldly leaps Webster Street with a curved bridgeway of shops, and ends on the west at Fillmore Street. Street signs are in both Japanese and English.

Tenants include the Japanese Consulate, manufacturers' showrooms, and retail stores with goods ranging from bonsai to jade and pearls. The 5-acre complex houses shops, restaurants, a theater, teahouses, tempura bars, the 15-story Miyako Hotel, and Japanese baths.

The Peace Plaza, containing a five-tiered, 35-foot Peace Pagoda with reflecting pool, is the hub of the Japan Center. A graceful wooden drum tower stands at the entrance to the plaza, and a copper-roofed walkway at the north end of the plaza connects the East and Kintetsu buildings.

Colorful festivals take place in the plaza. Most popular is the annual Spring Cherry Blossom Festival *(Sakura Matsuri)* held in April. This 7-day event spans two weekends, offering traditional Japanese music, dance, art, and tea ceremonies. *Aki Matsuri,* the annual fall festival, is a 3-day fête held sometime in September. *Tanabato,* or Star Festival, marks the weekend closest to July 7. One of the oldest and most romantic of Japanese festivals, it celebrates the yearly reunion of the mythical heavenly lovers, Vega and Altair. The celebration is joyously filled with colorful decorations, traditional songs, and graceful dance.

Inspired by the center and other urban renewal programs, residents of Japantown continue to revitalize this section of the city. In 1975, the Kyoto hotel opened at Sutter and Buchanan streets. The Buchanan Mall leading to the center's main entrance was completed shortly afterward. Dotted with flowering trees and unique fountains, the block-long mall is lined with an assortment of Japanese shops, restaurants, and businesses.

Only a mile from Union Square, Japantown and the Japan Center are easy to reach. From downtown, take MUNI No. 38 bus on Geary or No. 1, 2, or 3 and get off at Buchanan or Laguna. If you have a car, drive west on Geary to the center's garage entrance.

Golden Gate Park—a park for all seasons

San Francisco owes a great debt of gratitude to the late John McLaren, whose vision and perseverance in San Francisco's early years turned more than 1,000 acres of rolling sand dunes into a park. Today, Golden Gate Park is one of the great metropolitan parks of the world.

Park visitors benefit from an enlightened policy of operation; the park is meant to be used. You can walk, play, or picnic on the grass anywhere except the small plot of lawn surrounding McLaren's statue in Rhododendron Dell. The bridle paths, equestrian field, and bicycle trails are for public use; you can rent horses at the stables at Kennedy Drive and 34th Avenue and bicycles just outside the park in the 600 and 800 blocks of Stanyan Street.

The latest park fad is roller skating. On Sundays, the main road through the park, John F. Kennedy Drive, is closed to autos, making a perfect skating thoroughfare. Skating may soon be prohibited near the Strybing Arboretum, the Japanese Tea Garden, and the de Young Museum—areas too crowded for safe skating.

Shops around the park rent skates. Most have adults' and children's sizes, all require a deposit of a driver's license or major credit card.

The M. H. de Young and Asian Art museums, the Academy of Science, the concessions, the Arboretum, and the Conservatory close at night; otherwise the park is open 24 hours.

John F. Kennedy Drive takes you by many of the park's attractions; it's the entrance from the northwest corner. The nine-hole pitch-and-putt golf course located a short distance inside the park is open every day. To get to the clubhouse, turn left at the first intersection of Kennedy Drive after you leave the Great Highway.

The Chain of Lakes, a series of three artificial lakes, runs from north to south across the park near its western end. Largest of the three is North Lake (north of Kennedy Drive), dotted with several landcaped islands. The banks of Middle Lake (south of Kennedy Drive), are planted with camellias and Japanese cherry trees. South Lake, smallest in the chain, hosts large numbers of wild ducks.

North of Kennedy Drive and just east of the Chain of Lakes, the fences of the Buffalo Paddock are so carefully concealed by artful landscaping that buffaloes within the enclosure seem to be roaming at large.

Anglers will find an ideal practicing spot at the Flycasting Pool south of the drive. The cement-lined pool is divided into three sections—one for distance casting, another for accuracy, and a third for practicing difficult overhead casts.

As you approach Spreckels Lake, you'll pass some of the largest and oldest rhododendrons in the park. Planted on an island in the center of Kennedy Drive, they're at their best in May.

The lake itself is north of the drive. Its waters are usually freckled with wildfowl, and during summer the lake is used for sailing model boats. The San Francisco Model Yacht Club has its headquarters in the building just west of the lake.

Continuing east on Kennedy Drive, you pass 25-acre Lindley Meadow and tiny Lloyd Lake. A gravel path encircles the lake, leading to the "Portals of the Past" on its shore. The six white marble pillars that form the portals were the entrance to the A. N. Towne residence on Nob Hill. All that remained of the house after the 1906 fire, the pillars were later presented by Mrs. Towne to the park.

Stow Lake, largest of the park's manmade lakes, is the central reservoir for the irrigation system and also a popular recreation spot. Tree-lined walks border the lake, a road goes around it, and there's a snack bar near the dock where boats can be rented. Two footbridges lead to Strawberry Hill, a wooded island in the center of the lake. A 5-minute walk up a fairly steep slope puts you on top of the hill. The view from the summit reveals not only the park—a wide green swath through the west end of the city—but also the towers of the Golden Gate and Bay bridges, as well as the surf pounding the shoreline and, on clear days, the Farallon Islands, 30 miles out into the Pacific.

The Rose Garden, just east of Stow Lake Drive on the north side of Kennedy Drive, contains about 75 varieties of roses, including recent award winners.

The M. H. de Young Memorial Museum opened in 1895 after Michael de Young, publisher of the San Francisco *Chronicle,* proposed that the profits of the California Midwinter International Exposition of 1894 be used to house a permanent collection of art. The original museum buildings were torn down in 1926, and today's museum consists of two wings extending from either side of a 134-foot tower that faces a landscaped court. Both the Pool of Enchantment at the entrance and the bronze sun dial at the building's southeast corner are the work of sculptor M. Earl Cummings.

A special wing overlooking the Japanese Tea Garden was added in 1966 to house the Avery Brundage Collection of Oriental Art (now called the Asian Art Museum). On display are nearly 6,000 treasures covering 60 centuries of Asian civilization.

The museum houses extensive and varied art collections displayed in spacious galleries enclosing the court. Paintings include works by famous American and European artists. Though the Asian Art Museum is open daily from 10 A.M. to 5 P.M., the de Young is closed Monday and Tuesday; there is an admission charge.

The Japanese Tea Garden just west of the museum is open daily from 8 A.M. to dusk. Created in 1894, this 3-acre display of Oriental landscaping includes a moon bridge, a temple, Oriental gateways and lanterns, a large bronze Buddha, and a teahouse where Japanese women serve green or jasmine tea and cookies. In spring the cherry trees make the garden a fairyland of delicate blooms. Blossoms are at their peak around April 1. The admission charge (instituted in 1980) is slight.

The California Academy of Sciences grouping includes the North American Hall, with its collection of American mammals and birds displayed in their natural habitats; the African Hall, featuring an African water hole with giraffes, gnus, impalas, gazelles, zebras, and hartebeests grouped realistically around it; the Steinhart Aquarium; the Morrison Planetarium; the Wattis Hall of Man, featuring permanent life-size anthropological exhibits.

New in the Steinhart Aquarium is the Fish Roundabout. The first aquarium of its kind in the United States, the roundabout is a 100,000-gallon, giant ring tank. You stand on a platform in the center while sharks, tuna, and salmon swim around you.

The academy and the aquarium, open daily from 10 A.M. to 5 P.M. (later in summer), charges a small admission fee. There's an added charge for the Theater of the Stars planetarium's spectacular shows.

The Music Concourse, situated between the de Young Museum and the Academy of Sciences, is the setting for band concerts at 2 P.M. on Sundays and holidays (weather permitting). You can sit on terraces around the concourse or on benches.

Strybing Arboretum is a "must" for anyone interested in plants. Here in this self-contained, 60-acre world are about 5,000 species and varieties of plants from all over the globe, conveniently arranged according to geographical origin and carefully labeled.

The Arboretum, located along South Drive, is open from 8 A.M. to 4:30 P.M. on weekdays and from 10 A.M. to 5 P.M. on Saturday and Sunday; admission is free.

Conservatory of Flowers (open 8 A.M. to 4:50 P.M. daily) shelters another world. The atmosphere is warm and humid, the plants lush and tropical.

The conservatory houses many fascinating collections—bright crotons, large-flowered hibiscus, rare cycads, graceful ferns, exotic orchids. Along the path, among tall palms, are some of the largest and oldest philodendron plants under cultivation.

Be sure to look at the greenhouse itself. A replica of the conservatory at Kew Gardens, England, it was bought by James Lick, a San Francisco philanthropist. Its sections were transported from England around the Horn on a sailing ship. After the owner's death, the greenhouse was purchased by the city and erected in Golden Gate Park in 1878. The framework is wood, but the beams, unlike those of most greenhouses, are lami-

nated. If you look closely, you can see how short pieces have been fitted together to form the dome.

In Conservatory Valley between Kennedy Drive and the conservatory are many formal beds of annuals and bulbs. On the slopes behind these beds is a floral design in live plants that honors events of national or area importance.

Children's Playground, in the southeast corner of the park adjacent to the Sharon Building, is devoted to recreation. Neighborhood mothers bring their children here during the week, and sightseers visiting the park find that an hour or so of play gives their own youngsters a needed diversion. There is also a small animal farm.

Kezar Stadium, a municipal field, is used principally by local high school football teams. Through 1970, Kezar was the home of San Francisco's professional football team, the '49ers. Kezar Pavilion, the indoor stadium, is used for sporting events, including professional boxing and roller derbies.

Public transportation makes getting to the park easy. Just take the No. 38 Geary bus west on Geary Street to 10th Avenue, then transfer to No. 10 Monterey bus and get off at the de Young Museum complex.

Cars can park along most of the drives—there are few "No Parking" signs. On Sundays, auto traffic is restricted along Kennedy Drive.

The city's western perimeter

Fortunately for all of us, the Golden Gate National Recreation Area saved the existing greenbelts on both sides of the bay (see page 20). On the San Francisco side of the bay, a coastal fortification plan, developed in 1854, coincidentally protected much of the city's western edge from development by establishing a natural greenbelt from Fort Mason to Fort Funston.

Because of the dangerous undertow, most of San Francisco's waterfront is not safe for swimming. However, James D. Phelan Beach offers one of the few safe swimming areas in the city. At Baker Beach you'll find one of the huge coastal guns remounted in the Battery Chamberlain, and a small museum depicting the seashore defense system. For a look at Mile Rock Lighthouse, the Golden Gate Bridge, and the Pacific Ocean, take the northern turnoff from Point Lobos Avenue to Land's End. Besides a view, you'll see the shelled bridge of the USS *San Francisco,* torpedoed in 1942 at Guadalcanal.

Several other recreational activities are available, you can sun or fish from the beaches; golf among cypress trees; visit an art museum or a zoo; or stroll through historic Fort Point.

Fort Point National Historic Site, huddling under the southern end of the Golden Gate Bridge, is reached from Lincoln Boulevard. Here Colonel Juan Bautista de Anza planted a cross in 1775. In 1853 the Americans, on the site of an old Spanish fort, started work on this massive brick, iron, and granite structure built roughly along the lines of Fort Sumter in South Carolina. The fort, which never fired a defensive shot, has been abandoned since 1914.

(Continued on page 28)

WARM GLOW of nighttime Ghirardelli Square (above) invites visitors to explore delightful mélange of shops and restaurants now sprinkled throughout former chocolate factory.

PROUD VENDER (left) displays still-wriggling catch of the day. Fisherman's Wharf, spiced with old salts, sounds, and smells of the sea, still lures visitors and residents alike, seeking a walk-away crab cocktail, steamed clams, or a taste of its famous sourdough bread.

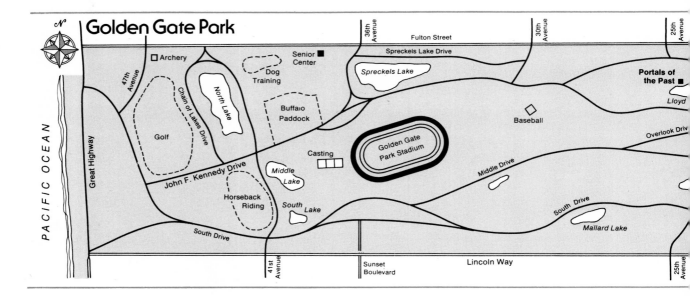

Golden Gate Park

. . . *Continued from page 26*

Its most serious adversary proved to be the weather. Wind-driven salt water and fog have rusted out iron balustrades and spiral staircases and have eaten into the mortar. If the Golden Gate Bridge's imaginative chief engineer, Joseph Strauss, had not ordered construction of a special arch over the fort, it would have been torn down to make way for the bridge in the mid-1930s.

Part of the Golden Gate National Recreation Area, the fort is open daily from 10 A.M. to 5 P.M. Guided tours reward visitors with unusual views of the bridge and the bay's shifting tides. For information call the National Park Service, (415) 556-0560.

Fort Funston, the western boundary of the Golden Gate National Recreation Area, offers a wheelchair-accessible loop trail with beautiful views and occasional picnic areas. You can watch hang gliders soar in the strong winds above the area's high cliffs. The fort is open from 7 A.M. to dusk.

Lincoln Park is at the end of El Camino del Mar, an extension of Lincoln Boulevard in the Presidio. Here you'll find a municipal 18-hole golf course and a fine art museum—the California Palace of the Legion of Honor. You'll see works by the great masters, a special collection of graphic prints, and, in the courtyard, Rodin's *The Thinker*. The museum is open daily from 10 A.M. to 5 P.M.

San Francisco Zoo ranks among the top city zoos in the United States. Adults as well as children will enjoy a visit. It's out at the edge of Ocean Beach (turn off the Great Highway at either Sloat Boulevard or Park Road) and is open daily from 10 A.M. to 5:30 P.M. You can easily walk around the zoo, looking through the fences at animals roaming in surroundings similar to their natural habitats. Or you can take the motor-drawn "Zebra Zephyr," which circles the entire zoo. Cars leave every half-hour near the main entrance, taking you on a 20-minute circuit.

Sigmund Stern Grove is an open-air wooded amphitheater just east of the San Francisco Zoo at 19th Avenue and Sloat Boulevard. The grove's annual Midsummer Music Festival features ten consecutive Sundays of free musical entertainment, from classical offerings to Gilbert and Sullivan. Concerts begin around 2 P.M., but come early to picnic.

The city's hills

San Francisco is famous for its many hills and the views that each affords. Some hills are more accessible than others (only a footpath reaches the summit of Mount Davidson, for instance), some are more interesting physically, and some provide exceptional views. Nob, Telegraph, and Russian hills, along with Twin Peaks, are probably San Francisco's best-known heights.

Telegraph Hill

At Lombard and Kearny streets, you pick up the road that climbs up Telegraph Hill to Coit Tower. Parking space at the top of the hill is limited, but with patience you can usually get a place. Or you can leave your car at a garage and board a MUNI bus. It will take you to the top and, if you prefer, you can walk down the footpath on the east slope of the hill.

Telegraph Hill gives good views of San Francisco's waterfront, Russian Hill, Nob Hill, the Bay and Golden Gate bridges, Alcatraz Island, Angel Island, Treasure Island and, on a clear day, some East Bay landmarks.

For an even loftier view, take the elevator (slight charge) to the top of Coit Tower (210 feet). Elevator operates from 11 A.M. to 5 P.M.

Coit Tower, dramatically lighted at night, is an easily recognized landmark against the city's skyline. It was

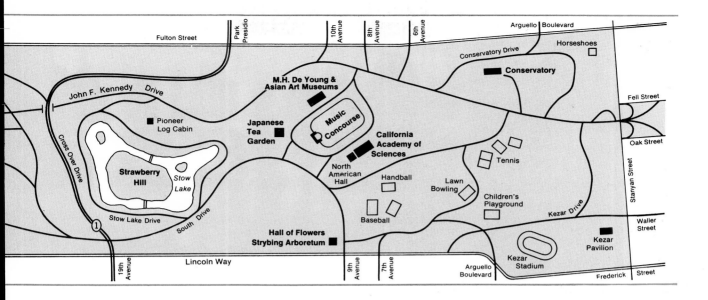

built in 1934 as a memorial to the city's volunteer firemen from funds left to the city by Lillie Hitchcock Coit, a great fire buff. The shape of the tower is often said to resemble a fire hose nozzle. Inside the fluted cylindrical column are murals done by artists in 1934 under the Work Projects Administration.

If you choose to walk down from Telegraph Hill, take the pathway that curves down the eastern slope. You will come to two sets of steps, one leading to Filbert and the other to Greenwich Street. Either stairway takes you down to Montgomery, a short distance below, and then drops down a long, steep flight to Sansome at the foot of the hill.

Russian Hill

Located west of Telegraph Hill, roughly between Hyde, Taylor, Vallejo, and Greenwich streets, is Russian Hill. In the immediate area you'll find small green parks, quaint cottages, and skyscraper apartment buildings. Here you can drive on two of San Francisco's most interesting streets. Filbert between Hyde and Leavenworth is one of the city's steepest streets; Lombard between Hyde and Leavenworth is the crookedest—the brick road coils down in snakelike fashion amidst bright hydrangea gardens.

Nob Hill

To reach the top of this hill, take the California or Powell Street cable car. If you prefer to drive, you'll find several parking garages on California, close to Mason.

The very top of the hill covers about three square blocks. Before the earthquake and fire of 1906, this small hilltop was the site of the city's grandest mansions. Only one survives: the imposing brownstone built by James C. Flood. Now the Pacific Union Club, it faces California, just west of Mason.

Two of San Francisco's most famous hotels, the Fairmont and the Mark Hopkins, stand atop Nob Hill at California and Mason. The luxurious Fairmont, the tallest building on the hill, has several restaurants, a spacious lobby, and a cocktail lounge at the top. You can reach the Crown Room in an outside glass-walled elevator or, if you prefer, in an inside elevator.

Across California is the Mark Hopkins Hotel, long known for the elegant Top of the Mark cocktail lounge. Panoramic views unfold from both the Crown Room and the Top of the Mark.

Next to the Mark Hopkins Hotel, at the corner of California and Powell, is the elegant Stanford Court Hotel, on the site of the Stanford mansion. Rebuilt and refurbished in turn-of-the-century decor, the hotel has a dramatic circular driveway entrance, accented with a round fountain and topped by an opulent stained-glass dome. The lobby, with its potted palms, reminds you of an early 1900s photo. A glass-enclosed restaurant and cocktail lounge look out on the city skyline.

Up the hill, at 1075 California Street, is the chic Huntington Hotel, with a renowned restaurant in the same building.

Three blocks west, at California and Jones, is Grace Cathedral, a study in Gothic architecture. Of particular interest are the interior murals, stained-glass windows, and the Ghiberti doors—gilded bronze panels that are a reproduction of the famous East Door of the Baptistry in Florence, Italy. Protected by guardrails, the doors are opened only on special occasions.

Across from the cathedral is the Masonic Temple, a spacious auditorium used for fine arts and musical productions. It is open to visitors Monday through Friday.

Twin Peaks

Situated in the center of the city, Twin Peaks are noted for their panoramic views of the Bay Area. Now a 65-

CITY LIFE seems far away when you're fishing near Fort Point (above), along Golden Gate National Recreation Area. Country's largest urban park, GGNRA stretches along city's waterfront from Fort Funston to Aquatic Park.

COUPLE STOPS a moment to savor serene surroundings of Golden Gate Park's Japanese Tea Garden (left). Graceful tiered pagoda highlights 3 acres of Oriental landscaping, with delicate blossoms, wandering pathways, cool pools.

acre park, their crests are popular lookouts. To get there, take Upper Market Street to Twin Peaks Boulevard.

Cathedral Hill, a redeveloped area of apartments and homes off Geary, is dominated by St. Mary's Cathedral, a stunning example of ecclesiastical architecture.

Streets that unlock the city

You'll make your own discoveries of some of San Francisco's most interesting byways. Here are a few of its famous (and some not-so-famous) streets, with an idea of what you'll find along them.

Market Street. San Francisco's best-known thoroughfare runs diagonally across the city from Twin Peaks to the Ferry Building. The strip of Market south of Union Square is a continuation of the downtown shopping area. Underneath Market runs BART, giving the street a new look—less traffic, wider sidewalks, new landscaping, and old-fashioned street lamps. At the foot of Market is the Ferry Building, partially obscured by the double-decked Embarcadero Freeway skirting the waterfront. Across the street is the Justin Herman Plaza, with its monumental free-form sculpture—the Vaillancourt Fountain, a walk-through design of 101 concrete boxes.

High-rise buildings accent Market Street's rejuvenation. The Crown-Zellerbach building, an impressive, 20-story green monolith, rises above a pleasantly landscaped park (popular with noon "brown baggers") at the corner of Market and Bush. At 555 Market Street you can stroll through colorful gardens at the Standard Oil Company Plaza; on weekdays you can go inside the 43-story building to view an exhibit on the history of petroleum. The Crocker Building (Post, Montgomery, and Market) towers 38 stories above its green mall.

At Market and New Montgomery streets stands a San Francisco landmark—the Sheraton-Palace Hotel. The reputation of this magnificent 8-story structure began with its opening in 1875. Built by silver king William Ralston, the building was severely damaged in the 1906 earthquake-fire; restoration was completed in 1909. The glass-roofed Garden Court dining room (a historical landmark) is a fine example of old San Francisco elegance—and a popular place for lunch or Sunday brunch.

Geary Street. A street of many faces, Geary runs west from Market, ending at Sutro Park near the ocean. On its way through town it passes by some of San Francisco's smartest shops, Union Square, the theater district, and the Japan Center.

Mission Street. Roughly paralleling Market through downtown, Mission takes an abrupt turn south after crossing Van Ness. It is primarily a warehousing area from its beginning at the bay, but it boasts one large tourist attraction—the historic U.S. Mint at 5th and Mission. Completed in 1873 and phased out of operation about 80 years later, the mint reopened as a museum in 1973. An outstanding example of Federal Classical Revival architecture, it's undergone extensive restoration and refurbishing. In the front section you'll see exhibits tracing the development of American money. The mint's

special coins and medals division operates in the rear. The landmark is open from 10 A.M. to 4 P.M. Tuesday through Saturday.

Se habla Espanol signs appear around the Mission District, with Duboce, Castro, Harrison, and 28th streets forming the perimeter. Walking around near Mission Dolores, you'll feel the strong Spanish influence. Mission Street once linked the village of Yerba Buena to this Franciscan outpost; now BART tunnels beneath it.

Mission Dolores, established in 1776, was the sixth of the California mission (Franciscan) chain. Its ceilings are decorated with Indian art, and the original bell and altar from Mexico remain. Be sure to walk through the garden cemetery, final resting place of many San Francisco pioneers. An impressive statue of Father Junipero Serra stands in the courtyard.

California Street. Taking off from Market at the Justin Herman Plaza, California extends all the way through town, avoiding much of the business traffic and ending at Lincoln Park. Along the way, you'll climb from the canyons of Montgomery's "Wall Street" through colorful Chinatown to the heights of Nob Hill, passing some of San Francisco's famous hotels, the Masonic Temple, and Grace Cathedral. It's a good street for catching outstanding views.

Union Street. Passing by the North Beach and upper Grant Avenue areas, Union becomes better known and less residential after crossing Van Ness. In pre-Gold Rush days, the district was known as Cow Hollow—it was, in fact, the city's dairyland. But its renaissance began in the late 1950s when ingenious merchants began reclaiming its vintage dwellings, cow barns, and carriage houses and converting them to a flourishing shopping area with galleries, boutiques, and restaurants.

Clement Street. A melting pot of ethnic life, Clement is trying hard to maintain its identity. This shopping area, not really frequented by tourists, has a little bit of everything—almost all authentic. Best known as a Russian neighborhood, it also harbors other European and Asian nationalities. Shoppers with string bags still barter with shopkeepers for the best-looking vegetables for the evening meal. Here you can learn belly dancing, eat at a vegetarian restaurant, or shop for fertilized red eggs, Indian pickles, or *piroshkis*. In some 50 establishments you'll find more than 16 national or ethnic cuisines, ranging from Indonesian to Italian fare.

Polk Street. In an afternoon you can explore on foot much of the 10-block length of Polk between Union Street on the north and Pine Street on the south. Sandwiched between the odds and ends emporiums are intriguing specialty shops, antique stores, galleries, and restaurants that give the street a reputation for both good eating and good shopping. Best times to shop are Tuesday through Saturday, from noon to 6 P.M. By 6 P.M. most of the restaurants near Union Street begin to open; they are usually crowded within an hour.

Sutter Street. Its name appropriate for today's shopping prospector, this 1.8-mile street runs from the financial district to the residential uplands and includes a rich lode of treasure in 8 blocks. Lined with grand and small hotels, specialty houses and boutiques, serious art galleries and import emporiums, fashionable restaurants and small cafés.

Outer Sacramento Street. This part of Sacramento has blossomed into a shopping sector reminiscent of Union Street. What was formerly a service area for Pacific and Presidio Heights residents is now a browsable, 7-block cluster of shops, galleries, and boutiques, many of them occupying turn-of-the-century clapboards. Interspersed among apparel, antique, art, gift, and home furnishings outlets are coffee houses, snack bars, restaurants, and a foreign film theater. Most shopping is between Broderick and Spruce streets.

The city's cultural side

San Francisco's cultural life began simultaneously with its financial history—in the 1850s. It is reported that the city's first classical concert was a trombone solo in 1850. From the beginning, local audiences were warm to actors and musicians; concert halls and theaters abounded, and performers were handsomely rewarded with gold. The city has never lost its zest for the arts.

The performing arts

Music and theater are not limited to legitimate stages. Sunday afternoon outdoor concerts are held in Golden Gate Park and, in summer, in the Sigmund Stern Grove (along Sloat Boulevard near 19th Avenue; see page 28).

San Francisco Symphony's regular season is December through May. Until the fall of 1980 their performances were held in the Opera House, but the symphony has moved to the Louise M. Davies Symphony Hall, located opposite the Opera House at Grove and Van Ness streets. Performances are Wednesday through Saturday nights plus Thursday afternoons. The symphony also plays pops concerts in July on Tuesday, Thursday, and Saturday nights.

San Francisco Opera's 11-week season opens in mid-September. Performances are Tuesday, Wednesday, Friday, and Saturday nights, as well as Sunday afternoons. "Spring Opera," in March or April at the Curran Theatre, features young American singers. "Dollar Opera" performances are held two weekends in early May at the Palace of Fine Arts Theatre.

Companies on tour also perform at the Opera House, Masonic Memorial Auditorium, Grace Cathedral, the Legion of Honor, San Francisco State University, and the Cow Palace. Check the Sunday newspaper's "Datebook" for listings.

San Francisco Ballet has two principal seasons. In December (during the Christmas holidays) they perform *The Nutcracker* in the Opera House. Spring season in the Opera House is the ballet's major offering. Get tickets at the Opera House box office.

American Conservatory Theatre, a repertory company whose season runs from early October into May, also presents a long-running show for the summer. The company performs at the Geary Theatre nightly except Sunday (matinees Wednesday and Saturday). Special productions play at the Marines Memorial Theatre.

Civic Light Opera productions start in April/May and continue into autumn at the Orpheum Theatre. Matinees are usually held Wednesday and Saturday; dark on Sunday.

A mélange of museums

Museum subjects range from history to wine; take your pick. Of the many museums in the city, here is a sampling.

African American Historical Society exhibits pertain to African and Afro-American history. Open Tuesday through Saturday from 1 to 5 P.M., it's at 680 McAllister Street; admission is free.

California Historical Society's 1896 red sandstone Whittier Mansion seems an appropriate headquarters for an excellent library and small museum. The library is open from 10 A.M. to 4 P.M. Tuesday through Saturday, and the headquarters is open from 1 to 5 P.M. on Wednesday, Saturday, and Sunday. It's located at 2090 Jackson Street; there's a small charge.

Chinese Historical Society of America has displays of early California mining activity and the building of the transcontinental railroad, as well as personal memorabilia. It's open 1 to 5 P.M. Tuesday through Saturday, except Christmas and New Year's Day; admission is free. The museum is in Chinatown at 17 Adler Place, just off Grant Avenue.

The Mexican Museum displays art from pre-Hispanic to the contemporary Mexican period. The museum is open 12 to 5 P.M. Tuesday through Sunday; closed Monday. For more information call (415) 621-1224. There is a fee.

The Octagon House, built in 1861 and restored in 1952 by the National Society of Colonial Dames, displays authentic furnishings. This elegant, unusual home is open 1 to 4 P.M. the first Sunday of each month and the second and fourth Thursdays. It's located at Gough and Union.

The Haas-Lilienthal House occupies nearly a block of San Francisco's Franklin Street. With its gables, intricate gingerbread, and four-story "witch hat" tower, it's a Victorian classic. Tour guides will escort you through the house Sundays and Wednesdays between 1 and 4 P.M. Tours begin every half-hour; small admission fee. The house is at 2007 Franklin Street near Broadway.

Wine Museum of San Francisco is the first of its kind in the United States. Paintings, sculptures, artifacts, and historical exhibits all relate to viniculture. The striking brick structure opened in January 1974. Located at 633 Beach Street near Fisherman's Wharf, it's open from 11 A.M. to 5 P.M. Sunday. There's no charge to visit this collection by the Christian Brothers and the Fromm family.

Looking at art

You'll find art galleries scattered throughout the city, but there are four main museums.

San Francisco Museum of Modern Art, on the third and fourth floors of the Veterans Building in the Civic Center, is the nucleus of modern art in the Bay Area. Traveling exhibitions add depth to the collection. Permanent acquisitions include works by Henri Matisse, Paul Klee, Alexander Calder, Jackson Pollock, and other noted artists. The museum is open from 10 A.M. to 6 P.M. on Tuesday, Wednesday, and Friday; 10 to 5 on Saturday and Sunday; and 10 to 10 on Thursday; it is closed on Monday. There is a fee.

Asian Art Museum's collection of treasures spanning 60 centuries is internationally acclaimed. You'll see bronze Hindu deities, sandstone Khmer figures, whimsical ivory and jade figures, fine porcelains, and silken scrolls. Open from 10 A.M. to 5 P.M., it's located in the M. H. de Young Memorial Museum, Golden Gate Park.

California Palace of the Legion of Honor is one of San Francisco's most splendid museums and sites. This neo-Classical edifice, set among green lawns, dominates the height of Land's End in Lincoln Park, in the city's northwest corner. Paintings span the 16th to the 20th centuries, with emphasis on 18th and 19th century French artists. The collection of Rodin sculpture is one of America's finest.

Free docent tours of permanent collections are given at 2 P.M. daily. Organ recitals are held Saturday and Sunday at 4 P.M. The museum is open from 10 A.M. to 5 P.M. Wednesday through Sunday; slight admission fee.

M. H. de Young Memorial Museum houses such treasures as Rembrandt portraits, El Greco paintings, Flemish tapestries, and many works by other major artists. The gallery of American art is a recent addition. Besides paintings and sculpture, you'll see displays of period furniture, porcelain, and silver. Exhibits include artifacts from Africa and Oceania.

Located in Golden Gate Park, the museum is open Wednesday through Sunday from 10 A.M. to 5 P.M.; admission fee. Guided tours are given daily.

GOURMET TIPS FOR CITY DINING

San Francisco menus are as international as the United Nations. With restaurants ranging from modest to expensive, the city has more than 2,600 places to dine. The quality and variety of cuisines—from Basque, Moroccan, or Hungarian delicacies to gold field creations—have made eating San Francisco's number one attraction.

San Franciscans take food seriously. Many arguments rage over the relative merits of a favorite restaurant. Proper atmosphere is almost as important to enjoyable dining as good food, and San Francisco establishments have met the challenge. You'll find elegant restaurants in grand hotels, cozy corners in family-run eateries, and salty atmosphere at Fisherman's Wharf.

The sea provides many traditional San Francisco delicacies—Dungeness crab, abalone, and Hang Town Fry (an oyster and egg dish favored by the 49ers). Other local favorites are the crusty sourdough French bread, green goddess salad, artichoke specialties, cheeses from neighboring counties, and California wines.

Because of the prominent international influence, you can expect to find Spanish and Mexican cuisines (they are different) competing for diners' attention with Chinese, French, and German food. You'll also discover Russian, Indian, Vietnamese, Italian, Korean, Filipino, Japanese, Greek, and Scandinavian menus.

Chinese cooking is in a class of its own; selection is the problem. Most is Cantonese, predominantly steamed and stir-fried foods, lightly seasoned. You'll notice the crisp vegetables. Sauces are light and delicate. Mandarin and Szechwan dishes are more highly spiced (sometimes volcanically) and usually stir-fried. Wine is often used in cooking.

Don't go to a Japanese restaurant with a hole in your sock, for you may be asked to remove your shoes. You may find yourself seated on the floor in order to eat from a traditionally low Japanese table, and your food might be cooked at the table. Your waitress will probably wear the traditional Japanese kimono.

Plunge right in and try *sushi* (a combination of rice with an endless variety of fillings). *Sukiyaki* is best known, but try *sashimi, tempura,* or *teriyaki. Saki* (the Japanese wine) is served warm.

Italian food is a never-ending series of courses. Go easy on each dish—otherwise, after antipasto, soup, salad, and pasta, you may find it difficult to eat your entrée.

French cooking needs little introduction. It's done imaginatively in San Francisco, where some of the most elegant restaurants feature French cuisine. Ask your waiter for house specialties.

Basque food centers around lamb. You'll probably eat boarding-house style with community serving dishes. A bottle of wine is served for every four people, and a bowl of fruit is your dessert.

Armenian, Jewish, Swiss, and Indian fare are only a sampling of the additional around-the-world discoveries in the city. Finally, you might want to end a meal at a coffee house, sipping an Italian *cappuccino* or an Irish coffee—both popular in San Francisco.

Many visitors to the San Francisco Bay area find Marin County the surprise treat of their visit. Marin's bay side is one of the most photogenic shorelines in California. Two ridges project like stubby fingers, forming a narrow horseshoe that encloses shallow Richardson Bay. The main Marin peninsula, with Mount Tamalpais in the background, faces across this small bay to the Tiburon peninsula and the low, offshore pyramid of Angel Island. Sausalito and Tiburon offer unusual shops, good restaurants, and lots of bay and boat watching. These two waterside centers have long been known as gathering places for artists, sailors, anglers, commuters, and visitors.

Across the Bay Bridge, crowded into a narrow strip between the water of San Francisco Bay and the low hills that rise to the east, the East Bay communities parallel the shoreline.

East Bay's attractions are plentiful. Discover Lake Merritt (in the heart of Oakland), handsome Oakland Museum, fine waterfront restaurants, California's largest university, and some of the state's finest parks.

The narrow belt of land south of San Francisco is divided into two distinctly different regions by a forested ridge of mountains that runs down its length. The bay side of the mountains is crowded with cities; the ocean side is sprinkled with peaceful farms, unspoiled beaches, and lightly traveled country roads.

Marin-on-the-bay

Sausalito is a hill town; Tiburon includes 10 square miles of salt water; Belvedere was once an island. But you catch only tantalizing glimpses of these bayside areas from U.S. Highway 101. For a real look, you must follow the slow roads along the shore east of the freeway. To absorb the special flavor of the Marin County communities, you'll want to browse through charming shops, stop at a seaside café, or stroll past harbors and nearby chandleries.

Sausalito's Mediterranean pleasures

Sausalito's setting has the quality of a southern European seacoast village. Its harbors are full of small vessels of varied sizes and shapes; its hillside-hung homes recall those of the Italian Riviera. Shops and restaurants are concentrated at the water's edge.

Before the time of the Golden Gate Bridge, Sausalito was the transfer point for Marin commuters. They came this far south by train and went on to San Francisco by ferry. These services stopped in 1937 with the completion of the bridge; however, commuter service has been revived. Modern ferries operate from the foot of Anchor Street.

Across the Golden Gate, North Bay seaside villages lure artists, sailors, and visitors. Windswept cliffs, virgin redwoods, stately mountains, and deer-dotted islands invite outdoor enthusiasts. East Bay discoveries include Oakland's downtown lake, a handsome museum, and next-door parks. Berkeley boasts California's largest university. South, along the peninsula, you'll find the way to San Jose, Stanford, amusement parks, and delightful foothill communities. Santa Cruz is ringed by mountains and a string of sparkling state beaches.

SEASIDE SAUSALITO hugs Richardson Bay at southern end of Marin County. Bridgeway, town's waterfront street, leads past shops and restaurants.

A short distance north of the Golden Gate Bridge, the road to Sausalito (Alexander exit) branches to the east. As you descend you have superb views of Raccoon Straits and Angel Island. Then the road drops, with abrupt turns, to Bridgeway, the waterfront main street of Sausalito. Along the way you'll get your first good look at the stair-stepped hill houses rising above you.

You can get a good view of the Sausalito terrain and the bay from the dining deck of the historic Alta Mira Hotel on Bulkley Avenue.

Sausalito is a town of small shops. The most complicated (and varied) shopping place is The Village Fair on Bridgeway not far from Plaza Viña del Mar. On its different levels are about 40 small specialty shops, some of which contain handcrafted goods and imports from Europe, Mexico, and India.

A walk south from The Village Fair along both sides of Bridgeway reveals one small shop after another, usually in refurbished, colorfully painted buildings. At the south end of town is a pier supporting several restaurants and a parking lot. From here, you get a marvelous view of Richardson Bay and San Francisco.

At the north end of town, on Bridgeway, is a curious industrial and maritime wasteland dotted with railroad remnants, ship hulls, abandoned shipways, old buildings, and scraps of roadways. Here, too, is the colorful and controversial houseboat community.

Turn to Tiburon

Tiburon sits on the shores of Richardson Bay, directly opposite Sausalito. To reach Tiburon, take U.S. 101 north from Sausalito to the Tiburon exit.

About a mile east of U.S. 101 on Tiburon Boulevard, watch for a handsome old Victorian (the Lyford House) standing off to the right in a cypress grove. This is headquarters for the 800-acre Richardson Bay Wildlife Sanctuary managed by the Audubon Society. About 8,000 birds are residents; as many as 30,000 more may stop by at peak migratory seasons. The sanctuary is open to visitors Wednesday through Sunday from 9 A.M. to 5 P.M., except holidays. The Lyford House is open Sundays from 1 to 4 P.M., September through June. Guided nature walks take place Sunday mornings at 9. There is a slight visitor charge.

Follow Tiburon Boulevard to the water and park in one of several parking areas. Main Street's first block is Tiburon's downtown: shoulder-to-shoulder shops, art galleries, and waterside restaurants.

Old St. Hilary's Church and Wildflower Garden on Esperanza Street is a good example of carpenter's Gothic; it's open from 1 to 4 P.M. Sunday and Wednesday, April through September. Beach Road will take you over Belvedere Lagoon past the yacht club and the old, shingled headquarters of the Belvedere Land Company, in business since 1889.

Commuters ferry from Tiburon to San Francisco (Ferry Building) during the working week. Ferries also operate between San Francisco, Angel Island, and Tiburon daily during the summer; weekends and holidays the rest of the year. For information call the Red and White Fleet (415) 546-2810.

Roaming through Marin

Small towns are grouped near Marin County's main north-south thoroughfare—U.S. 101. Many lodge in canyons west of the highway. San Rafael extends down to the bay, and you can take a bridge across the bay to Richmond, on its east side.

Mill Valley got its name from a historic saw mill which still stands in skeleton form. The charming public square in the center of town evokes memories of England. From here you can see the meandering streets and the steeply gabled roofs of lovely homes tucked in the hills surrounding the town. At the botanical gardens on Edgewood Avenue, you walk among native California plants in a natural environment.

Marin's most traveled east-west road is Sir Francis Drake Boulevard. Starting from its junction with State Highway 17 just west of the Richmond-San Rafael Bridge, it threads its way from U.S. 101 west to the Point Reyes Peninsula. Along its route you'll pass the towns of Ross, a treasury of stately homes with an Art and Garden Center, and San Anselmo, once the junction for railroad lines throughout Marin. Like a medieval French castle, the San Francisco Theological Seminary dominates the southern hillside. Near Fairfax, to the west, are the lovely lakes of Bon Tempe, Lagunitas, Alpine, and Phoenix—ideal for picnicking, hiking, and horseback riding.

In San Rafael you'll find a replica of Mission San Rafael Archangel, founded in 1817; Boyd Park and Museum; the Marin Historical Society Museum; and to the east, on San Pablo Bay, a fishing village and swimming beach.

Nestled in a group of hills just north of San Rafael is the imaginative, domed Marin County Civic Center, designed by Frank Lloyd Wright. It's open daily and there's no charge to look around. Here, also, stands the Veterans' Memorial Auditorium-Theater, a center for performing arts.

Situated in the rolling hills of northern Marin County, Novato's residential areas belie its early Spanish settlers. Nine miles west of Novato is the Marin French Cheese Company, a good place to watch cheese being made on weekday mornings, when the factory is busiest. Tours are given daily; call (707) 762-6001 for information.

Each fall the Renaissance Pleasure Faire, an Elizabethan festival, is held on the meadows south of State Highway 37. At this replica of an English country fair, you'll find food, drink, crafts, and entertainment—both on stage and off. For information, write to Renaissance Pleasure Faire, P.O. Box B, Novato, CA 94947.

High to low: Marin's parks

Ranging from an island in the bay to one of the bay area's tallest peaks, Marin's parks are a varied lot. Marin, curiously, has greater extremes of climate than the counties farther north, principally because Mount Tamalpais and the high ridges leading up to it form a sharp barrier against sea fogs.

Marin Headlands—a bay view

Minutes north of San Francisco lie the Marin Headlands, now part of the Golden Gate National Recreation Area. Plummeting from bare-crested hills into deep water all along its length, the westerly section of Marin Headlands stretches from the Golden Gate Bridge to Point Bonita. Here you'll find protected coastal valleys, windswept beaches, former army forts, abandoned artillery bunkers, and magnificent views of San Francisco, the Golden Gate Bridge, and the Pacific Ocean.

If you seek solitude—take a hike. The Miwok, Coast, and Tennessee Valley trails begin in the headlands and traverse the coastal hills. Rodeo Beach and Kirby Cove offer fine grounds for a group outing or family picnic. These beaches afford sweeping ocean views, but their waters are not safe for swimming.

The Marin Headlands Hostel, situated off Fort Barry Parade Grounds, offers day and overnight facilities for a slight fee.

Point Bonita Light Station perches on the eroding tip of the Golden Gate's north side. A prime weather station and warning point for the bay, it's a reliable gauge of the comings and goings of the summer fog bank. The first sounding device installed here in 1856 to help befogged mariners was an army sergeant, charged with firing a muzzle-loading cannon at half-hour intervals whenever the weather demanded. At the end of 2 months, he was exhausted and had to petition for relief. An unearthly electronic racket does the job now. Once closed to visitors, the light station plans to open for touring. Call (415) 561-7612 for information.

Fort Cronkhite is the outermost of three sentinel forts on the north side of San Francisco Bay. Reasons for visiting are several: rockhounds roam Cronkhite's gravelly shore in search of jadeite and jasper, especially in winter; the summer crowd comes to bask in the lee of bluffs that offer some protection from the prevailing westerlies; and people who like to watch seabirds fly have a superior arena.

Though no public transportation provides service to the headlands area, it is easily accessible by car. Immediately north of the Golden Gate Bridge, take the Alexander Avenue exit off U.S. 101. Two entrances are available: one over Conzelman Road along the coastal cliffs, and one through the tunnel into Rodeo Valley. Watch the signs carefully or you may end up heading back across the bridge. From the north take the last (unmarked) exit to your right before crossing the bridge.

Angel Island State Park

Part of the fun of going to Angel Island is the way you get there. A tour boat of the Red & White Fleet (pier 43½) at San Francisco's Fisherman's Wharf or ferry service from Tiburon or Berkeley (summer only) will deliver you to the island in the morning and pick you up in the afternoon. Or you can make the trip in a private boat.

At Ayala Cove, the entrance to Angel Island, you'll find picnic facilities, beaches for sunning (no swimming is allowed), and a grassy softball field. Bike rentals are available (summer only), or you can take along your own. You'll find posted maps of hiking trails. If you take the sightseeing tour of the island, you'll pass through former military installations.

Mount Tamalpais—for the view

"Mount Tam" is the keystone of four park units that have common boundaries. A finger reaches down to sea level at Muir Beach, but the main body of the park drapes across the upper slopes of the 2,571-foot mountain. You'll find a labyrinth of hiking and equine trails.

Picnic grounds are at the Bootjack area on Panoramic Highway leading up from Mill Valley, near the park headquarters; campsites are at Pan Toll and still higher at East Peak. The large parking area at East Peak is as far as cars can go. Paths lead up the last couple of hundred feet to the summit.

For campers: Pan Toll Campground, with unimproved sites a short stroll beyond the parking area, is heavily booked from spring through autumn.

(Continued on next page)

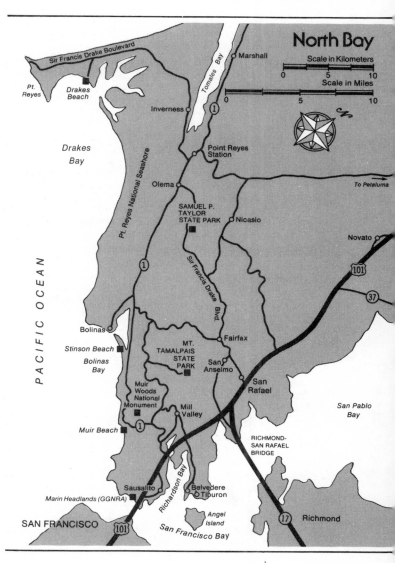

. . . Continued from page 37

For hikers: Trails offer endless variety of terrain and distance. You can pick up a trail map at park headquarters; trails are clearly posted and well groomed.

Muir Woods: Closest redwoods to San Francisco

Always cool and green, the 502-acre national monument named for naturalist John Muir preserves a stand of virgin coast redwoods (*Sequoia sempervirens*) at the foot of Mount Tamalpais.

For a leisurely walk, follow the ½-mile, sign-guided Bootjack Trail. Redwoods and Douglas fir tower above the forest floor. You will also find tanoak, alder, buckeye, and California laurel, from which one type of bay leaf finds its way into spice jars.

The central part of the park and most of its paths are on a relatively level stretch of forest floor. If you want to do some exploring off the main trail, consider the two trails that climb high up the canyon wall to lookout points and a panoramic view to either side of the Golden Gate.

Muir Woods, part of the Golden Gate National Recreation Area, is open daily during daylight hours. No camping or picnicking is allowed.

You can reach the woods by way of State 1 and the Panoramic Highway. The road into the park, like all those flanking Mount Tamalpais, is narrow and winds tortuously up the long grade from sea level.

Oakland: East Bay's major city

Though Oakland's "big city" reputation may not equal San Francisco's, some Oakland attractions can match, or even exceed, those of its fabled sister.

The third largest city in Northern California, Oakland is an important industrial center with the second largest Pacific Coast shipping port. The city prides itself on its recreation areas, international airport, impressive sports complex, and exceptional museum. Here, too, is the headquarters of BART—the Bay Area Rapid Transit system. Berkeley, also on this side of the bay, contains California's largest university, plus some of the Bay Area's finest parks.

For an overall view of the Oakland area (including the nearby cities of Alameda, Piedmont, and Berkeley), take a narrated bus tour, operating between Memorial Day and Labor Day. The 2½-hour ride begins at Jack London Square daily (except Monday) at 1 P.M.

Knowledgeable volunteers offer free walking tours through Oakland's landmark areas Wednesday and Saturday afternoons. Call (415) 273-3234 or 273-3831 for information. To explore the area yourself by car, follow the bright blue "Scenic Tour Oakland" signs, starting with Jack London Square.

For additional information, write to the Oakland Convention and Visitors Bureau, 1830 Broadway, Suite 1105, Oakland, CA 94612, or call (415) 839-9000.

Riding BART is an experience for everyone. Moving from underground stations to elevated tracks, shining BART cars streak from Richmond and Concord on the north to Fremont on the south, and underneath the bay through San Francisco to Daly City. Visit BART Headquarters (800 Madison Street) for a route map.

Oakland's International Airport, within minutes of downtown, is served by interstate and major U.S. carriers. Limousine and bus service is available to Berkeley, downtown Oakland, and San Francisco.

The Port of Oakland, Northern California's leading shipping center, is the country's largest container port. It's fun to drive through this beehive of activity and watch cargo from all over the world being unloaded. The new 140-acre Seventh Street Terminal is probably the easiest to reach, though you can watch the ships pass in and out of the Oakland Estuary from Jack London Square.

Each Thursday, from April through September, the Port of Oakland offers harbor boat tours. Leaving from Jack London Square four times each Thursday, the 1½-hour tours are free; for reservations call (415) 444-3188.

Downtown Oakland

Oakland is getting a face-lift. Construction has already started on a 14-acre, multimillion-dollar complex—Chinatown/Hong Kong USA—with shopping arcades, high-rise towers, and a hotel. Another area, Victorian Row, will house boutiques, offices, and restaurants in a 2-block area of refurbished old homes.

A favorite recreation spot for Oakland and other East Bay residents, Lake Merritt is a 155-acre body of salt water right in the heart of the city. The Y-shaped lake is encircled by a 122-acre park strip and a main thoroughfare. Green lawns and cool shade greet you as you turn off Grand Avenue and enter Lakeside Park to sample its variety of activities.

The oldest waterfowl refuge in the country is an area on the northeast arm of the lake. The refuge was set aside in 1870 for the protection of the ducks and other waterfowl that flock to the lake. Between November and April, the bird count here may climb as high as 5,000. You can buy a bag of grain and feed the birds, or watch them any day at 3:30 P.M. being fed by park naturalists.

The Camron-Stanford House, an Oakland landmark at 1418 Lakeside Drive, is the last Victorian on the shore of Lake Merritt. Built in 1876 for $15,000, it later served as the Oakland Public Museum for 57 years. When the new museum opened, the stately Victorian was painstakingly restored as an example of ornate Victorian design and lifestyle. You can tour the building Sunday from 1 to 5 P.M., and Wednesday from 11 A.M. to 4 P.M. Docents provide detailed descriptions.

Other activities around the lake include a children's fairyland, gardens, lawn bowling and putting greens, summer band concerts, and boating facilities. The sailboat clubhouse near the wildlife refuge has launching ramps for sailboats and motorboats. On the west shore of Lake Merritt is the main boathouse, where you can rent canoes, rowboats, and sailboats. Launch trips around the lake leave at frequent intervals during the day.

QUEEN QUAFFS *goblet of mead (right) at Renaissance Pleasure Faire. Each year costumed "royalty" and visitors imbibe Elizabethan music and merriment in Marin countryside.*

WINDSWEPT HILLS, *plummeting cliffs, steel blue waters welcome day hikers to wildly beautiful Marin Headlands (below). Just north of Golden Gate and cosmopolitan San Francisco, these open, rugged lands are a protected part of Golden Gate National Recreation Area.*

For excitement, try Oakland's museum

Oakland's handsome museum covers four square blocks alongside and beneath an evergreen park. The three-tiered complex is constructed so that the roof of each level becomes a garden and terrace for the one above. To enter the museum at 10th and Fallon streets, on the south shore of Lake Merritt, you walk down, not up.

The basic concept of the museum is not only intriguing but, in many ways, unique. Three different disciplines—history, natural science, and art—are combined in one museum displaying its treasures as environments. In the Cowell Hall of California History, you'll see actual rooms—kitchens, parlors, offices out of the past—or vivid displays suggesting a historical period, such as the time of an election campaign, the Gold Rush era, or the 1906 earthquake. Visitors to the Natural Sciences gallery take a simulated walk across California's eight biotic zones re-created through imaginative lifelike exhibits.

The museum is open daily except Monday; admission is free. There's parking beneath the museum, which is located at 10th and Oak streets, one block from the Lake Merritt BART station. For recorded information, call (415) 834-2413

Pause for history at Jack London Square

Oakland's waterfront, the birthplace of the city, begins at historic Jack London Square, a 10-block area located on the Oakland Estuary at the foot of Broadway. Here, around landscaped malls, are shipping wharves, marina docks, restaurants, and shops.

Of special interest is the First and Last Chance Saloon, a weathered and rustic old building located on the edge of the square at 50 Webster Street. Built in 1880 from the remains of a whaling ship, the building was first a bunkhouse for oystermen and later a saloon. A favorite boyhood hangout of California author Jack London, the saloon is filled with photos and mementos of the era. It's open from 1 P.M. to 2 A.M. daily except Sunday. Ask the bartender about its history.

Oakland sports complex

The Oakland-Alameda County Coliseum complex is two separate circular structures—an outdoor stadium and an indoor arena. At the outdoor stadium you can watch professional baseball; in the arena, ice hockey, basketball, stage shows, and civic and cultural activities take place. The coliseum complex is well designed—every seat is comfortable and provides a good view. Adjacent to the arena floor is an exhibit hall for trade, boat, home, and car shows.

The coliseum is just east of the Nimitz Freeway. Take the Hegenberger or 66th Avenue exit to the spacious parking lot, or take BART to the Coliseum station.

Knowland Park: home of the zoo

Animals—real ones and sculptured ones—welcome visitors to the Oakland Zoo, located in Knowland Park. One observation point allows you to look a Bengal tiger right

in the eye. From across a narrow moat, you can toss peanuts to Malaysian sun bears. Children are welcome to pick up goat kids and piglets and to pet a baby llama.

To reach the zoo, take the Golf Links Road turnoff from MacArthur Freeway (Interstate Highway 580).

A look at Victorians

Many of the Oakland area's old homes are dilapidated, and many have been torn down, but a few choice examples of Victoriana remain.

Dunsmuir House, in southern Oakland, is a notable product of Victorian wealth and taste. The 37-room estate cost a cool $350,000 in 1899. The house and its 48-acre grounds are open to the public on Sundays from noon to 4 P.M. Golden Gate Park designer John McLaren did the landscaping; that alone is worth a visit. The house is located at 2960 Peralta Oaks Court; there's a nominal admission charge.

The McConaghy Estate, just south of Oakland in Hayward, looks much as it did in 1886. The 93-year-old farmhouse estate, authentically renovated and refurbished, is now open for touring Thursday through Sunday from 1 to 4 P.M. for a slight admission fee. The McConaghy Estate is about ½-mile west of State 17 at 18701 Hesperian Boulevard (next to J. F. Kennedy Park); it is also served by the A.C. Transit bus service.

More visual treats around town

A few other buildings deserve at least a "pass-by." The Paramount Theatre of the Arts (2025 Broadway) was an opulent movie palace in the 1930s. Carefully restored, it is now a center for concerts, as well as symphony and ballet performances. On the 4700 block of Lincoln Avenue are two architectural treasures: the Mormon Temple and the Greek Orthodox Church. For a parkside stop, visit the Morcom Rose Garden at Jean Street off Grand Avenue. And for stargazing, ascend Mountain Boulevard to the Chabot Science Center on Friday or Saturday evening for a 7:30 show (small admission charge).

Berkeley backs up to a university

Dating back to the 1800s, Berkeley achieves its fame and notoriety from one of the world's largest educational institutions—the University of California. It's an inviting place to park your car and walk around. Telegraph Avenue, just south of the campus, has a 4-block stretch (between Bancroft and Dwight ways) where street artists and skilled artisans display their wares.

University of California—Bear country

The University of California's Berkeley campus—some 1,232 acres of it—spreads up into the hills and surrounds sections of the town. University buildings, espe-

cially Sather Tower (the Campanile), punctuate the landscape.

For a magnificent view of the campus, the whole East Bay area, and San Francisco across the water, take the elevator 175 feet up the 307 foot Campanile, then climb 25 feet to the observation tower. Open daily between 10 A.M. and 4:15 P.M., the ride costs 10 cents—just as it did in 1923.

To take a walking tour of the campus, pick up a self-guided tour map outlining the nearly 2-mile walk (about 1½ hours) at the Visitor Center in the Student Union at the end of Telegraph Avenue. Escorted tours leave there at 1 P.M. on weekdays.

You'll want to see the California Memorial Stadium (seating capacity: over 76,000) where the Golden Bear football team plays out its fall schedule; pace across the 133-foot stage of the Greek Theatre, a beautiful amphitheater presented to the university by Phoebe Appersen Hearst in 1903; linger on the footbridges that cross Strawberry Creek, a thin stream that becomes fairly boisterous after the first rains; and visit the Botanical Garden (located near the stadium in Strawberry Canyon), a 30-acre tract of more than 8,000 different plants, including rare rhododendrons, cacti, and succulents.

One architectural highlight is the university's art museum: a sculpture in itself with its jutting balconies, staggered levels, interesting angles, open galleries, and ramps—all arranged around an open central gallery. Museum hours are 11 A.M. to 5 P.M. Wednesday through Sunday (closed Monday and Tuesday); admission is free. Three floors of prehistoric animals and fossils fill the Museum of Paleontology; the Lowie Museum of Anthropology rotates exhibits depicting the life of man; and the Bancroft Library displays paintings of 18th and 19th century California life.

Lawrence Hall of Science, built as a research facility for science education, has exhibit areas housing dozens of colorful, do-it-yourself displays demonstrating scientific principles on a child's level. Youngsters operate complex electronic equipment and control preprogrammed experiments. Open daily, the complex is on North Canyon Road, reached from Gayley Road on the east side of the campus or from Grizzly Peak Boulevard, a scenic route that follows the crest of the East Bay hills. There's a moderate admission charge.

Berkeley's performing arts

If you're an avid theatergoer, you'll enjoy the intimate atmosphere and the professional excellence of the Berkeley Repertory Theatre. Now entering its 13th season, the nationally recognized company takes the stage in a brand-new, 400-seat house at 2025 Addison Street off Shattuck. Each year the company offers two seasons—fall and summer—featuring anything from classical *Hamlet* to new works like *Dracula, A Musical Nightmare*. Tickets are in the $5 to $10 range, depending on the night; for information call (415) 845-4700.

From early July to late September enjoy Shakespeare under the stars at the Berkeley Shakespeare Festival (now in its seventh season) in John Hinkel Park on

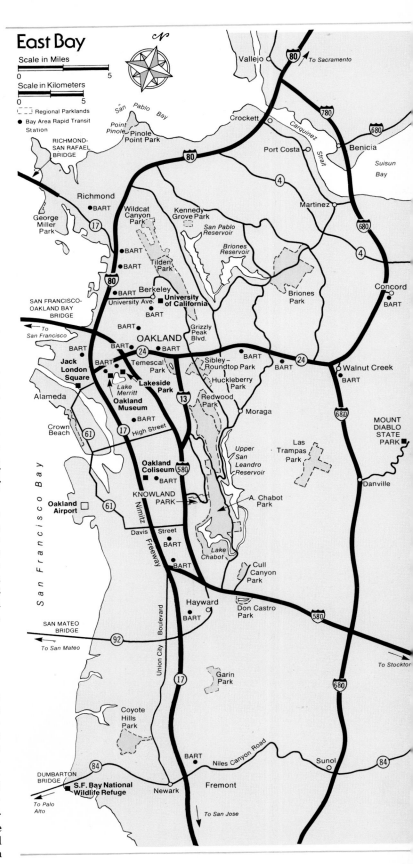

STUDENTS FLOOD SPROUL PLAZA on
noontime break at U.C. Berkeley (above). Sather
Gate and Campanile are familiar landmarks
at California's largest university campus.

OVER OAKLAND MUSEUM ROOF spills
a terraced hillside park (left), open to three
gallery levels and linked by wide stairway
to courtyard below.

Southampton Road off Arlington Avenue. For schedule information call (415) 845-0303.

Berkeley Stage Company, now over 5 years old, offers experimental works at their theater at 1111 Addison Street. For schedule and ticket information call (415) 548-4728.

East Bay parks

In the low hills that rise behind the East Bay cities, 51,600 acres of beautiful countryside have been set aside for recreational use. About 4,600 acres of San Francisco Bay beach and swampland in Alameda and Contra Costa counties have also been incorporated into the East Bay Regional Park System. Some of the parks are small, some large; some are highly developed, some relatively untouched and primitive. Many miles of hiking and bridle trails lead through unspoiled woods and fields. Picnicking, swimming, fishing, boating, and archery are offered at most of the parks, which are primarily designed for daytime use. Three areas allow overnight camping.

Parks of particular interest are Tilden (Environmental Education Center, model railway, Little Farm, merry-go-round, golf course), Temescal (one of seven East Bay parks that offers swimming, picnicking, hiking, fishing), Redwood (redwood groves, heated outdoor swimming pool at Roberts Area), Chabot (marina, horse rental, overnight camping), Crown (beachcombing, annual sandcastle contest), Point Pinole (bicycling, hiking, fishing from 1,225-foot pier in San Pablo Bay), Shadow Cliffs (swimming), Coyote Hills (ancient Indian shellmounds, nature programs, bicycling), and Black Diamond Mines (historical area).

For detailed information and a free brochure on all the parks in the region, write to the East Bay Regional Park District, 11500 Skyline Boulevard, Oakland, CA 94619.

A new wildlife refuge

Fringing the levees that stretch along the south end of San Francisco Bay is the recently established 23,000-acre San Francisco Bay National Wildlife Refuge.

An interpretive center at the refuge headquarters in Fremont near the Dumbarton Bridge toll plaza is open Wednesday through Sunday, 10 A.M. to 5 P.M. A trail overlooking the salt marsh and diked ponds encircles the refuge headquarters hill. For schedule information on nature walks, film programs, and slide presentations, call (415) 792-0222.

Up Mount Diablo

Mount Diablo's summit provides exceptionally fine views. On a clear day you can see the Sierra, Mount Lassen, San Francisco, and the inland waterways of the Central Valley. Because such an expanse of California is visible, Mount Diablo has been the surveying point for Northern and Central California since 1851.

Diablo's main peak is only 3,849 feet in elevation; however, it seems higher because it rises so abruptly. Occasionally during the winter the conical peak gets a coating of snow.

A state park covers a portion of the area with 80 campsites, group camping facilities, and about 250 picnic sites. You'll find a number of good hiking trails. The park is open all year; day-use hours are 8 A.M. until dark. You can reach Mount Diablo from Interstate 680 at Danville.

Along the Carquinez Straits

Seen from the Carquinez Straits, Port Costa is just a tuck in the rolling Contra Costa hills. Yet from the late 19th century to the early 1930s, this town of 300 people was one of the West's busiest grain-shipping ports. To save the town from encroaching decay, a community redevelopment effort began in the 1960s. No longer a gallimaufry of deserted docks and abandoned structures, Port Costa now offers a charming new face. Around Main Street you'll find an ornately refurbished hotel, antique shops in restored shipping docks, and boutiques and restaurants in converted warehouses.

To reach Port Costa take the Crockett exit off Interstate 80. It's a 3-mile drive south of Carquinez Bridge.

At Martinez, east of Port Costa, is the John Muir Historic Site. You can follow Pomona Street from Port Costa or take Interstate 80 to State Highway 4. Follow State 4 to Alhambra Avenue and turn left under the overpass. The John Muir home is about 100 yards beyond the overpass to the left.

Tours of the house start every hour from 1 to 4 P.M., Wednesday through Sunday. There's a small admission charge for visitors over 15 years of age.

Across the strait is Benicia, California's state capital in 1853-54. Once a thriving port, today it is quiet. Many of its weathered buildings house antique shops. The two-story State Capitol Building (built in 1852), still stands, now restored as a state historic park.

The Benicia Chamber of Commerce (737 1st Street), open weekdays, has maps and a walking-tour booklet.

The Peninsula

Geographically, Palo Alto lies at the end of the San Francisco Peninsula, but the cities of Mountain View, Los Altos, Sunnyvale, Santa Clara, and San Jose—though farther south—are generally considered part of this south-peninsula region. At the southern tip of the bay, this area is the scene of heavy industry. Moffett Naval Air Station is located here, along with many electronics firms, chemical companies, and a variety of large and small businesses.

Several main routes run down the peninsula from San Francisco, so you can actually drive to the southern tip of the bay without encountering a single stop light. State Highway 1 skirts the ocean, Skyline Boulevard (State Highway 35) follows the ridge of the mountains, and Junipero Serra Freeway (Interstate 280) runs along the east side of the mountain spine. The Bayshore Freeway (U.S. 101) and El Camino Real (State Highway 82) pass through population centers that edge the bay.

Traveling the Bayshore

There are many highlights on the peninsula and the Bayshore Freeway provides rapid access to them.

Candlestick Park is a stadium that huddles along the edge of Candlestick Point, on the bay side of the freeway, 8 miles south of San Francisco. The stadium is in use almost all year: the San Francisco Giants play baseball from mid-April to late September, and the San Francisco '49ers play football from September to December.

The Rod McLellan Company, the world's largest hybrid orchid grower, offers daily tours at 10:30 A.M. and 1:30 P.M. You'll see scientific labs and lush tropical grounds at the headquarters at 1450 El Camino Real in South San Francisco.

The Cow Palace, a huge, strangely named sports arena, is on Geneva Avenue in Daly City. This is the site of the Grand National livestock exposition, horse show, and rodeo—an event that draws large crowds every fall. You can also attend basketball games, circuses, prize fights, big conventions, and concerts in its vast arena.

San Francisco International Airport spreads along the edge of the bay east of the highway near San Bruno. Three terminals accommodate over 20 million air travelers who pass through the airport annually.

Bay Meadows Race Track, next to Bayshore Freeway in San Mateo, is where horses compete 200 racing days a year. Times and admission vary according to type of racing. Call (415) 345-1661 for information.

Allied Arts Guild, at Arbor Road and Creek Drive in Menlo Park, offers a glimpse of the early, more leisurely Spanish California. The 3½-acre site is part of the once-vast Spanish land grant, El Rancho de las Pulgas (Ranch of the Fleas). The barn and sheep sheds of the old ranch still stand but now house crafts shops. Buildings containing a variety of shops preserve the Spanish Colonial theme of the original ranch. The dining room opens at noon for luncheon; tea is served from 3 until 4:30 P.M. Reservations are advised; call (415) 324-2588.

Sunset Magazine and Books (Lane Publishing Company), in Menlo Park, welcomes visitors to its editorial and business offices. The two buildings are located at Willow and Middlefield roads (between Bayshore Freeway and El Camino Real). Hostesses offer conducted tours Monday through Friday at 10:30 and 11:30 A.M. and 1, 2, and 3 P.M. You will see the kitchen where recipes are tested before they are published, and you can stroll through the extensive demonstration gardens of outstanding trees, shrubs, and flowers native to sections of the Pacific Coast.

Ames Research Center, in Mountain View, gives fascinating tours through its large wind tunnel, flight simulation facilities, and flight operations hangar at Moffett Field. Tours are offered by reservation only; phone (415) 965-6497 for information.

Stanford University—the elegant "Farm"

University Avenue, Palo Alto's main street, crosses El Camino Real on an overpass southeast of Menlo Park. West of El Camino Real, University becomes Palm Drive, the approach to Stanford.

At the entrance of the Quadrangle at the end of Palm Drive, the Stanford Guide Service Information Center has an assortment of maps (one outlines a tour of the campus) and descriptive material. The center is open daily from 10 A.M. to 4 P.M. Guided tours leave daily at 11 A.M. and 2 P.M. from the center.

An easily visible campus landmark is the 285-foot tower of the Hoover Institution of War, Revolution, and Peace. An elevator goes to the top where you get a visual orientation of the campus. Call (415) 497-2053 for hours.

You'll want to see the Memorial Church, dedicated in 1903 and completely rebuilt after the 1906 earthquake. The large, ornate church is decorated with Venetian mosaics, most striking of which are reproductions of "The Sermon on the Mount" on the front façade and Rosselli's "Last Supper" in the chancel. Unless services are in progress, the church is open to visitors from 10 A.M. to 5 P.M. daily.

Located on Lomita Drive and Museum Way, northeast of the Medical Center, is the Stanford University Museum of Art. Among the museum's permanent exhibits are galleries of ancient Oriental, Egyptian, and primitive art, baroque paintings, and early Californiana. Of particular interest are an extensive Rodin collection, and the Stanford Collection, with exhibits of family photographs and paintings, Leland Stanford Jr.'s boyhood collection of toys and artifacts, and other memorabilia. Hours are weekdays (except Mondays) from 10 A.M. to 4:45 P.M., weekends from 1 to 4:45 P.M. Admission is free.

San Jose: A growing city on the bay

One of the nation's fastest-growing cities, San Jose was founded in 1777 with a population of 66. It remained a small town, taking a back seat to San Francisco, until the early 1950s when industry moved in.

The San Jose/Santa Clara Valley Information Center, conveniently located near the San Jose Municipal Airport, is a helpful guide to the area's attractions. Roadside signs direct travelers to the center (1788 Technology Drive), at the convergence of U.S. 101 and State 17, near Brokaw Road.

The center is open daily, 9 A.M. to dusk, May to September; and 11 A.M. to 5 P.M. weekdays, 9 A.M. to 5 P.M. weekends, during the rest of the year.

For a recorded message on what to do and see in the San Jose area call (408) 293-4678, or write to the San Jose Visitors Bureau, 1 Paseo de San Antonio, San Jose, CA 95113.

FunBus Sightseeing Tours offer individual and group trips to major points of interest in the Santa Clara

Valley. Tours operate daily, except Christmas, and leave from the FunBus terminal at the information center. Pickups at major hotels in the area can be arranged; reservations are suggested. For more information, call (408) 279-3336.

Downtown San Jose—a changing scene

If you have not been to San Jose recently, you're in for a surprise. With the help of a major urban renewal program, this city—more than 200 years old—is blossoming into a pleasant mélange of old and new. An exciting center of performing arts and a new convention center serve as the cultural anchor for the downtown renaissance. Park Center Financial Plaza, Paseo de San Antonio mall, and nearby San Jose State University attest to continuing commitment to downtown development.

The new engenders a growing respect for the old. The Chamber of Commerce offers a self-guided, history walk past some of downtown's architectural treasures. Included are the Peralta Adobe (San Jose's oldest building), a handsome Romanesque-revival building now housing the city's art museum; the site where A.P. Giannini, Bank of America founder, was born; and the multidomed St. Joseph's Catholic Church, now over 100 years old.

The Center of Performing Arts, designed by Frank Lloyd Wright's Taliesen West Foundation, brings theater, music, and dance into the heart of San Jose. The 2700-seat theater with its bold stucco façade is home of the San Jose Symphony, the San Jose Civic Light Opera, and the stage for visiting performing arts companies. The center is located at 225 Alamaden Boulevard between San Carlos Street and Park Avenue.

Paseo de San Antonio offers a green space for walkers, sitters, and picnickers. A stroll along the 3-block, brick-paved pedestrian mall (between Market and 3rd streets) reveals grassy knolls, fountains, sculpture, and outdoor cafés.

Parks and gardens are sprinkled throughout the San Jose area. Visitors can smell the roses, peer at animals, meditate in a temple, or hike through a rugged canyon. Children enjoy Kelley Park with 150 acres of grassy hills and tree-shaded picnic sites. In the park's 2-acre Happy Hollow and Baby Zoo, youngsters can pet and feed small animals and watch bear, tiger, and leopard cubs at play. Also located in the park are the Japanese Friendship Gardens, featuring a teahouse, picturesque footbridges, miniature maple groves, and a pagoda. To reach Kelley Park, take the Story Road exit off U.S. 101 and continue 4 blocks south.

San Jose's museums—from the Old West to Egyptian art

To catch a glimpse of turn-of-the-century San Jose, visit the historical museum. Not a typical museum, this city-run complex consists of ten full-size structures reconstructing the San Jose of the 1890s. Stroll through the restored lobby of the Pacific Hotel, gaze at a 115-foot electric light tower, or stop at Dashaway Stables, where a blacksmith shoes horses. The museum is located at 635 Phelan Avenue near Senter Road.

The San Jose Museum of Art, housed in a state historic landmark at Market and San Fernando streets, is best known for its exhibits of post-War modernists and contemporary American art. Hours are 10 A.M. to 4:30 P.M. Tuesday through Saturday, noon to 4 P.M. on Sunday; admission is free.

The Rosicrucian Egyptian Museum (with an art gallery, library, and planetarium) displays authentic artifacts from Egypt, Babylon, and Assyria. Here you can examine mummies and jewelry, walk through a replica of a pharaoh's tomb, and enjoy the gardens highlighted by an obelisk, a sphinx, and murals. Admission to the museum at 1342 Naglee Avenue is free; there is a charge for planetarium shows.

Around San Jose

A potpourri of attractions in the greater San Jose area includes everything from a mystery house and theme parks to a prestigious observatory, a historic mission, fine wineries, and a bevy of appealing shopping centers.

The Winchester Mystery House, 4 miles west of the city at the Winchester Road exit off Interstate 280, is a state historic landmark. Sarah Winchester, heir to her father-in-law's gun fortune, was an eccentric who believed that if she stopped adding rooms onto her house, she would die. The 160-room house, now refurnished, is a memorial to her obsession. Tours cover 6 acres of Victorian splendor—the house, museum, and extensive gardens—daily from 9 A.M. for a moderate charge.

University of California's Lick Observatory, 20 miles southeast of San Jose, is reached by a winding narrow road that climbs to the summit of 4,209-foot Mount Hamilton. Visitors are welcome every Saturday and Sunday (except national and university holidays) from 1 to 5 P.M. Guide service is provided at no charge. Of particular interest is the 120-inch reflector telescope, the second largest in the world.

Mission Santa Clara de Asis, eighth in the chain of California missions, was founded in 1777 along the banks of the Guadalupe River. After several locations and structures, the present site was selected and the church constructed in 1825. One hundred years later, fire practically destroyed the mission; however, in 1929 a concrete replica was completed.

You'll see a few original remnants: a cross, dating back to the founding, stands in a protective covering of redwood in front of the church; a bell, given by the king of Spain in 1778, still tolls in the tower; and a magnificent crucifix hangs above a side altar. Now part of the campus of the University of Santa Clara (on the Alameda), the mission is open daily.

Wineries are not new to the Santa Clara Valley. Settlers have planted grapes here since the 1800s. Now, of the more than 50 "hidden" wineries in the area, 32 offer tours. You can see how wine is made, question vintners about their wines, and, best of all, test the wines yourself in open tasting rooms. For detailed information on wineries in the area, see the *Sunset* book *Guide to California's Wine Country.*

Shopping is a San Jose pastime. The Santa Clara Valley offers abundant shopping centers ranging from boutiques and specialty shops in settings of early California to a well-patronized flea market.

Over 2 million visitors yearly find their way to The Flea Market at 12000 Berryessa Road off U.S. 101. With its labyrinth of over 1,800 booths, it's a weekend bargain hunter's paradise. The Pruneyard makes shopping easy, with its fountains and open plazas set amidst early California architecture. If you cannot find that "special" gift, try the Eastridge Shopping Center with over 160 stores—the largest enclosed shopping mall in the western United States.

Los Gatos and Saratoga—two foothill charmers

Nestled in the foothills of the Santa Cruz Mountains, the neighboring towns of Los Gatos and Saratoga have a country village charm. Here you'll find good shopping in a variety of tiny boutiques and restaurants, parks for picnics, rambling old houses, and wineries to tour. To reach these attractive towns, take the State 17 turnoff southwest from U.S. 101 in San Jose. Saratoga is 4 miles northwest of Los Gatos.

Old Town Los Gatos is a lively collection of shops, studios, restaurants, and theaters housed in a converted elementary school. Most stores are open Tuesday through Sunday; most restaurants serve lunch and dinner daily. Other galleries and antique stores are scattered around the town's main streets.

Hakone Gardens, tucked into the hills just behind Saratoga, is an unexpected bit of the Orient. Formerly a private garden established in 1917, it is now a city park, open daily from 10 A.M. to dusk. Follow Big Basin Way west about a mile to reach the gardens.

Through the mountains

Skyline Boulevard (State 35) will take you along the mountain spine of the peninsula. Interstate 280 runs just east of the mountains. The Santa Cruz Mountains, a spur of the Coast Range, stretch from the Crystal Springs area to just below Santa Cruz, east of Monterey Bay. Standing 2,000 to 3,000 feet high, these mountains receive heavy rains in the winter, which help to produce the forests of Douglas fir, pine, madrone, maple, alder, bay, and the towering, shadowy redwoods that make this a shady retreat.

Attractions along the way

You'll pass by Crystal Springs Reservoir, which holds the water supply for San Francisco. Toward the southern end of the reservoir, Interstate 280 intersects Cañada Road. If you take Cañada north, you see the Pulgas Water Temple at the southern tip of the reservoir. The temple marks the end of the Hetch Hetchy aqueduct, a 162-mile pipeline that begins at an impoundment on the

Tuolumne River in the northern section of Yosemite National Park. It's a good place for picnicking, strolling, or just watching the waters surge past.

Also on Cañada Road is the Filoli estate (once the Roth estate), an elegant Woodside residence built in 1900. The house, its extensive secluded grounds, and beautiful gardens were given to the National Trust for Historic Preservation. After restoration, the gardens were opened for public viewing. There is a moderate admission fee. For more information, call (415) 366-4640.

Parks farther south include Huddart Park, Sam McDonald Park, San Mateo County Memorial Park, Pescadero Creek County Park, and Portola State Park. All are to the west of Skyline; some have overnight camping.

Where Skyline Boulevard meets Saratoga Gap, a left turn on State 9 will take you to Saratoga, or you can turn right and take State 9 through the San Lorenzo Valley to the coast, where it meets the Coast Highway (State 1) at Santa Cruz. State 9 is the valley's Main Street.

Big Basin Redwoods State Park, the first preserve of redwoods ever set aside as a state park, is today one of the most visited forest parks in California. The Big Basin junction is about 6 miles down State 9 from Skyline; it's 8 miles from the junction to the park.

A trail connects Big Basin with the newer Castle Rock State Park, just south of the junction of state highways 35 and 9.

Take a ride on the Roaring Camp & Big Trees Railroad

One-half mile south of Felton, you can board a steam train at a quaint old depot for a 5-mile-loop trip through thick redwood groves. You can stop over at Bear Mountain for picnicking and hiking and return on a later train.

Steam passenger trains leave Felton daily at 11 A.M., 12:15, 1:30, 2:45, and 4 P.M., June through Labor Day. Trains run daily the rest of the year, except Christmas, on a reduced-run schedule. Fares are moderate.

Roaring Camp trains run right alongside Henry Cowell Redwoods State Park, their whistles the only disquieting note in the cathedral-like stillness of a mature grove of redwoods and Ponderosa pines. The 4,000-acre park has two streams, good for winter steelhead fishing and inviting for summer swimming and wading.

The scenic coast highway

The most picturesque route down the peninsula is State 1. The Coast Highway follows the shoreline closely, staying away from large cities. You won't make good time on this road, but if you enjoy the ocean, beaches, hills, and windswept bluffs, this will be the most enjoyable route.

The San Mateo Coast State Beaches, with headquarters at Half Moon Bay, are a collection of nine beaches

TWIST, TURN, LOOP, AND GLIDE on
roller coaster (above) at Marriott's Great America,
just north of San Jose.

*SANTA CRUZ waterfront (above) attracts Bay
Area residents in summertime. Fish from the
long pier, try deep-sea trolling, or enjoy the beach.*

*FRAMED BY ROLLING HILLS, Stanford University's
Memorial Church (below) exudes scholarly calm.
Church dominates 17-acre quadrangle of sandstone
buildings that forms heart of campus.*

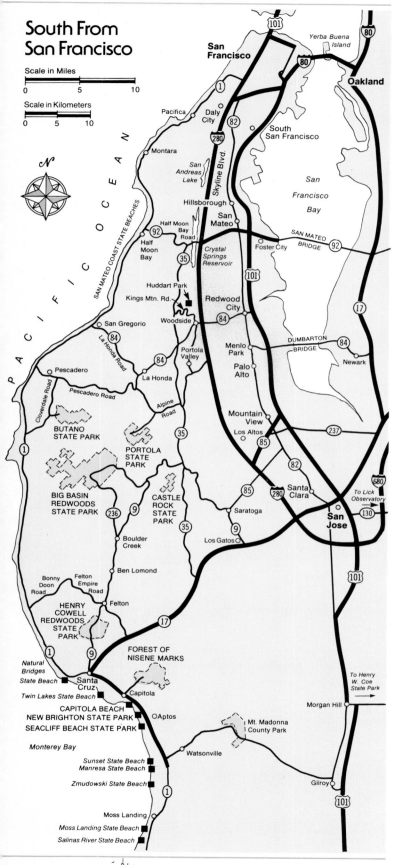

South From San Francisco

Scale in Miles
0   5   10

Scale in Kilometers
0   5   10

scattered along 50 miles of the San Mateo County coast and administered as a single park unit. Often foggy in summer, these narrow beaches, lying below low coastal bluffs or steep cliffs, are popular for strolling, picnicking, sunbathing, shallow wading, and surf and rock fishing. The currents are too dangerous for safe swimming though.

North to south the beaches are Thornton, Gray Whale Cove, Montara, Half Moon Bay, San Gregorio, Pomponio, Pescadero, Bean Hollow, and Año Nuevo (an elephant seal and sea lion reserve). All beaches except Thornton are accessible from State 1.

Butano State Park is 7 miles from Pescadero Beach. Here, you can hike, picnic, or camp. Easiest access is from State 1. In addition to dense forests of Douglas fir and redwood, you'll find a creek and a small fern canyon. Three major trails traverse the park's 2,186 acres; from Outlook Trail you get a good view of Año Nuevo Island just off the coast.

Santa Cruz retains its Victorian style

The town of Santa Cruz, at the north end of Monterey Bay and at the mouth of the San Lorenzo River, has undergone some real cultural ferment since the Santa Cruz campus of the University of California was established here in 1965. The city, known for its stunning Victorian architecture, is also a good base for exploring nearby beaches.

At the waterfront, you can fish off the long municipal pier, go deep-sea fishing, enjoy the ocean beach, or try the attractions and rides of a vintage boardwalk.

Pacific Avenue, the main street of the downtown area, is a shopping delight. Now a tree-shaded mall, it's full of crafts shops and interesting restaurants. A star attraction is Cooper House, the former County Courthouse that is now a restaurant-shopping complex.

Tree-Sea Tour, a 29-mile sightseeing route, has blue and white signs marking principal points of interest. To guide you, the Santa Cruz County Convention and Visitors Bureau provides a pamphlet, with map, many interesting facts about way points, and motel and restaurant listings. Copies are available from the bureau's office at Church and Center streets. Here, too, you can get your own walking guide of the city's Victorians.

Mission Hill—site of California's 12th mission, founded in 1791—is where the city began and where you'll find the largest concentration of "gingerbread" architecture. At the Reliquary (a small museum) attached to the replica of the mission, you can get a pamphlet on the history of Mission Santa Cruz and the surrounding buildings. The oldest building in town is across School Street from the mission. This adobe once served as a guardhouse for Spanish soldiers accompanying the clergy.

Visit the University of California at Santa Cruz (on High Street in the sloping hills above the city), and take a walk through this innovative campus in the woods. There's a visitor kiosk just inside the entrance where campus activities are listed. You can pick up free, detailed campus maps and directions for guide-yourself tours through the forested campus.

Southeast of Santa Cruz, Capitola was one of California's first beach resorts, dating back to the late 1880s. Today it sparkles with new shops, galleries, and attractive restaurants. You'll find most of the new spirit along Capitola Avenue. Shops sell arts and crafts, antiques, books, coffee, tea, and imported goods.

At 2545 Capitola Road, the Antonelli Brothers' Begonia Gardens feature a begonia show from June through October, and a large, year-round selection of ferns and house plants.

To reach Capitola, take State 1 southbound to the Capitola exit. Northbound on State 1, take the Capitola/Soquel exit.

The beach parks

The coast in the Santa Cruz-Capitola area is dotted with excellent beach parks. Most of them have clean, wide beaches and are popular with swimmers, surfers, and surf fishermen. The water is warmer here than along the coast farther north, and the surf is usually gentle.

Within the Santa Cruz city limits, Natural Bridges Beach State Park is an excellent surf fishing, swimming, and picnicking park. Its beautifully arched bridges were a favorite subject of painters and photographers. Today only one remains.

Twin Lakes Beach State Park, also within the city limits, is a favorite with local residents. Camping is not permitted, but there are firepits for day-use picnicking. One lagoon in the park is a wildfowl refuge; a second is an 850-berth small craft harbor.

Campsites are available at New Brighton and Sunset state beaches. Seacliff State Beach offers trailer hookups, as well fishing from an unusual pier—a 435-foot cement ship, *Palo Alto.* Zmudowski, Moss Landing, Salinas River, and Manresa beaches are day-use parks.

FOR FAMILY FUN—PICK A PARK

When you ask children where they like to go on the peninsula, three theme parks usually rank high on their list. But adults as well as children enjoy spending several hours, if not a whole day, at any one of them.

Marine World/Africa USA covers a 65-acre stretch of tidal flats east of the Bayshore Freeway and south of the San Francisco airport. To date, over 7 million visitors have come to the sprawling, well-landscaped refuge to see over 2,000 land, air, and sea animals in both natural and performing settings.

Seven spectacular shows and 60 other attractions allow you to watch lions, elephants, tigers, whales, dolphins, and other exotic animals in action. A narrated rubber-raft safari cruise winds through facsimiles of the Amazon jungle and the African veldt—created as much for the animals populating the shores as for the people viewing them.

One of the biggest thrills for children is the Whale of a Time playground. Here they can crawl through a sea of balls, slide down the Birdie Glide, and ride the Rope Romp.

To reach Marine World/Africa USA, take the Ralston Avenue/Marine World exit from U.S. Highway 101. The park is open daily in summer from 9 A.M. until dusk; weekends, and holidays during the winter; and Wednesdays through Sundays in the spring and fall. All entertainment and activities, except the elephant and camel rides, are included in a single admission price.

Marriott's Great America, just 3 miles north of the San Jose airport, has drawn millions of visitors to its gates since opening in 1976. Inside the 100-acre park, you'll first encounter Carousel Plaza with the world's largest two-level merry-go-round. The plaza opens onto five Americana theme areas: Hometown Square, County Fair, Yukon Territory, Yankee Harbor, and Orleans Place. All rides, shows, shops, and restaurants are keyed to a particular theme area.

Live entertainment and visitor participation reign. Spirited musical revues appear in the Great America theaters, and special films flicker on the world's largest motion picture screen—seven stories tall and 100 feet wide. Each year, visitors discover new shows and events, including live entertainment by popular musicians.

If you're a thrill seeker, dare some of the park's 125 rides. Two of the most popular are The Demon, a twin-looped, subterranean, corkscrew roller coaster, and the Tidal Wave, a 360° loop roller coaster which attains a speed of 55 miles per hour in three seconds.

To reach Great America, take the exit marked with its name from either U.S. 101 or State Highway 237. The park is open daily in summer, and on weekends during spring and fall. A single admission fee includes all attractions.

Characterized by white beaches, craggy rocks, pounding surf, and twisted cypresses, the Monterey Peninsula juts into the Pacific Ocean south of Monterey Bay. Here you can view one of the most spectacular shorelines along the Pacific coast, explore carefully preserved historic Monterey, browse through the shops of charming Carmel, and drive through the densely wooded Del Monte Forest.

The peninsula's ocean setting conditions its weather. Summer months are likely to be overcast; you can expect morning or late evening fog. In autumn, the days are warm and the sky crystal clear. Rain is frequent from December to March; but even in January, the wettest month, there will be crisp, sunny days.

On the peninsula you'll find numerous accommodations, ranging from old hotels to modern motels. For a list of places to stay, write to the Monterey Peninsula Chamber of Commerce and Visitors and Convention Bureau, P.O. Box 1770, Monterey, CA 93940, or call (408) 649-3200.

State Highway 1, from north or south, runs directly through the heart of the Monterey Peninsula. If you want to follow the coastline, exit from the highway and follow the 17-Mile Drive (see page 54).

South of the peninsula, on State 1, the area is sparsely populated. On your way to San Simeon, site of Hearst Castle, you'll pass through Big Sur country, with the ocean on one side and the Santa Lucia Range on the other. Inland, U.S. Highway 101 will take you to Soledad, Pinnacles National Monument, Salinas, San Juan Bautista, and up to Gilroy and Morgan Hill—developing areas for the winegrowing industry.

Monterey: Mexico's last bastion

Juan Rodriguez Cabrillo, a Portuguese explorer sailing for Spain, discovered Monterey Bay in 1542, and Sebastian Vizcáino visited the bay in 1602. But it was not until 1770 that the area was settled. On the south shore of the bay, Gaspar de Portolá and Father Junipero Serra established the first of Spain's four California presidios and the second of the Franciscans' 21 Alta California missions. One year later Father Serra moved the mission to its present site on the Carmel River.

Until the middle of the 19th century, Monterey was California's liveliest and most important settlement. Beginning the century as the Spanish capital of Alta California, it became the Mexican capital in 1822 and the American capital in 1846. After the discovery of gold in 1848, San Francisco took over as California's number one city. Monterey's 20th century role centers around its tourist and waterfront attractions.

A historic past, a scenic setting, intriguing shopping at Cannery Row and Carmel, cypress-lined 17-Mile Drive, and renown as "the world's golf capital" attract visitors to the Monterey Peninsula. Cliff-hugging Highway 1 sweeps south along dramatic Big Sur coastline to castle at San Simeon. Inland, side trips lead to missions and monuments; Salinas, birthplace of John Steinbeck; and a cluster of wineries.

BIG SUR'S DRAMATIC COASTLINE rises almost vertically from ocean into Santa Lucia Mountains. Bixby Creek Bridge on State Highway 1 crosses inlet 260 feet above water.

Monterey Peninsula

The old Spanish and Mexican village of Monterey echoes in today's modern town of 27,000. Many buildings constructed before 1850 still stand, most in good repair. Over ten of these buildings and sites are preserved in Monterey's State Historic Park, near the downtown and wharf area. Stop first at the old Custom House near Fisherman's Wharf for a map that guides you past many of these venerable structures (see page 56).

The annual spring Adobe Tour includes a number of these buildings, but the tour focuses special attention on buildings not normally open to the public. Check with the chamber of commerce for schedule and ticket information.

Along the waterfront

The Municipal Wharf stretches into Monterey Bay from the foot of Figueroa Street. Here you can watch commercial fishing boats unload anchovies, cod, kingfish, herring, salmon, sole, and tuna. Seven fish-processing plants share space at the end of this wharf. If you don't mind getting your feet damp, you can watch from doorways as workers clean and pack fish. Municipal Wharf is the best place for pier fishing (the catch ranges from sunfish to tomcod) and for viewing Monterey spread along the crescent-shaped bay.

Fisherman's Wharf, around the Monterey Marina, 4 blocks west of Municipal Wharf, has novelty shops, a commercial aquarium, an art gallery, excursion boats, several restaurants, and a broad, expansive plaza reminiscent of old Monterey. Sport fishing boats leave from here early every morning.

Near Fisherman's Wharf, at One Portola Plaza, is the handsome Monterey Convention Center. This three-level complex complete with meeting rooms, ballrooms, and the 500-seat Steinbeck Forum lecture hall, can accommodate over 2,500 people. Its spacious art-filled lobbies, landscaped plazas, and expansive bay views make it worth a visit. Flanked by a resort hotel and shopping plaza, the center brings new vitality to old Monterey.

Cannery Row's old canneries are still there, monuments to the sardines that mysteriously vanished from Monterey Bay near the end of the 1940s. But the row is not the same street Steinbeck described in *Cannery Row* as "a poem, a stink, a grating noise."

Today as you enter Cannery Row, you drive under the covered conveyor belts that once carried the canned fish from the canneries to the warehouse. Many of the old buildings have been renovated. You can browse through art galleries, antique shops, and boutiques, or eat at one of several restaurants. Some reminders of Steinbeck's novel remain—at 800 Cannery Row are the weathered clapboards of Doc Rickett's Western Biological Laboratory; across the street is Wing Chong's, the "Lee Chong's Grocery" of the book; and down the block is the Bear Flag Inn.

Around the corner from Cannery Row, at 101 Ocean View Boulevard, is the American Tin Cannery. Once the site of a large tin can factory, the refurbished building houses boutiques, antique shops, restaurants, and specialty stores in an airy, skylit indoor mall.

Presidio of Monterey

Founded in 1770 by Gaspar de Portolá, the Monterey Presidio is a subpost for the 22,000-acre Fort Ord Area; the site of the Defense Language Institute, West Coast Branch (where 24 languages are taught); and the Training Center Human Research Unit.

The main gate is at Pacific and Artillery streets, near where Sebastian Vizcáino landed in 1602 and Father Junipero Serra and Captain Portolá founded Monterey in 1770. A drive up the Corporal Ewing Road to the motor pool will take you to a life-size statue of Father Serra and a splendid view of Monterey Bay.

West of the Father Serra monument is a memorial to Commodore John Sloat, who in 1846 declared Monterey a possession of the United States.

Naval Postgraduate School

Just east of downtown Monterey, alongside State 1, are the grounds of the old Del Monte Hotel, once one of the most elegant resorts in California. In 1947 the hotel was purchased by the U.S. Navy and in 1951 it became the Naval Postgraduate School.

Visitors may stroll through the campus daily between 9 A.M. and 4 P.M. The grounds contain more than 1,200 exotic trees, Del Monte Lake, and landscaped gardens. The hotel buildings remain, now converted into classrooms and offices. Hermann Hall boasts handpainted ceilings, wrought-iron chandeliers, and a now-unused fountain that extends along one wall from floor to ceiling.

To reach the school, turn onto Aguajito Road from State 1; then turn right on 3rd Street to the main entrance.

Music in Monterey

One of the musical highlights on the Monterey Peninsula is the yearly Jazz Festival. Since it began in 1958, the September festival has followed the same highly successful formula: two afternoon and three evening concerts, along with such appealing fringe benefits as pre-concert rehearsals and the chance not only to hear but also to see at close range quite a few of America's best-known jazz musicians.

Despite the lighthearted informality that prevails at the Monterey County Fairgrounds, the audience becomes serious and attentive when the performance starts. Everyone comes to listen.

Admission to the fairgrounds (located about 2 miles east of Monterey, just off State highways 1 and 68) is limited to ticketholders for the day's concerts. Because the festival is so popular, it's advisable to order tickets in advance. For information on dates and ticket prices, write to Monterey Jazz Festival, P.O. Box JAZZ, Monterey, CA 93940. Season tickets are sold April 1 to June 30. Single performance ticket sales start in August.

Jack's Peak Park—behind Monterey

Jack's Peak Regional Park, a 550-acre area in the coastal hills behind Monterey, is open daily from 8 A.M. to

dusk. You can picnic in the pines, take a hike, or just enjoy the splendid views.

A mile-long loop trail to the top of the peak begins at the park's parking lot. You walk along the west side of the mountain, catching grand views of Carmel, Point Lobos, and Carmel Valley. The return takes you across meadows on the east side of the mountain.

To enter the park, leave State 68 at Olmstead Road, opposite Monterey Peninsula Airport, and go south 2¼ miles to Jack's Peak Park Road. Turn right to the parking lot at the road's end. Bike lanes are marked along the occasionally steep access roads.

Pacific Grove— a butterfly town

The Methodists founded Pacific Grove in 1875 when they held the first of many seashore camp meetings here. Incorporated in 1889, the town was corseted with ordinances strictly regulating dancing, drinking, and public bathing. Today's Pacific Grove is more relaxed.

Three annual events draw crowds to Pacific Grove: the Victorian House Tour in April, the Feast of Lanterns in July, and the Butterfly Parade in October.

The Monarch butterfly (*Danaus plexippus*) is the Pacific Grove symbol. Starting in October, thousands of Monarchs arrive to winter in a 6-acre grove of "Butterfly Trees" (follow the signs at the end of Lighthouse Avenue).

Point Pinos Lighthouse, just north of the intersection of Lighthouse and Asilomar avenues, has stood at the entrance to Monterey Harbor since 1855. On the first floor of the lighthouse is a Coast Guard historical museum open to the public from 1 to 4 P.M. Saturday and Sunday. Surrounding the light station is a Coast Guard reservation, where deer roam protected and anglers fish from the rocky shoreline. The original lighthouse of granite and mortar was rebuilt of reinforced concrete after the 1906 earthquake. Automation is planned for the future so the crew of two will no longer have to check hourly on the light, radio, and foghorn.

The Museum of Natural History, at Forest and Central avenues, displays animal, vegetable, and mineral life of the Monterey Peninsula. Of particular interest is the relief map of the peninsula and bay. You can see the

---

FORE!

Few places in the world have as many beautiful golf courses as the Monterey Peninsula. No wonder it's called the "golf capital of the world."

Some of the courses are by the shore, some in the valleys; each has individual challenges, and all offer great adventure for player or spectator. The 16th hole at Cypress Point (private course) is one of the most talked about in the world; golfers must drive over 220 yards of undulating ocean to reach the green.

Peninsula hotels and motels often offer golf packages. Check with your travel agent for details. Below is a listing of courses:

Carmel Valley Golf & Country Club, 8,000 Valley Greens Drive, Carmel, CA 93923; (408) 624-5323; 18 holes; 6,756 yards (championship), 6,401 yards (regular); reciprocal arrangements with members of other private clubs.

Corral de Tierra Country Club, Corral de Tierra Rd., Salinas, CA 93908; (408) 484-1112; 18 holes; 6,532 yards; reciprocal arrangements with members of other private clubs.

Fort Ord Golf Course, North-South Rd., Fort Ord, CA 93941; (408) 242-5651; two 18-hole courses; 6,966 yards (bayonet), 6,239 yards (blackhorse); military and guests only.

Laguna Seca Golf Club, York Rd., Monterey, CA 93940; (408) 373-3701; 18 holes; 6,310 yards; public.

Monterey Peninsula Country Club, Box 2090, Pebble Beach, CA 93953; (408) 373-1046; 36 holes; 6,400 yards (shore course), 6,450 yards (dunes course); reciprocal arrangements with members of other private clubs.

Naval Postgrad School Golf Course, Box 665, NPS, Monterey, CA 93940; (408) 646-2167; 18 holes; 5,680 yards; military and guests only.

Old Del Monte Golf Course, 1300 Sylvan Rd., Monterey, CA 93940; (408) 373-2436; 18 holes; 6,175 yards; public.

Pacific Grove Municipal Golf Course, 77 Asilomar Blvd., Pacific Grove, CA 93950; (408) 375-3456; 18 holes; 5,493 yards; public.

Pebble Beach Golf Course, The Lodge at Pebble Beach, Pebble Beach, CA 93953; (408) 624-3811; 18 holes; 6,806 yards (championship), 6,389 yards (regular); semiprivate (reservation required 2 weeks ahead for busy periods).

Peter Hay Par 3 at Pebble Beach, The Lodge at Pebble Beach, Pebble Beach, CA 93953; (408) 624-3811; 9 holes; public.

Rancho Cañada Golf Club, Box 22590, Carmel, CA 93922; (408) 624-0111; 36 holes; 6,613 yards (west course), 6,401 yards (east course); public.

Spyglass Hill Golf Course, Box 787, Pebble Beach, CA 93953; (408) 624-3811; 18 holes; 6,810 yards (championship), 6,277 yards (regular); semiprivate.

great chasm of Monterey Bay, which plummets 8,400 feet, deeper than the Grand Canyon. The museum is open daily.

Perkins Park, winding along Ocean View Boulevard, includes a protected beach and Lover's Point, a good place for picnicking and watching scuba divers explore the underwater world. A short distance east of the beach is Point Cabrillo, where Stanford University maintains the Hopkins Marine Laboratories. Ideal weather and water conditions allow extensive research in hydrobiology.

Asilomar State Beach fronts the ocean side of the Monterey Peninsula. The adjoining conference grounds are often used for large group meetings. If you cannot find hotel space on the peninsula, rustic and comfortable rooms are sometimes available at Asilomar. The beach here is perfect for hiking.

17-Mile Drive

Contained within 4,280-acre Del Monte Forest, the 17-Mile Drive is an exceptionally scenic route. For 17 miles you drive through thickly wooded areas and see spectacular views of Monterey Bay's breathtaking, rocky shoreline. At any of the four entrance gates (fee is $4 per car) you'll be given a map of the route showing points of interest. It's easy to drive this 17-mile route— just follow the yellow line.

Along the drive stand weathered Monterey cypresses, whose branches and foliage have been dramatically distorted by the sea winds. At Seal and Bird Rocks are black cormorants, sea ducks, sea gulls, and leopard or harbor seals. Between the shore and the rocks, sea lions roar.

Though overnight camping is not allowed within the Del Monte Forest, you can picnic in specified areas. Fishing is permitted from Fanshell Beach north; hunting is not allowed.

Along the peninsula's south shore is Pebble Beach. Here is the famous Pebble Beach Golf Course (one of six courses within the forest), The Lodge at Pebble Beach (a resort hotel), and exclusive homes.

If golf is not your game, note that the Pebble Beach Equestrian Center offers more than 34 miles of beautiful bridle paths. Or, as a spectator, you can watch polo and rugby matches, championship tennis, the Concours d'Elegance (a rally of vintage cars), the famous Crosby Pro-Am Golf Tournament, or any of the other public events scheduled at Pebble Beach each year.

Carmel-by-the-Sea

Since its first settlement, Carmel has prided itself on remaining a simple village by the ocean. Even today, houses have no street numbers and mail delivery is nonexistent—everyone goes to the post office. Down-

town there are no billboards, no large retail signs, and at night no flood lighting and almost no street lighting. On the side streets you see no curbs, no sidewalks.

But this lack of commercialism attracts tourists. The sidewalks are crowded on weekends, and the main street is jammed with cars. Now Carmel's motto seems to be, "If you can't beat 'em, join 'em."

Shopping. This is a village of shops—more than 150 of them, mostly small. And the shopping is good. Specialties are casual clothing for both men and women, often from Scotland, England, Ireland, or Italy; art and crafts work of all kinds, much of it created locally; decorative imports from Mexico, Sweden, France, Italy; basketry, pottery, furniture from Japan and Hong Kong. Shopping is a pastime in Carmel.

Carmel has always respected its artists, writers, and craftspeople. Many serious artists who live here display their works in downtown galleries. The Carmel Art Association maintains a sales gallery on Dolores Street.

Festivals. One of the yearly attractions here is the Bach Festival, held each July in Sunset Center. Entering its 43rd season, the 2-week festival brings some of the world's finest musicians to the Monterey Peninsula.

Throughout the year, the Sunset Center coordinates other music, dance, drama, and film festivals. Here, too, the Friends of Photography's Sunset Gallery exhibits the work of contemporary American photographers. The center is located on San Carlos Avenue between 8th and 10th avenues.

Lodging. Carmel has several hotels and a large number of motels, inns, and guest cottages; yet advance room reservations are advisable, especially during such events as the Bach Festival.

Architecture. In exploring Carmel, you'll see a variety of architectural styles. Early rough summer cabins have given way to Hansel and Gretel-type structures and Monterey-style adobes. Fronting the ocean are some modern homes, including one designed by Frank Lloyd Wright.

Carmel's beaches were made for walking

Carmel's classically beautiful beach is ideal for walkers and, in good weather, sunbathers. The beach is unsafe for swimming, but most bathers find the water too cold anyway. On Scenic Drive, which runs along the water, you will see dark, gnarled cypresses, sparkling white sand, and crashing surf. At the southern end of the beach, the shoreline becomes rocky and pocked with tidepools.

South of the village limits, at the end of Scenic Drive, the beach becomes Carmel River State Beach. Here you can picnic around a beach fire or splash in the lagoon of Carmel River.

Carmel Mission Basilica

South of the town, just off State 1 at Rio Road (or follow Junipero Avenue south), is Basilica San Carlos Borromeo del Rio Carmelo. Fully restored through the efforts of craftsmen, benefactors, and clergy, the mission

(Continued on page 57)

CATWALKS AND CLAPBOARDS *are still part of Monterey's famous Cannery Row (above). Converted cannery shops lure visitors with a cornucopia of salt-water treats, from taffy to seasoned antiques.*

LONE CYPRESS *(right) clings precariously to craggy outcrop at lookout point along exclusive 17-Mile Drive. Tourists enjoy unobstructed views of rocky shoreline and crashing waves.*

DOE TIPTOES DELICATELY *past rapt golfer (below). Championship golf courses designed to fit in between land and sea make Monterey Peninsula a golfer's paradise.*

MONTEREY'S PATH OF HISTORY

Many Spanish-style adobes were constructed during the early 1800s to accommodate the 2,000 residents of Monterey. When New England seamen arrived, they modified the Spanish colonial design and created the "Monterey style"—two-story adobes with a balcony. Although many of the old buildings have disappeared, some buildings have been preserved and are maintained as the Monterey State Historic Park; most of them are open daily.

These historical structures are close to the downtown area and the harbor. A good place to start is at the Custom House near Fisherman's Wharf.

The Custom House, at 1 Custom Plaza, is the oldest government building on the Pacific Coast. Here the United States flag was officially raised for the first time by Commodore John Sloat in 1846. This building was the collection center for revenue from foreign shipping until 1867, when it was abandoned. Today, the interior has been restored; inside is a display of early ships' cargo. The plaza with its adobe walls and benches is reminiscent of early California.

The Pacific House, at 8 Custom House Plaza, dates back to 1847. This building was first used by the U.S. Quartermaster for military offices and storage; later it housed a tavern; now it's a museum. The first floor contains exhibits of California history and the second floor a collection of American Indian artifacts.

Casa del Oro is so named because of the unverified story that the building was once used as a gold depository. A general merchandise store in the 1850s, Casa del Oro stands at the corner of Scott and Oliver streets and displays trade items from early Monterey days.

California's First Theater, built in 1846-47, at the corner of Scott and Pacific streets, is open daily except Monday. Each week a theater group presents 19th century plays. The old bench seats are still there, and walls of the barroom are lined with old theatrical mementos.

Casa Soberanes, at 336 Pacific, is a private residence not open to the public. But it is an excellent example of "Monterey-style" architecture.

Colton Hall, on Pacific Street, was built in 1847-49 and is the largest and most impressive of the old buildings. A museum on the second floor displays early government documents.

The Larkin House, which dates back to 1835, is an excellent example of "Monterey-style" architecture. The two-story adobe, surrounded on three sides by a balcony, was built by Thomas Larkin, U.S. Consul. Many of the furnishings are original pieces. This home, at the corner of Jefferson Street and Calle Principal, is open to the public. Visitors are taken on a 35-minute guided tour daily except Tuesday.

Casa Gutierrez, at Calle Principal near Madison, is a typical adobe home of the Mexican period. Now it's a Mexican restaurant.

The Cooper House, at the corner of Polk and Murray, is the former home of Captain John Cooper, a trader and half brother to Thomas Larkin. The Department of Parks and Recreation is working to open it to the public.

The Stevenson House, named for Robert Louis Stevenson, who lived in this building during his short sojourn in Monterey in 1879, dates back to the late 1830s. At 530 Houston Street, the restored building devotes several rooms to Stevenson's personal mementos. The house is open for guided tours.

The Royal Presidio Chapel of San Carlos de Borromeo was founded in 1770 by Father Junipero Serra. The original, hastily constructed mud structure was rebuilt with a baroque façade by Father Serra's successor in 1794. A simple wooden cross sits atop the chapel. Inside are several statues and Stations of the Cross dating from the founding of the chapel. The chapel, on Church Street, is still in use; visitors are welcome.

The U.S. Army Museum, in the Presidio of Monterey, exhibits military items from early Spanish days to the present. The museum is open Thursday through Monday.

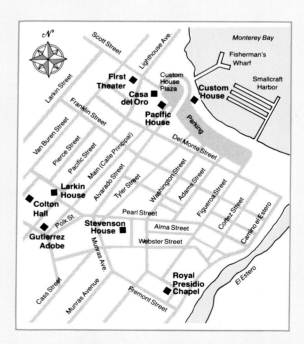

. . . Continued from page 54

provides one of the most authentic and picturesque links to early California history. The mission is open to visitors Monday through Saturday from 9:30 A.M. to 4:30 P.M., Sunday from 10:30 A.M. to 4:30 P.M.

In the mission museum are the original silver altar pieces brought by Father Junipero Serra from Baja California and the restored refectory of Father Serra. Behind the mission is a cemetery where 3,000 Indians are buried. Inside the mission is Father Serra's final resting place.

Point Lobos State Reserve

On State 1 just south of Carmel stands 1,500-acre Point Lobos State Reserve, one of the most beautiful spots on the California coast. Its broken coastline encompasses 6 miles. At this magnificent meeting of land and sea you can hike, picnic, explore tidepools, sun on the beach, or fish.

Around the headland and shoreline, low tides expose rocky pools teeming with marine creatures. Colonies of sea urchins, sea anemones, starfish, and hermit crabs are a few of the more conspicuous inhabitants. Remember that Point Lobos is a nature reserve; tidepools are for looking only. On prominent rocks you will see sea gulls and, on Bird Island, cormorants and brown pelicans.

If you visit Point Lobos in November, you might see the California gray whale, which travels close to shore here on its annual 12,000-mile migration to Baja California.

Point Lobos is open only during daylight hours. There are picnic sites, but camping and fires are not permitted. There is a nominal admission fee.

Carmel Valley

South of Carmel, the Carmel Valley Road turns east from State 1 and heads inland along the Carmel River. Driving through the valley, you'll pass artichoke fields, fruit orchards, strawberry patches, rolling hills, and grazing cattle. Right off State 1, on Carmel Valley Road, is The Barnyard—a shopping complex built around the popular Thunderbird Bookshop. The collection of shops, boutiques, galleries, and restaurants housed in eight rustic barns attracts many visitors.

Carmel Valley is a vacationland. Its weather is sunny, warm, and clear—ideal for such outdoor sports as fishing, hunting, horseback riding, tennis, and swimming. Near the mouth of the Carmel Valley, spanning both sides of the Carmel River, are two championship golf courses—available for public play. The Carmel River holds an abundance of trout, and, during the annual spawning season, steelhead fishing is excellent. In the nearby Santa Lucia Mountains, you can hunt wild boar and deer.

At the Carmel Valley Begonia Gardens, 15,000 begonias form a massive wheel of color in the summer. The Korean Buddhist Temple also welcomes visitors. It lies west of the Farm Center off Robinson Canyon Road.

The Hidden Valley Opera's 300-seat theater is just off Carmel Valley Road about 10 miles inland from State 1 (just west of the Carmel Valley Village shopping area). For information and reservations write to the Hidden Valley Opera, Box 116, Carmel Valley, CA 93924, or call (408) 659-3115.

Hikers, joggers, and horseback riders enjoy the 540-acre Garland Regional Park, about 8 miles inland from State 1 along Carmel Valley Road. More than 7 miles of park trails amble over forested hills and riverside meadows. Maps of the area are available at the park ranger's office. You can camp at Riverside Park and Saddle Mountain Recreation Park.

Hotels and motels are more than places to spend the night; all offer a variety of interesting activities. For a list of accommodations and facilities available, write to the Carmel Valley Chamber of Commerce, Box 288, Carmel Valley, CA 93921.

South along the coast

The dramatic 30-mile drive along State 1 to the Big Sur area takes about an hour from Monterey and Carmel. The road south dips and rises, clinging precariously to the seaward face of the Santa Lucia Mountains as it follows the rugged coastline.

As you drive south from Carmel, you cross the dramatic Bixby Creek Bridge, 260 feet above the creek bed. Park your car and walk out to observation alcoves for a

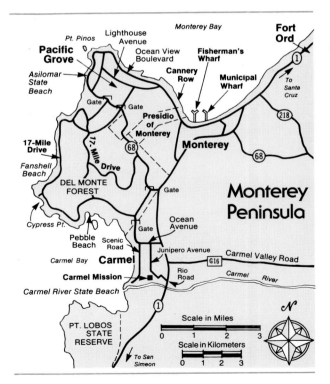

DOLL HOUSE architecture of Carmel restaurant (above) provides whimsical setting for intimate afternoon lunch or tea. Tourists throng Ocean Avenue, town's main street, on weekends the year around.

GLOWING POPPIES accent classic grace of Carmel Mission Basilica (left). Churchgoers and visitors alike delight in leisurely walk through mission's courtyard.

view of the surf, beach, and headlands. You'll pass a cliff-perched eating place—Rocky Point Restaurant—and Point Sur Lighthouse, rising on a headland of rock. Every 15 seconds a warning flashes that can be seen 25 miles out to sea.

Though the road is two lanes with narrow shoulders, vista turnouts are numerous. You can stop for a roadside picnic (Big Sur has a few small grocery stores) or a leisurely lunch at one of Big Sur's restaurants, take a stroll in the redwoods or a walk on the beach, do some shopping or gallery browsing. The Coast Gallery (center for local artisans) maintains two showrooms inside redwood water tanks. You can dine at Ventana Restaurant, a resort with rental condominiums and a gift shop.

Enjoy Nepenthe, 3 miles south of Pfeiffer-Big Sur State Park. The restaurant's redwood pavilion, designed by a student of Frank Lloyd Wright, sits 800 feet above the sea and affords a superb view of southern Big Sur. The original core building was the honeymoon "cottage" built in the 1940s for Rita Hayworth by Orson Welles. Nepenthe opens every day at noon. Besides being a restaurant, it has become an informal social-cultural center for the Big Sur region.

For more information on Big Sur's establishments and facilities, write to the Chamber of Commerce, Big Sur, CA 93920.

State parks along the way

Some of the finest meetings of land and water occur in three state parks along the coast. Two of the parks offer camping, but you have to walk in to one.

Andrew Molera State Park has 2,088 acres encompassing the lower section of the Big Sur River. Because it's closed to motorized vehicles, park your car off the highway and walk in to a designated camping area. Here you'll find somewhat primitive arrangements for about 50 campers. A network of fire-control roads makes it easy to get around in this preserve of redwoods, rocky bluffs, meadow land, and beach.

Pfeiffer-Big Sur State Park is one of the most popular of the state's nonbeach parks. Though the park isn't large, its trails give access to 300,000 acres of back country in Los Padres National Forest and the Ventana Wilderness. (Permits to enter the wilderness should be requested at least 2 weeks in advance from the District Ranger, Los Padres National Forest, 406 S. Mildred, King City, CA 93930.)

The park's campgrounds are likely to be crowded, especially in summer or on weekends. You can picnic, hike, swim, or fish upstream in the river. Hotel-type rooms and housekeeping cabins are available at Big Sur Lodge, Big Sur, CA 93920.

Pfeiffer Beach, south of the park entrance, is reached via narrow Sycamore Canyon Road from State 1. A scenic gem, the beach is open daily from 9 A.M. to 6 P.M.

Julia Pfeiffer Burns State Park's attractions include a dramatic waterfall, redwood groves, and vantage points for viewing gray whale migration. You'll also find 2 miles of scenic coastline and high country extending up canyons laced with trickling creeks. There's no camping, but you can picnic, hike, or stroll along the cliffs. The park is open in summer and during spring and fall weekends.

San Simeon: A castle fit for kings

The Hearst San Simeon State Historic Monument, a collection of mansions, terraced gardens, pools, sculpture, and exotic trees, occupies 123 acres atop a spur of the Santa Lucia Mountains. The focal point, designed by Julia Morgan, is *La Casa Grande,* a 137-foot-high structure resembling a Spanish cathedral. Its imposing ridge-top position gives it the aspect of a castle when viewed from afar.

In 1922, construction began on *La Casa Grande,* William Randolph Hearst's private residence. Hearst called the estate *La Cuesta Encantada*—The Enchanted Hill. Money was no object—Hearst imported furniture, antiques, Gothic and Renaissance tapestries, fine wood carvings, French and Italian mantels, carved ceilings, silver, Persian rugs, and Roman mosaics.

San Simeon is located on State 1, about 96 miles south of Monterey. Getting there has never been easy, entailing a long trip on the twisting highway. Bus tours leave for the historic monument from Monterey. For schedule information call or write the Monterey Peninsula Chamber of Commerce (see page 51). Three separate tours, each about 2 hours long, are conducted through the estate. Reservations (always required during the busy season) are available at Ticketron outlets. Tour prices are moderate, but there's a separate charge for each tour. All tours begin at the foot of Enchanted Hill; you board a bus for the ride up the hill.

Inland side trips

Two inland routes parallel the coastal highway and offer sights well worth seeing. U.S. 101 heads south through the valley of the Salinas River; State Highway 25 crosses the San Benito River in the coastal range.

Pinnacles National Monument

At Pinnacles National Monument, spires and crags—remains of a volcanic mountain—rise to 1,200 feet above the canyon floors and present a sharp contrast to the surrounding smooth countryside.

The best way to appreciate fully the extraordinary features here is to hike some of the trails. On the east side, short, easy trips lead through the cave area around Bear Gulch, near the visitor center and picnic area. The High Peaks Trail is strenuous; Juniper Canyon Trail makes it easier to reach High Peaks from Soledad.

On the Soledad side of the monument, you walk into the narrow defile between the overhangs of Machete Ridge and The Balconies. Huge boulders close the caves to natural light (be sure to carry a flashlight). You will have to crawl, stretch, duck, and squeeze along for a few hundred feet until you come to daylight and the other end of the cave. Children should not go in the caves alone—slippery places, low ceilings and dropoffs are hazardous in the dark.

Pinnacles National Monument is just off State 25, 32 miles south of Hollister. You can also reach the Pinnacles along U.S. 101 by turning onto State Highway 146 at Soledad and following the narrow, winding road 14 miles to the camping and picnic area. Fall through spring are the best months to visit the monument; the summer months are hot.

Campgrounds are at Chalone Creek and Chaparrel, with group camping at Chalone Annex.

Soledad mission ruins

A turn westward off U.S. 101 just south of Soledad will take you past a frame and adobe building on your right. This is Los Coches, former headquarters of a large ranch, part of the lands of Mission Nuestra Señora de la Soledad.

A half-mile drive west of Los Coches, and a turn to the north, will lead you to the mission ruins. Here, the thirteenth mission in the California chain was founded by Father Fermin Lasuen in 1791. With the nearby Salinas River to irrigate the dry fields, crops flourished and lush pastures amply fed horses and cattle.

But this same river would be the mission's nemesis. Recurring floods destroyed adobe walls, and epidemics killed Indians and missionaries. By the 1830s, the mission personified its name—"loneliness"—with only a handful of faithful remaining within its desolate walls. When resident friar Father Sarría died in 1835, the mission was officially closed. Winds, rains, and sun reduced "Our Lady of Solitude" to its present state of crumbling walls on windswept beet fields. A modern chapel stands in its place.

From the mission ruins, you can backtrack to U.S. 101 or take the back roads to Carmel and Monterey. Drive south up the steep Arroyo Seco Road, following its turn in a westerly direction to Paloma Creek Road. This is a dirt road—unsatisfactory for traffic for 24 hours after rain. Wind 18 miles through range land dotted with oaks, eucalyptus, sycamores, and pines, and you'll be back on the paved Carmel Valley Road.

Mission San Antonio de Padua

Named for Saint Anthony, Mission San Antonio de Padua was founded in 1771 by Father Junípero Serra. Though somewhat isolated in the middle of a military reservation, the mission rewards the persistent traveler who takes the time to find it. Almost completely restored, it unfolds in grand style amid an oak-studded valley. To reach it, exit U.S. 101 at King City and follow County Highway G14 to Jolon, a distance of 18 miles.

Mission San Antonio de Padua is reminiscent of missions during the days of the padres. In place of the crumbling adobe walls you might expect, you'll see replicas of buildings that existed in the prosperous years between 1771 and 1830. Some of the original tiles still cover the roof.

Besides the mission itself, you'll see a water-powered grist mill, a tannery, the original wine vat, early mission art, and replicas of mission equipment.

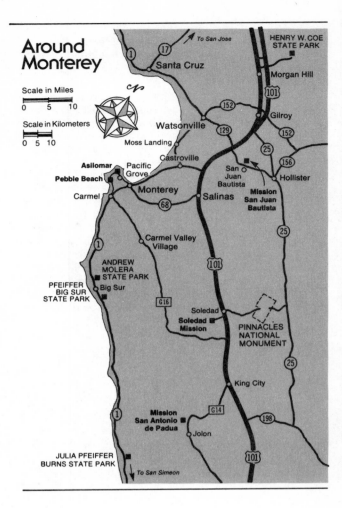

Around Monterey

Scale in Miles
0 5 10

Scale in Kilometers
0 5 10

In & around Salinas

Salinas, the heart of the "salad bowl of the world," is the birthplace of Nobel and Pulitzer prize-winning novelist John Steinbeck (1902–1968). His home, a two-story Victorian on Central and Stone streets, has been restored and opened as a restaurant. Downstairs is the Best Cellar gift shop offering local crafts and a selection of the author's works.

Salinas and the surrounding valley provided much of the local color of Steinbeck's novels. Visit the John Steinbeck Library at 110 W. San Luis Street to see exhibits of original manuscripts, photographs, letters, and tapes having to do with the author's life and works.

One of the oldest buildings in town, the Boronda Adobe at West Laurel Street and Boronda Road, preserves the authentic mood of an early California rancho.

Built in 1848 by José Eusebio Boronda, the adobe graces the meadows above Alisal Slough. Now a state historic landmark, the estate is open to the public. The façade typifies the detailing of the Monterey colonial style, and the house is architecturally linked with the

Larkin House in Monterey. Inside you'll find a wealth of original furnishings, photographs, and artifacts depicting California's Mexican period. Admission is free. For additional information, call the Salinas Chamber of Commerce, (408) 424-7611.

The wild West is alive and well in Salinas when the rodeo comes to town. Held each third weekend in July, the Salinas California Rodeo is the main event in a week-long celebration of parades, barbecues, and hoe-downs. Over 700 competitors round up for accolades and prizes in California's largest rodeo. You'll see the best men and women of modern rodeo buck wild broncos and bulls, rope wily calves, wrestle steers, and race around barrels. The action never stops—there is also thorough-bred racing, trick riding, and even gunfights. When you've eaten enough sawdust, settle down to the cheerful strains of bluegrass fiddling at Salt Flats Hoe-down. For ticket and schedule information, contact the California Rodeo Office, P.O. Box 1648, Salinas, CA 93902.

From Salinas it's only a few miles to the Monterey Peninsula or to Castroville (the artichoke capital) and Watsonville on State 1.

Mission San Juan Bautista

About 21 miles north of Salinas, 3½ miles off U.S. 101, lies Mission San Juan Bautista. After its founding in 1797 by Father Lasuen, the mission grew spiritually and financially. The mission's success reflected its founding friars' energy and zeal. Father Felipe del Arroyo, a linguistic whiz, preached to the Indians in seven dialects, teaching them everything from the simplest ways of the white man to the writings of Plato and Cicero. His counterpart, Father Estevan Tapis, was an ebullient music man. By depicting different musical parts in brightly colored notes, he taught choral music to the Indians and formed choirs that continued his legacy for forty years.

Now a state historic park, San Juan Bautista presents a carefully restored chapter of early California history. Once a crossroads of stagecoach travel, the old mission village declined after the railroad pushed south from San Francisco. But in 1933 San Juan Bautista was named a state historic park, and the flavor of old San Juan was preserved. Construction of the present mission building began in 1803 and reached completion in 1814. The carefully restored buildings still overlook the valley much as they did. Down in the town, though, new shops, galleries, and other attractions are moving into the old frame buildings that stand shoulder-to-shoulder along Third Street.

At La Calavera, on Washington Street, a resident troupe presents plays stocked with early California history on Friday and Saturday evenings.

Mexican holidays begin in December. The typical *Las Posadas* procession and fiesta take place nightly from mid-December until Christmas Eve.

Nearby camping spots include Fremont Peak State Park, a rich historic and botanical area 11 miles south of San Juan Bautista on the San Juan Canyon-State Park Road. Fourteen miles east of Morgan Hill on East Dunne Avenue is Henry W. Coe State Park, little known and usually uncrowded. Seasonally blessed with good wild-flower displays, the park is at its best in spring and in autumn after the first rains.

Try the Hecker Pass wineries

Stretching along U.S. 101 from Morgan Hill to Gilroy, then west along State Highway 152 toward Hecker Pass, is a group of wineries clustering like so many grapes on a vine. Once known almost solely for their robust jug wines, these wineries are rapidly expanding their bill of fare to include a wide selection of varietals.

Wine tasting is leisurely paced in the Hecker Pass region of vine-filled bottomlands, golden hills, oak knolls, and meandering creeks. Not all wineries are open to the public, but some offer informal tasting, others more formal tours ending in elegant tasting rooms. If you go in October, you'll have a good chance of seeing the picking and crushing. Here is just a sampling of what you'll find.

Bertero Winery, set back from State 152, is one of the oldest in the area. In its handsome pavilionlike tasting room you'll sample Barbera, Cabernet Sauvignon, Pinot Noir, and Zinfandel, as well as whites, rosés, and sherries.

Fortino Winery, along State 152, has a spacious tasting room and gift shop—a good place to pick up a red, white, or rosé for a picnic in the country.

Thomas Kruse Winery, west of Bertero, offers informal tours, tasting rooms, and picnic grounds. Set in a classic wooden barn, the winery offers an uncommon list of wines—sparkling whites from Zinfandel, dry rosés from Cabernet Sauvignon, Pinot Noirs, and Grignolinos.

Kirigin Cellars sits on one of the oldest properties in Hecker Pass but has one of the newest wineries. North of State 152 and west of U.S. 101, the winery offers group tours, pleasant tasting rooms, and pine-shaded picnic grounds. Try a sample of their Chablis, French Colombard, Cabernet Sauvignon, and a dessert specialty, Vino de Mocca.

For a more complete listing of the area's wineries see the *Sunset* book *Guide to California's Wine Country*. To reach the wineries, leave U.S. 101 at Morgan Hill; just south of town, take Watsonville Road roughly 7 miles to the junction with Hecker Pass Highway (State 152). Besides wineries you'll find picturesque towns, parks, and picnicking spots in this area.

About 14 miles north of Morgan Hill is Henry W. Coe State Park. It was once a working ranch, and the park's headquarters occupy the old ranch buildings, perched high at 2,600 feet. When wildflowers bloom, scores of would-be Monets flock to the park's rolling grassy hill, canvas in hand. Here you'll find picnic tables and a few campsites. Expect a day-use fee.

To the west in the hills lies Mount Madonna County Park at the Hecker Pass summit. Like Henry W. Coe State Park, this area developed from a one-time working ranch. Cattleman Henry Miller once owned it, then bequeathed its formal gardens to posterity.

Roads meander through oak-dusted hillsides at the park's upper elevations, where you may spy a few diffident albino deer. The entrance to the park is from State 152; there is a day-use fee.

The North Coast

Sheer cliffs, pounding waves, rocky headlands, and offshore rocks characterize much of the northern shoreline. A national seashore, pocket beaches, and coastal inlets invite hikers, backpackers, and anglers. The oceanside highway passes by Fort Ross (former Russian fur trading outpost), old fishing ports, weathered farms and fences, and forested campgrounds. Mendocino, an artists' mecca, is a center for old inns; Eureka, a Victorian lumber town, lies among redwood groves. Just north is the stillness of the Redwood National Park.

Stretching almost 400 miles from San Francisco Bay to the southern border of Oregon, the virtually unspoiled Northern California coastline delights visitors. Photographers record the beauty of whitecapped waves pounding against rugged shores; anglers contest with fighting steelhead in mighty rivers emptying into the sea; campers choose between parks ranging from sandy dunes to dense forest; and crowds of urbanites flock to unique rural festivals.

Heading north across the Golden Gate Bridge, you can reach the coast either by way of U.S.Highway 101, an inland route until meeting the ocean at Humboldt Bay, or by the slower, scenic route—two-lane State Highway 1. Numerous back country roads connect these two major highways before they join at Leggett, just south of the redwood-lined Avenue of the Giants.

It would be impossible to list the chief attractions of this section of Northern California; everyone makes a personal discovery. Hikers may want to roam the vast open spaces of Point Reyes National Seashore. California's history takes on a new dimension when you view the wooden outpost of the Russian fur traders—Fort Ross. The charms of artistic Mendocino and its bustling fishing and lumbering neighbor, Fort Bragg, rank high among coast attractions. To the north, the mighty coast redwood makes spectacular daytime viewing as herds of Roosevelt elk munch in meadows fringed by titans.

Weather is usually foggy and cold along the coast during the summer; winter brings clear, warm days. Old-fashioned inns with modern accouterments dot the coastline and complement the often stark climate with a warm, intimate atmosphere. In any month, the North Coast provides a dramatic meeting of land and sea.

The Marin beaches

As far as mariners are concerned, the Marin County shore from Point Reyes to the Golden Gate has very little to recommend it. For them it is a treacherous obstacle to San Francisco, composed of sea fogs, howling winds, reefs, and shoals. But for those who are shorebound, it is something else: good rock fishing, good wave-watching, good rock-hounding and good clamming. In its shallow bays, the hardy enjoy good swimming.

Only one remote beach is more than an hour from San Francisco. Some of the shore is hardly 15 minutes away. In spite of its proximity to the city, Marin's coast has not been subjected to any permanent overcrowding, mainly because the terrain slopes skyward in many places. Lack of further development has been somewhat assured by the recent creation of parks along all but a handful of miles of shoreline.

SILHOUETTED STROLLERS, dwarfed by massive cliffs, make tracks along stark Sonoma coastline. Low tide's gentle waves scallop beach's shimmering sands.

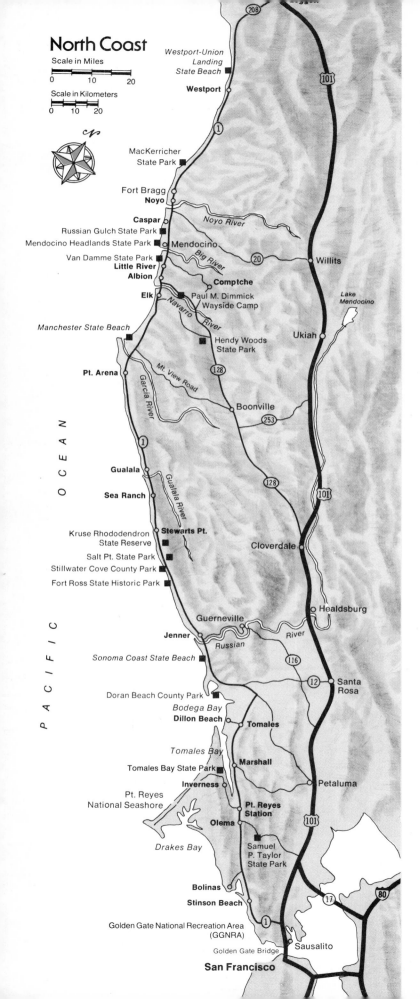

North Coast

Scale in Miles
0 10 20

Scale in Kilometers
0 10 20

208

101

Westport-Union
Landing
State Beach

Westport

1

MacKerricher
State Park

Fort Bragg
Noyo

Noyo River

Caspar
Russian Gulch State Park
Mendocino Headlands State Park **Mendocino**

Van Damme State Park
Little River
Albion

Big River

20

Willits

Comptche

Elk   Paul M. Dimmick
Wayside Camp

Navarro River

Manchester State Beach

Lake
Mendocino

Ukiah

Hendy Woods
State Park

Pt. Arena

Mt. View Road

128

Garcia River

Boonville

253

1

Gualala

Gualala River

Sea Ranch

128

101

Kruse Rhododendron
State Reserve   **Stewarts Pt.**

Salt Pt. State Park
Stillwater Cove County Park
Fort Ross State Historic Park

Cloverdale

Healdsburg

Guerneville

Jenner   *Russian River*

Sonoma Coast State Beach

116

12   Santa
Rosa

Doran Beach County Park

Bodega Bay
Dillon Beach   **Tomales**

Tomales Bay

Marshall

Tomales Bay State Park

Inverness   Petaluma

Pt. Reyes
National Seashore

**Pt. Reyes
Station**

Olema

Drakes Bay   Samuel
P. Taylor
State Park

101

Bolinas

Stinson Beach

Golden Gate National Recreation Area
(GGNRA)

17   80

1

Golden Gate Bridge   Sausalito

San Francisco

O C E A N

P A C I F I C

Marin's shores from the north end of the Golden Gate Bridge are practically all open to the public as part of the Golden Gate National Recreation Area (which extends as far north as Olema). The land is a mixture of former army forts, ruggedly undeveloped open areas, and once-private ranch lands.

Stinson Beach is not only the name of a small town, but also a day-use park now part of the Golden Gate National Recreation Area. The park runs mostly south of town. Fishermen do well with ling cod, cabezone, and blenny at several rocky points toward the park's south boundary. Just opposite the town entrance is a 4,500-foot ocean swimming beach, its waters warmed by the shoal of Bolinas Bay. Swimming is permitted from late May to mid-September when lifeguards are on duty and the weather most temperate. The park, which attracts over a million visitors annually, is open from 9 A.M. to one hour after sunset; admission and parking are free. For weather and traffic conditions call (415) 868-1922.

Audubon Canyon Ranch, 3 miles north of Stinson Beach, is a good place to watch the courtship rituals of the great blue herons who rendezvous here every March. Bring binoculars or use the ranch telescopes to watch these, along with graceful white egrets. Most birds are gone by August.

Bolinas, sitting just across the mouth of a small lagoon from Stinson Beach, is a tiny town that doesn't try very hard to attract visitors but gets them anyway. Duxbury Reef, a principal cause of Bolinas's popularity, sets up the proper conditions for surfing, tidepooling, clamming, and rock fishing. Striped bass feed at the mouth of the lagoon. Each end of the town's east-west main street dips down to a beach access. The one nearest Stinson Beach serves bass fishermen and surfers; the westerly end is closest to the foot of Duxbury Reef.

Point Reyes National Seashore

U.S. Weather Bureau statistics cite Point Reyes as the foggiest and windiest station, bar none, between Canada and Mexico. Summer weather is often foggy and windy—so bring warm clothing.

The Point Reyes peninsula is an ideal place for an August, September, or October outing. The peninsula reaches another peak from February to late July when wildflowers bloom in the moist and mild climate. Limited lodging restricts the area as a vacation spot. Bear Valley has a few campgrounds, or you can camp at Samuel P. Taylor State Park (about 6 miles southeast of Point Reyes Station) or at a private campground near Olema.

Point Reyes is an island recently separated (geologically speaking) from the mainland by the San Andreas Fault, running northwest-southeast for about 600 miles. As a result of earthquakes, the land on the west side of the fault at Point Reyes has moved northward as much as 20 feet.

Though his log is lost, most historians believe Sir Francis Drake arrived in 1579 aboard his ship, the *Golden Hinde,* in the area just below Point Reyes—now Drakes Bay. His was the first landing on this continent by an English explorer.

In 1962, Congress declared the 64,000-acre Point Reyes area a national seashore because of its dramatic natural and historic significance.

Just 50 miles up the coast from San Francisco, Point Reyes can be easily reached from U.S. 101 and Sir Francis Drake Boulevard or State 1. It's divided into two distinct areas. You reach major beaches and dairylands through Inverness to the north; the Bear Valley trails and hilly forest of Inverness Ridge through park headquarters near Olema off State 1.

Drakes Bay: Home for the *Golden Hinde?*

A long and gentle curve facing almost due south, this bay has a wide, flat, sandy beach abutting steep sandstone bluffs all the way from Point Reyes on the west to a point next to Bolinas on the east. The one break in the arc is the mouth of Drakes Estero, a clutching hand of water that cups oyster beds in its palm.

Although some historians believe Drake brought his ship into Bodega Bay, Bolinas Bay, Tomales Bay, or San Francisco Bay, the prestigious Drake Navigators Guild claims a stronger case for Drakes Bay. Whether or not the argument is ever resolved by some dramatic new turn (like the discovery in Bolinas Lagoon of what might have been Drake's fort), the bay is a pleasant place to stroll the beach, hike, fish, or watch whales.

The Kenneth C. Patrick Visitor Center adjoins the parking lot. Sheltered picnic tables allow you to sit and watch waves when the weather gets too raw for strolls along the beach. On good days, beautifully symmetrical breakers plunge ashore.

At the end of the point, the 107-year-old Point Reyes lighthouse is now open to visitors. The light is open daily (subject to weather conditions) from 10 A.M. to 5 P.M. To check, call the station at (415) 669-1534 or the Bear Valley Information Center at (415) 663-1092.

Limantour Beach and Estero (east of Drakes Beach) is the other spot on the seashore where wading and swimming are usually safe. Sun and stroll or watch the bird life; the estero is one of the few Pacific coast marshes not seriously altered by man. On summer weekends (July 4 to Labor Day) a shuttle bus runs between the Limantour parking area and the Bear Valley trailhead, making it possible to hike and ride through this region.

Point Reyes Bird Observatory is the only full-time ornithological field research station on the continent. You'll see land birds, shore birds, and waterfowl on the south end of the peninsula the year around. Take Mesa Road from Bolinas.

Point Reyes Beach, southwest of Inverness on the Sir Francis Drake Highway, is ruler straight, steep faced, current ridden, wind scoured; it has a haunting, austere beauty. Solitude and astonishingly high surf are rewards for your visit. Sometimes big waves roll up from distant storms during a spell of warm weather that comes nearly every February. Picnicking then is better than during almost any other month of the year. Water and rest rooms are available. Pounding surf at Point Reyes and McClures beaches makes them too dangerous for water activities.

McClures Beach, at the northern end of the peninsula, is usually deserted because the access trail is steep and narrow. There's no swimming here but plenty of rocks for shelter from the wind.

Bear Valley trails

Headquarters to the national seashore is a mile west of Olema at the old Bear Valley Ranch. The Information Center, open daily from 8 A.M. to 5 P.M., has maps, trail guides, nature books, and schedules of nature programs. Here you'll also find a seismograph registering any quiver of the San Andreas Fault. Near headquarters is a self-guided tour of Earthquake Trail and an authentic replica of a Coast Miwok Indian Village. At the nearby Point Reyes Morgan Horse Farm, self-guided tours and interpretive talks are offered at the stables.

Bear Valley trailhead is gateway for over 100 miles of trails for hikers, horsemen, and bicycle riders to enjoy. Some run through fir groves and meadows to the sea, others lead steeply up to panoramic vistas of the entire peninsula. You can spend an hour or days just roaming. Reservations are necessary at four hike-in camps. To obtain a permit, register at the headquarters.

No fees or permits are required for day hiking, but there are a few rules: don't bring animals on the trails, carry your own water, and stay back from the cliffs. Winds often pick up, so it's a good idea to carry a jacket.

To Tomales Bay for gapers

Its skinny profile and the sheltering bulk of Inverness Ridge make Tomales Bay a tranquil alternative to the oceanic edges of Point Reyes.

Tomales Bay State Park, just north of Inverness, is not a part of the national seashore but includes some fine stretches of pleasant sandy-bottom coves—Shell, Pebble, Heart's Desire, and Indian—offering the warmest and quietest salt-water swimming on the Marin coast. Rockier stretches below sandstone bluffs support fair-sized populations of rock cockles. In addition to its shoreside charms, the park is a preserve for the Bishop pine, which flourishes on the peninsula but is absent on the adjacent mainland.

Around on the east side of the bay is a county boat launch just south of the point where State 1 bends inland toward the town of Tomales. Beach areas all along the bay are accessible for cockling or the winter run of herring. You can buy oysters from one of the commercial growers in the town of Marshall.

Dillon Beach, a raffishly charming commercial establishment and summer village right at the mouth of Tomales Bay, is almost due west of Tomales on a spur road. Clamming for gapers on a low-tide island, fishing of various sorts, and swimming (for the hardy) are popular.

Sonoma's lovely coastline

Shorter and less developed than the Mendocino coast, its more famous neighbor to the north, the Sonoma coastline begins at Bodega Bay and runs north to the mouth of the Gualala River. Its principal attractions are a series of beach parks, awesome scenery, and Fort Ross, last surviving sign of the 19th-century Russian settlements in California. The Sonoma coast divides into three distinct parts—two lengths of coastal shelf divided by a spate of steep hills marching into the sea. The shelves extend from Bodega Bay to Jenner on the south, and from Fort Ross to Gualala on the north. Overnight accommodations are scarce; it's wise to arrange lodging in advance.

Around Bodega Bay

The Bodega Bay-Jenner segment of the Sonoma coast is the most developed and easiest to view. A gently sloping shelf permits State 1 to run along a series of sandy beaches, only a little over an hour from San Francisco by way of Petaluma.

Bodega Bay, discovered by Spanish explorers in 1775, provides the only protected small boat anchorage of any size between San Francisco and Noyo in Mendocino County. Both charter and commercial boats operate out of Bodega, chasing salmon from May to October and bottom fishing when salmon are scarce. If you're in Bodega in the early afternoon, watch a party fishing boat unload the day's catch.

Perch feed in the lagoon shoals, especially along the west shore. A few gaper clams lurk along the shores, but most of them cluster offshore on a lowtide island. Outside the lagoon surfers can get up and ride toward the spit, starting at a point 400 yards east of the breakwater. Rock fishermen work the jetties and exposed side of Bodega Head. Parents and active children can romp endlessly in the rolling dunes that run all the way from the head north to Salmon Creek.

Doran Beach County Park occupies most of the curving sand spit that reaches across the bay toward Bodega Head, forming the inner lagoon where the moorages are. The outer beach is good for long strolls and rock fishing—sometimes for surfing. Inside, a boat launch adjoins the U.S. Coast Guard station. Camping is toward the tip.

Westside County Park adjoins a moorage in the lee of Bodega Head. In essence, it is a pair of parking lots, one for boaters and one for campers. Besides a launch ramp, it offers shore fishing for perch and quick access to Bodega Head's scenic beauties. You'll find picnic tables and trails down to open beaches.

Sonoma beaches—for variety

Small beaches, rocky headlands, and massive offshore rocks characterize Sonoma Coast State Beach. A collection of beaches and coves extends along State 1 from the village of Bodega Bay to the mouth of the Russian River, with over 14 miles of almost uninterrupted ocean shoreline in state park lands. Beachcombers and anglers find this stretch of coastline fascinating. For a park brochure, stop at the entrance station at Bodega Dunes or at park headquarters just to the north.

Bodega Head, the state beach's southernmost unit, is now public property. Here you can park your car and view the coast north as far as Fort Ross, south to Point Reyes. One mile north is Bodega Dunes, a state campground with over 100 units.

Salmon Creek is 1½ miles north of the town of Bodega Bay. Near the parking lot, Salmon Creek forms a summer wading pond. After fall rains break down the bar, it becomes a spawning stream for salmon and steelhead. Local surfers, night smelters, and surf fishers use the outer beach. Sand dunes roll away to the south, crisscrossed by foot and bridle paths.

Other beaches unfold in quick succession. Most are pockets of sand interrupted by outcrops of rock, good for surf or rock fishing.

Duncan's Landing is a dangerous section of coast. A large sign looms in front of a barbed wire fence, noting that a number of persons have been swept to their deaths in a pounding sea by unexpectedly high waves. Yet, there's plenty of safe rock fishing in these parks. On sandy beaches, surf fishing and dip-netting for smelts are good. Duncan's Cove, just in the lee of the point, is one of the most productive day smelt beaches in the region.

Wrights Beach, north of Duncan's Landing, is a camping unit of Sonoma Coast State Beach and a picnicker's favorite, as much for its broad, sandy strand as its facilities.

Goat Rock Beach is more than one thing—a protected cove, a long, sandy beach reaching out to form the mouth of the Russian River, and a sandy length of river bank. The road to it forks off State 1 near a long, upgrade crest and descends across nearly a mile of meadows to arrive at sea level. The northern end of the park is a popular daytime beach offering good smelt fishing in summer and steelheading in the winter.

From Jenner north, the coast is wilder, rockier; there are no easy returns to inland highways for many miles.

A Russian fort

Fort Ross is about 13 miles north of Jenner, where State 1 finally comes down from elevations that are either awe-inspiring or terrifying, depending on the density of the sea fog and the reliability of the driver. You see the stout, wooden buildings sitting high on the headlands before you reach them. The parking lot turnoff is just beyond the park.

A state historic park, Fort Ross was originally the North American outpost for Russian fur traders in the 19th century. During their reign the Russians and Aleut hunters wiped out the sea otter herds to the point of extinction, with help from American and British competitors. The Aleuts, skilled at hunting Alaskan otter herds, were deadly efficient. Fleets of two-man kayaks would form a circle and then start constricting the perimeter.

(Continued on page 68)

VISITORS INVADE stout wooden walls of Fort Ross (above), perched high on sunny headlands overlooking Pacific Ocean. Once an American outpost for Russian fur traders, fort is now state historic park.

WOOLLY SHEEP SCURRY across Mendocino County road (above). Bucolic scene is common in area where quiet ranches dot rolling pastures and sheep raising is still lucrative.

. . . Continued from page 66

When the animals surfaced to breathe, they were harpooned. Or hunters would take a live pup and use its distress cries to lure adult otters into range.

In recent years arsonists have plagued Fort Ross. In 1970 the Commandant's House burned. Within a year, two more fires blackened the seven-sided blockhouse, devastated the little chapel, and severely damaged the stockade. Painstakingly restored, the fort now looks much as it did.

A small museum within the Commandant's House contains artifacts from the Indian-Russian-American era.

Walk by the Call Ranch (privately owned and not open to the public), home of the owners of Fort Ross from 1873 to 1903, to get a beautiful view of the beach below, once the site of a profitable shipping business. Rockhounds forage in the gravelly shore, and divers work the rocks north and south in quest of abalone.

There is a slight fee for visiting the historic buildings and using the adjacent park and picnic grounds. The fort is open from 10 A.M. to 4:30 P.M. Park hours are sunrise to sunset.

The northern beaches

From Fort Ross to Mendocino, the coastal shelf is generally narrow but gently sloping, sometimes wooded but mostly covered by meadow grass. Take along a picnic basket; eating places are few.

Immediately north of Fort Ross the land is privately held as part of the Timber Cove development. Walk around to the seaward side of the hotel to look at sculptor Beniamino Bufano's last finished work—a monument to Peace—that overlooks both land and sea.

Stillwater Cove County Park, 3½ miles north of Fort Ross, opened its cove and creek-front location for day use in 1975. A favorite of scuba divers, the park has tables, a canyon trail, and the old Fort Ross schoolhouse.

Salt Point State Park, midway between Jenner and Stewarts Point, is worth a stop, whether or not you plan to camp, picnic, or comb the beach. At the point you'll find open and secluded sites for camping, deeply cut coves rewarding to scuba divers (there's an underwater park here), small stands of pygmy pines and redwoods, and miles of hiking trails. This rich environment made Salt Point a pioneer unit in the state's marine park system.

Kruse Rhododendron State Reserve is at its best from April to June when plants are in bloom. You can wander along paths through more than 300 acres set aside to preserve shrubs as high as 20 feet. Sorry, no picnic facilities.

Stewarts Point and Sea Ranch show great architectural diversity. Stewarts Point's general store, hotel, and schoolhouse are late 19th or early 20th century vintage. At Sea Ranch, a private development just up the road, you'll see strikingly modern trendsetting vacation homes designed to blend with the landscape. The ranch's restaurant/lodge complex typifies the design approach that you'll see reiterated in many houses in the meadows and hills north to Gualala.

Gualala is an old lumber port between Anchor Bay and Sea Ranch. The county park occupies the headland and spit, forming the south side of the Gualala River and marking the northern boundary of Sonoma County. You can camp beside the river in which Jack London liked to cast for steelhead. Gualala has motels and the noble old Gualala Hotel, built in 1903, with a frontier-style bar, genteel dining room, and a few rooms to let. St. Orres, a small inn outside of town, is vaguely reminiscent of Fort Ross in its Russian-inspired architecture. The dining room offers fine coastal views.

Mendocino's magnificent coast

The spirit of independence still flourishes in Mendocino County. On December 31, 1974, some citizens of Mendocino "seceded" from the state and formed their own "state"—Northern California. The news elicited no official comment from Sacramento except one wry remark by a veteran observer that "the county's departure, if it ever goes, would scarcely be noticed, at least not until the fog lifted."

Foggy it may be during the summer, but Mendocino's 19th century charm and scenic beauty draw thousands of visitors yearly and a regular influx of new residents. Urbanization doesn't threaten yet; narrow, crooked roads help preserve its relative remoteness, and towns are still small and spaced well apart.

Blue sea and white surf contrast with deep green forests and weathered gray barns. In the 100 miles from Gualala to Rockport, the mood changes around every headland, making this a photographer's field day. Even the gap-toothed fences are appealing.

For most visitors the heart of this rugged coast is the short distance from Mendocino to Fort Bragg. At either end of this stretch, you'll find less deep sea fishing, less Victoriana, and less tourism but more expansive beaches for driftwood hunters and surf fishermen.

Highways and byways are more prevalent on this part of the coast than farther south. The southern boundary of the county lies only 125 miles north of San Francisco, the northern edge only 250 miles. And yet a weekend can often mean more hours on the road than on the beach. (For a delightful loop drive, head east from Mendocino to Comptche, north to State Highway 20, and west to Noyo, just below Fort Bragg.) Most visitors find they need at least three days to linger leisurely in comfortable old inns, browse among art galleries, and picnic on pebbly beaches.

State 1 clings to the seaward edge of Mendocino County. Much of it is two lanes, within a mile of the sea and almost always in sight of it. Dipping and twisting across sharply ridged country and around deep coves, the highway takes you across the mouths of Mendocino's many rivers and creeks.

To reach the Mendocino coast you can join State 1 at its Leggett junction with U.S. 101 north of Fort Bragg or come up the Sonoma coast.

Two other routes provide easy access. State Highway 128 meanders north and west from Cloverdale on U.S. 101, passing through miles of rolling orchard and vineyard country before becoming a winding path through towering redwood forests. You pass through several hamlets along the 57 miles of well-paved, two-lane highway. State 20 is more direct and the area it passes through, less inhabited. The highway leaves U.S. 101 at Willits and joins State 1 just south of Fort Bragg-Noyo. Paralleling the route of the Skunk train, you'll travel 35 miles through fine stands of redwoods and Douglas fir. Watch for logging trucks on any road.

Accommodations center around the Mendocino-Fort Bragg area of the coast. You have your choice of old-time establishments or modern motels.

Inns in Little River, Elk, and Westport, as well as a hotel and several inns in Mendocino, recall the past (see page 77). If you wish to stay at one of these places, reservations are essential. Reservations are also advisable at motels in Fort Bragg and Mendocino. For a list of accommodations, write Mendocino County Chamber of Commerce, P.O. Box 244, Ukiah, CA 94582.

Weather is variable. Your best chances for a good outing are in May and early June when blooming azaleas and rhododendrons are plentiful and summer traffic is not, or during September and October when the weather is balmy and the roads and campgrounds are less crowded. Tourist season runs from Memorial Day to Labor Day, even though the coastal fog bank often descends during summer months.

The rainy season begins around mid-October; most of the annual rainfall of 35 inches occurs between December and May. Winter days are usually in the 40°F/4°C to 50° F/10°C range; summer temperatures often get into the 70s.

Beach parks and campgrounds

Getting down to the shore or back into the forest is mainly a matter of getting to the public beaches scattered along the coast from Gualala to Fort Bragg. Ranging from flat, sandy coves to tunneled headlands, most of them have fine camping or picnicking facilities and abundant scenery.

(Continued on page 71)

SMILE, IF YOU CALL A MAN A *HAIREEM*

Like the Hawaiians with their pidgin and the cockneys with their rhyming slang, some of the people of Boonville speak a colorfully unique dialect. It's called Boontling, and when a real Boonter speaks it, there's an uneven lilt and a touch of humor that run all through the more than 1,000 words of the vocabulary.

Boonville, with a population of about 1,000, lies at the southern end of picturesque Anderson Valley in Mendocino County. It's no problem to find your way to the coast on State Highway 128 from Boonville, but if you ask directions of one of the oldtimers in town he might give them to you in Boontling and watch your surprise. It's a game they play, and one of the reasons the language developed.

Rumors are it had its beginnings in the Anytime Saloon, and evolved mainly from a desire to exclude outsiders. Some say it was a parent's form of pig Latin.

Boontling grew up in Boonville in the late 1880s when the men would meet in town and try to *shark* (stump) each other with a new Boont word. Origins of some words have been lost, for Boontling developed as a spoken language and has only recently been written. But the oldtimers have passed along most of the words to the new generations, and several logical patterns are apparent in word formation.

All through Boontling, names have become descriptive nouns, and a spirit of fun prevails. Those who speak it today do so strictly to entertain each other. These are some of the words they use:

A *Charlie Walker* is a photograph, after the one-legged photographer from Mendocino who took Boonville family portraits. A big mustache is a *Tom Bacon*—named for the man who could reputedly wrap his handlebar around his ears. Horace Greeley's name is used for any journalist, but especially to signify a newspaperman.

A *relf* is a rail fence, a *hairk* is a haircut, a *haireem* is a "hairy mouth" or dog, and *skipe* is a clergyman, from sky pilot. If you add the word "region" to these, a *hairk region* becomes barbershop and a *skipe region,* a church.

The remainder of Boontling is made up mostly of words or phrases whose connotation is immediately clear to a Boonter. *Featherlegged* means a know-it-all and comes from the strutting barnyard cocks. *Trashmovers* (big storms) tell something of winter problems in a rural community.

It's not easy to hear Boontling because Boonters speak it mostly to each other. But if you buy a cup of coffee or a sandwich in town, take a good look at the receipt. Across the bottom may be written: "Our Gorm is Boll, our Zeese is hot; some regions de-Hig you, but we will not." One hint: *Boll* means good.

BEHIND THE RED DOOR, Heritage
House (below) epitomizes charm and warm
hospitality of north coast inns.

FISHING BOATS SNUGGLE UP to peaceful dock
(above) during golden moment at Noyo harbor,
fishing center of Mendocino County.

HEADLANDS FRONT CLASSIC VIEW of quaint
Mendocino (below), California's answer to a New
England coastal village.

... *Continued from page 69*

Manchester State Beach has the first generous sand beach in Mendocino County and the last one south of Fort Bragg. Its 7 miles of wide shore run most of the distance between the Garcia River and Alder Creek. Middling good for sand castles, the beach is far roomier than its minimally developed campground, sheltered behind dunes from the frequent winds. To the south you see Point Arena's lighthouse, the most powerful light on the west coast; closed to visitors.

Van Damme State Park, on scenic Little River, offers campsites, reasonably safe (but cold) swimming, and biking or hiking trails. One trail leads to an ancient pygmy forest of stunted conifers in the southeast quarter of the park. Its beach is a pleasant wayside stop but only a minor introduction to the main park on the inland side of the highway.

Mendocino Headlands State Park, whose splendor needs no superlatives, begins at the mouth of the Big River as a sandy beach, loops west beneath the bluffs as a wall of rock, and then broadens to cover the flat fields of the headlands, as well as their wave-swept edge. Heeser Drive, a loop road west of Mendocino town, circles along the edge of the bluff and down to the beach. This is a highly sculpted shore, with wave tunnels, arched rocks, narrow channels—even a few lagoons. Tidepoolers should have a "look but don't touch" attitude, and skin divers fare well. Watch an unusually picturesque surf pound its way ashore; the outermost point contends for honors as the finest wave-watching spot on the coast. Because offshore rocks or shoals temper the fury of onrushing swells, safe vantages are only a few feet away. At the north end of Heeser Drive, a public fishing access adjoins calmer seas.

North of Mendocino, another undeveloped unit in the state park system is Caspar Headlands State Reserve. When the tide's out, you can picnic on a small beach.

Russian Gulch State Park looks back across a broad bay at Mendocino from the next headland to the north. It offers a compacted replay of the sheltered beach at Van Damme and the exposed headlands at Mendocino. A creek cutting out of the gulch pauses in a low, sandy spot so children may splash around in safety, and then slips into the sea in the lee of a craggy, lofty headland. A blowhole just north of the main overlook only works during storms.

From its dramatic edge, the main body of the park runs deeply inland; protected campsites nestle in the mouth of the canyon. It's an easy hike upstream to a lacy waterfall set amidst a forest underlaid with beds of ferns.

MacKerricher State Park begins north of Fort Bragg where Pudding Creek empties into the sea. Greatly enlarged in 1972, its headlands, beaches, surf, heavily forested uplands, and small lake for fishing and boating make it the most versatile of the parks. A road wanders down to the shore between a rocky beach to the south and sandy beach to the north, which runs all the way from the main parking area to Ten Mile River. Chief reasons for heading out along the dunes are smelt fishing or driftwood hunting. You can get to the Ten Mile River end of the beach from an old logging road off State 1.

Like Van Damme and Russian Gulch to the south, MacKerricher is popular and, despite three campgrounds, rarely has campsite vacancies in summer. For information on any of these parks, write to Department of Parks and Recreation, Mendocino Area State Parks, P.O. Box 440, Mendocino, CA 95460; call Ticketron for reservations.

Inland to Boonville

About 30 miles inland from the windy Mendocino coast lie the quiet ranches and hillside pastures of the Anderson Valley. Boonville, largest town on State 128 between Cloverdale and the ocean, was settled in the 1850s. Locals still make their living growing apples and raising livestock.

Special events are scattered throughout the year. In the spring when apple blossoms and native western azaleas color the valley pink and white against sheep-cropped, green hills, it's time for the local art show (March), the wildflower festival (April), and "Buck-a-roo Days," a rodeo in June. In July, sheep raisers gather to exchange gossip, compete for prizes, and feast on barbecued lamb. Held under tall shade trees at the Mendocino County Fairgrounds, this event attracts many visitors.

In the fall and winter, steelhead run in the Navarro River, and roadside stands sell the valley's fine apples. September is the month for the County Fair and Apple Festival; reminiscent of old-time fairs, it draws visitors from all over the West.

Camp and parks dot the roadside. Paul M. Dimmick Wayside Camp, a 12-acre redwood park between the highway and the river, makes a handy base for both trailer and tent campers. Forested Hendy Woods State Park has two camping areas, a stream for summer swimming and fishing, and stands of virgin redwoods.

From Mendocino to Fort Bragg

From Little River on the south to Fort Bragg on the north, Mendocino County reaches a sort of high point. These miles are the most populous, the most popular with tourists, and contain the two principal towns and the major fishing harbor. Progress is so complete that State 1 has been straightened and widened, bringing Mendocino and Fort Bragg within 15 minutes of one another. However, the best plan is not to hurry. There's variety to savor.

Mendocino: New England revisited

Almost startlingly in contrast to its time and place, this small cluster of wooden towers and carpenter's Gothic houses contains a contemporary society of artists and artisans. They share a view south across the mouth of the Big River and west across the grassy headlands to the sea. Amble through the numerous galleries and see how resident artists translate such scenes in oils, wood blocks, and water colors.

Settled as a mill town in 1852 by timber baron Henry Meiggs, Mendocino may look like a Cape Cod relic, but its weathered buildings are bursting with life. Park your car as soon as you get to town. Streets are short, narrow, and easily jammed by vehicle traffic. The terrain is good for biking.

A walking tour will take you to the Mendocino Art Center (heart of the coastal art renaissance), past homes of long-dead lumber barons, to art galleries, book stores, unusual shops, and coffee houses. Be sure to notice the Old Masonic Hall with its intriguing rooftop sculpture of Father Time braiding a maiden's hair.

Fort Bragg—for fish and flowers

Just up the road is the harbor town of Noyo, sportfishing center of Mendocino County. Charter boats operate out of a deep cove just inside the mouth of the Noyo River. Private boats go in free at a public launching ramp; charters go out for a half-day of salmon fishing. Fishing season runs from June until the first week in October (weekends only after school starts). Some of the best seafood restaurants are on the Noyo flat.

Fort Bragg, largest city on the coast between San Francisco and Eureka, was first settled as an army post in 1857, then resettled with the construction of its first sawmill in 1885. Paul Bunyan Days (Labor Day weekend) bring big crowds to watch modern loggers perform axe throwing, pole climbing, and log rolling. You can tour the Georgia-Pacific Museum, hop aboard the strangely named "Skunk" train for an 80-mile round trip through redwood groves to Willits on U.S. 101, take a walking tour of the town, picnic and fish (slight fee) at the Fort Bragg Trout Farm pond from noon to dusk, or visit the Mendocino Coast Botanical Gardens, a lavish, 47-acre display of plants and bulbs. On most summer weekends, you can enjoy an afternoon of music in the gardens. (Gardens are open daily 9 A.M. to 6 P.M.; there's a moderate charge.) For winter schedule and concert information, call (707) 964-4352.

Beyond Fort Bragg the coastal shelf narrows to next to nothing, then nothing. Weathered Westport's New England-style houses have changed little since the heyday of lumbering. Shore fishing is productive at Westport-Union Landing State Beach and South Kibesillah Gulch Coast Angling Access Area. A pair of unpaved parking lots alongside the highway give access to several hundred yards of vertical shore. Tiny Westport has a restaurant, grocery store (with gas pumps), café, and modest hotel.

The Redwood Highway

Before the Gold Rush brought a surge of new population to Northern California, a vast forest of the world's tallest trees—the coast redwood or *Sequoia sempervirens*—blanketed an area up to 30 miles wide, ranging 450 miles from the Santa Lucia Mountains south of Monterey northward into a corner of Oregon. The oldest known coast redwood was 2,200 years old when cut in the 1930s.

Civilization's demands have left only small parts of the forest primeval. The majority of the remaining redwoods are located along U.S. 101 from Leggett north to Crescent City. These giants grow naturally in no other part of the country.

The Avenue of the Giants, a 33-mile, alternate scenic route (254), roughly parallels U.S. 101. Winding leisurely through a cathedral-like aisle of 300-foot-high trees it offers a closer view of these "ambassadors from another age." The entrance is at Sylvandale, about 6 miles north of Garberville. The avenue ends about 5 miles north of Pepperwood (30 miles south of Eureka). Numerous turnouts and parking areas allow for "neck-craning"; trails lead you through tranquil glens and along bucolic river banks. If you take U.S. 101, you'll miss these sylvan glades, public campgrounds, picnicking and swimming facilities, and a few small towns on the way.

Logging still thrives, and visitors are not encouraged at harvesting areas. But you can visit demonstration forests, stop by reforestation displays, or visit the Pacific Lumber Company (one of the world's largest mills) at Scotia. At the main headquarters you get passes for self-guiding plant tours on weekends. For more tour information call (707) 764-2222.

Squirrel-Redwood Bus Tours offers a narrated guide to the Avenue of the Giants. From June 15 to September 15, buses leave Garberville four times weekly; some include nature walks and visits to neighboring lumber mills. For more information call (707) 986-7526.

Weather is variable in redwood country. The finest season is autumn, when the crowds thin out, the air turns brisk, and the seasonal show of color brightens the countryside. Wildflower season along the coast often extends from March until August, but April to June is the best period. Expect rain and fog in summer; redwoods grow in moist climates.

Eureka, the major city in the redwoods, is one of the cooler places in the nation from June until October. From this city north to the Oregon border, the weather is much the same as the Mendocino coast. South of Eureka, after U.S. 101 cuts behind the coast hills, you experience an entirely different kind of climate. Because the mountains screen out the cooling ocean air, summers can be warm and dry.

Accommodations in redwood country are somewhat limited. More motels and hotels line this highway than appear along the Mendocino coast, but traffic is correspondingly heavier. Eureka and Arcata have a number of motels between them, but during summer's tourist peak, it's wise to have advance reservations. Without reservations you'll have a better chance of finding a place to stay in Orick (southern gateway to the Redwood National Park) or in Crescent City. Roadside motels and inns are scattered along the road between Willits and Eureka. Ukiah, at the southern extreme of the area, also offers a number of motels. Camping is very popular during the summer.

Pick a park

The best of the remaining coast redwoods are preserved in the Redwood National Park and in several state parks along the Redwood Highway section of U.S. 101. Parks are busy throughout the summer, offering informative naturalist programs, nature hikes, and evening campfires. If you're of the school that believes a family visiting the redwoods ought to have a square mile or so to itself, plan your trip in the off season.

South of Eureka, scenic attractions and the highway play tag with the South Fork of the Eel River. Sprawling Humboldt Redwoods State Park is the main attraction, but there are other good spots for campers. Several of the smaller parks contain awesome stands of old-growth redwoods and are frequently less crowded than the more publicized Humboldt groves. Standish-Hickey State Recreation Area, just north of Leggett, has plenty of camping but only one mature redwood among dense forest. Picnicking is popular at Smithe Redwoods State Reserve, a little farther north. You can hike to a waterfall or take a footpath down to the Eel River. The Benbow Lake State Recreation Area, south of Garberville, features picnic and limited camping facilities.

Richardson Grove State Park is relatively small (about 800 acres), but you can't fail to find it—the Redwood Highway goes right through it. Here are swimming holes along the Eel River's South Fork and highly developed campgrounds. Ten miles of trails make good hiking. Although it can be wet and chilly in the winter, Richardson Grove is open the year around. In winter, silver and king salmon and steelhead trout attract many fishermen.

Humboldt Redwoods State Park is scattered along most of the length of the Avenue of the Giants and the Eel River. Acquired piece by piece, the park complex now ties together more than 70 memorial groves. It begins unobtrusively at the Whittemore Grove across the river from the highway; take Briceland Road at Redway. Beyond Miranda, the groves are fairly continuous to the junction of the South Fork and the main Eel, with major breaks at Myers Flat, Weott, and the freeway overpass that has cut a tremendous swath between Founders Grove and California Federation of Women's Clubs Grove. At Burlington, in a dark copse of second growth, an all-year campground adjoins the park headquarters. Rangers give information on camping and picnic facilities in other parts of the park and, in autumn, tell where to see the best color display.

Highlights of the park include the Founders Tree, for many years considered the world's tallest (364 feet before a broken top brought the figure down to 347); the solemn depths of the Rockefeller Forest; the wide pebble beach of the Eel, where you can stand back and look at redwoods from top to bottom instead of being encircled and overwhelmed; and Bull Creek flats, where you can sit underneath the soaring trees and bask in the silence or stroll down to the site of the present "tallest" tree, Giant tree, and Flatiron tree.

Grizzly Creek Redwoods State Park, a small, secluded area along the Van Duzen River, is highly prized by picnickers and campers because of its climate, often warmer and less foggy than parks right along the coast. Its 234 acres include a virgin redwood grove, more than a mile of river front, hiking trails, and improved campsites—but no grizzlies. Summer trout fishing is fair to good; steelheading is good from mid-February to mid-April. The park is 18 miles east of U.S. 101 on State Highway 36.

For more information on these parks, write to California Department of Parks and Recreation, District 1 Headquarters, 3431 Fort Avenue, Eureka, CA 95501.

Eureka: A Victorian city

Lumbering and fishing built Eureka, largest city in Humboldt County, and are still its main industries. Sniff the air: the odors come from docks along Humboldt Bay or pulp mills south of town. Eureka is a midway point between San Francisco and Portland; you'll have to get off the main highway and drive through town to enjoy its charms. Here you'll discover many motels, a delightful Tudor-style hotel, and several fine restaurants well known for their seafood. For maps, stop by the Eureka Chamber of Commerce, 2112 Broadway, on your way into town. During the summer, the chamber offers a 5-hour bus tour of the area's attractions, including lunch and a bay cruise; price is moderate and reservations are a must. For more information call (707) 442-3738.

Fort Humboldt State Historic Park, constructed in the 1850s and abandoned as a military post in 1865, is a half-mile off U.S. 101 on the southern edge of Eureka. Open daily from 9 A.M. to dusk, a small museum behind the park headquarters gives a brief history of the fort where Ulysses S. Grant spent several months just prior to his resignation from the army. On display is a selection of equipment used for turn-of-the-century logging near a reconstruction of a typical logger's cabin. On a clear day the view of Humboldt Bay is outstanding.

Sequoia Park (Glatt and W Streets) is a woodland oasis in the heart of Eureka. On these 52 acres, you'll find one of the best forests in this region. You can walk leafy trails past ferns and streams, stop at a zoo and children's playground, or feed ducks the remains of your picnic lunch. A shady haven on rare warm days, it's equally pleasant when the weather is cool and foggy.

Victorian-sighting is excellent in Eureka. Except for downtown thoroughfares, the town retains much of its original character. Brightly colored turrets, spires, and gables show up well against the often-stark sky. Most homes are well preserved or are being renovated. The largest concentration of Victorian homes is south of Seventh Street between C and K streets. Called the "queen" of Victorians, the flamboyant and much-photographed Carson Mansion is on M Street between Second and Third.

Now a private men's club, the mansion looks much as it did when completed by lumber baron William Carson in 1886. Decide for yourself whether it is the "finest example of Victorian Gothic architecture" or an "architectural monstrosity." The smaller house across the street was also built by Carson as a wedding gift for his son. The carriage house, connected by a walkway, houses an interior decorator's studio.

A self-guided tour highlights other examples of Victorian architecture throughout Eureka. Tour maps are available at the Eureka Chamber of Commerce.

Eureka's Old Town has come to life. Spurred by a concentrated redevelopment program, this once decaying waterfront district now boasts budding restaurants, speciality shops, new businesses, even a community art center.

Major renovation has focused on Second Street between C and M streets. At Second and F streets, Old Town Square features an open-air gazebo and meandering fountain. For some blocks in each direction you can glimpse restored vintage buildings.

Around the corner from Old Town Square the Humboldt Cultural Center (422 First Street) was a mercantile store in the 1870s. It now houses shows by local artists and craftspeople. Another popular stop is the Art Center, G and Second streets, which offers art supplies, gifts, and two galleries.

Also located in Old Town is the Clarke Memorial Museum at Third and E streets. The museum features extensive collections of Victorian, maritime, and pioneering relics, plus an outstanding native American exhibit.

Humboldt Bay

Just beyond the waterfront section of downtown Eureka and almost concealed from the highway is Humboldt Bay, largest deep-water port between Portland and San Francisco. You can explore the harbor on an old ferry, study the bay's birdlife, go boating and fishing, or beachcomb along the great stretches of sand guarding the harbor's narrow entrance.

Getting around the bay is easy when you take a narrated cruise leaving several times a day from the foot of C Street. You'll see bay highlights and hear a brief history of the area. Watch the commercial fishing fleet coming into the harbor with nets still dripping from their catches or the large ocean freighters loading pulp on the peninsula.

Six boat ramps and two hoists make it easy to put your boat into the water. You'll find public ramps at several points: at the Eureka Mooring Basin, on the North Spit before the Coast Guard station, and at Fields Landing on South Bay. You can rent a skiff or charter a boat at King Salmon and use hoists and a ramp for a nominal fee.

Crossing the bridge to Samoa takes you over Woodley and Indian islands. Marshy Indian Island, part of the Humboldt Bay National Wildlife Refuge, is the site of the northernmost egret/heron rookery on the Pacific Coast. In a small grove of cypress, you may see hundreds of roosting birds, massed like a feathery white cloud. A sign at Samoa marks the turnoff to the Cookhouse, where you dine family style at one of the last lumber camp cookhouses operating in the West.

From Samoa you can continue along the North Spit across Mad River Slough to Arcata, where a self-guiding architectural tour takes you back to the time of Bret Harte and the heyday of gold mining. A few miles north of Arcata, the Azalea State Reserve bursts into bloom around Memorial Day. Trails lead you among masses of overhanging blossoms. Take the North Bank Road from either U.S. 101 or State Highway 299.

Picturesque Trinidad, settled in 1850, is one of the oldest towns on the north coast. Just minutes north of Eureka, this former whaling station is now a bustling fishing village. Colorful boats dot its sheltered harbor, and nearby Trinidad State Park offers day-use facilities. Fishing expeditions, gift shops, restaurants, and motels make Trinidad an inviting diversion at the north end of the bay.

A valley loop

A 73-mile trail loops through pastoral Mattole Valley to the sea and back into the redwoods. You can begin at Ferndale, about 15 miles south of Eureka.

Ferndale's freshly painted look is a study in carpenter's Gothic. Here you'll find some of the coast's best-preserved Victorians, from small white cottages to intricate gingerbread mansions. A stroll down Main Street reveals a menagerie of artisans working in stained glass, metal, even custom shirt design. Here, too, are antique and crafts shops, a western saddlery, several galleries, and a couple of restaurants worthy of a lunch stop. At the annual art festival in May, displays of arts and crafts line Main Street. The village also hosts the county fair in August.

For an overall town view (and a steep uphill climb), try 30-acre Russ Park. Take Ocean Avenue east from Main Street; your hike starts just west of the Catholic cemetery.

Driving over Bear River Ridge, you coast downhill through manicured pastures and finally reach the shore.

Heading back inland you'll pass through Petrolia, site of California's first drilled oil wells, and Honeydew, one of California's smallest towns. The village consists of a general store, gas station, and post office—all under one roof. Back in the redwoods, the road slants down to Bull Creek through Rockefeller Grove, meeting U.S. 101 about 2½ miles north of Weott.

Redwood National Park

A representative segment of old-growth redwood and the outstanding coastal scenery in Northern California are now being protected so that, generations from now, people will be able to view the magnificent trees and the plant and animal life which they nurture.

Stretching from above Crescent City at the north to below Orick to the south, Redwood National Park contains 106,000 acres (48,000 were added in 1978) of some of the West's finest scenic and recreation areas. Park headquarters is located in Crescent City; a visitor information center is in Orick. Scheduled for 1980 completion is a new activity center near Prairie Creek Redwoods State Park. The center will help day-use scenery seekers and backpackers effectively plan their national park visit.

A tour service offers bus trips highlighting Humboldt's north coast attractions. Starting from Trinidad, stops include selected state parks and sections of Redwood National Park. Reservations are suggested; price

(Continued on page 76)

SAND FLIES as young equestrians (left) trot onto sunny beach near Trinidad for a brisk bareback run.

LACED IN GREEN, majestic coast redwoods (Sequoia sempervirens) *stand tall (right) in soft morning light of Richardson Grove State Park.*

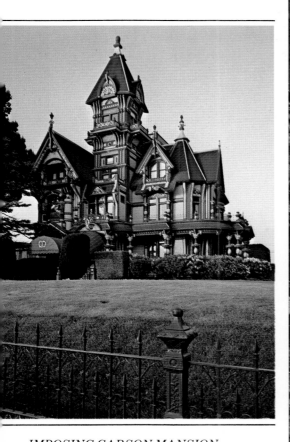

IMPOSING CARSON MANSION (above) is incongruous blend of turrets, gingerbread, gables, moldings. Built in 1886 for lumber baron William Carson, Eureka mansion now houses private men's club.

Redwood Coast

Scale in Miles

0   5   10   15

Scale in Kilometers

0   5   10   15

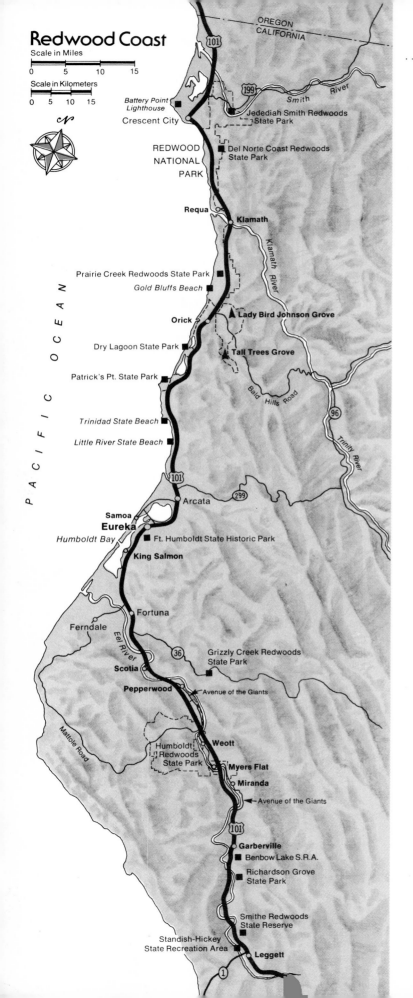

. . . Continued from page 74

is moderate. For more information call Northcoast Redwood Tours (707) 677-0334 or (707) 677-3470.

Klamath, at the mouth of the Klamath River, is well known for fine salmon and steelhead fishing. You can take a 64-mile jet boat trip up the river just to view the scenery. Tours leave one mile north of Klamath, on U.S. 101, from June 1 to the end of September.

Lady Bird Johnson Grove is located along the Bald Hills Road 2 miles east of U.S. 101 (just north of Orick). A half-mile trail will take you to the site where Mrs. Lyndon B. Johnson dedicated the national park on November 25, 1968.

Tall Trees Grove, home of the skyscraping sequoias, runs along Redwood Creek just west of Bald Hills Road. The tallest tree is 367.8 feet high and 14 feet in diameter. Primitive camping is available.

At one time the only way to see the world's tallest trees was a 17-mile round-trip hike along the creek. Now the park's new summer shuttle service takes you within a mile of these ancient giants. Every hour from 9 A.M. to 4 P.M. daily, passenger vans leave from the parking area 7 miles up Bald Hills Road to carry hikers to the grove's trailhead. The walk in is mostly downhill to the river. Once you reach the grove, a sign points out the world's tallest known tree.

Three parks within a park

Included within the Redwood National Park are three long-established state parks (Prairie Creek, Del Norte, and Jedediah Smith). In addition to being the nucleus of the national park, at present these parks have the only established camping. Federal recreation permits are not valid in the state parks, and summer reservations are a must for the 350-plus campsites.

Much of the redwood forest acreage of the state parks consists of memorial groves purchased by the Save-the-Redwoods League with donations from private individuals. Supplemented by state funds, this money is used to acquire more redwood groves and enlarge the parks.

Prairie Creek Redwoods State Park is a favorite of many campers. It does have more than its share of special wonders: a handsome creek, a herd of native Roosevelt elk, the wide expanse of sand at Gold Bluffs Beach (tent camping available), and scenic Fern Canyon. About 100 inches of rain falls on Prairie Creek most years, giving it rain-forest overtones; but high ground to the west protects it from most of the chilly ocean winds and fog. Hiking the more than 100 miles of trails (including one for the blind and a self-guided nature walk) is the best way to explore the park's interior. Two campgrounds offer a total of 100 sites.

Del Norte Coast Redwoods State Park lets you enjoy both a drive through rugged inland forest on U.S. 101 and vistas of Pacific shore from high turnouts south of the wooded section. Damnation Creek Trail will take you on foot through the dense forest to the ocean where the giant redwoods grow almost to the shore. From April to July, you'll see outstanding displays of rhododendrons and azaleas. Del Norte has excellent camping facilities at Mill Creek Campground.

Jedediah Smith Redwoods State Park is 9 miles northeast of Crescent City on U.S. 199. At the northernmost end of the Redwood National Park, Jedediah Smith presents views of skyline ridges still tightly furred with giant redwoods. The highway runs through hilly Tyson Grove and the National Tribute Grove (just two of 18 memorial groves in the park) and then out onto a magnificent flat, where some of the most imposing redwoods soar above vine maple, salal, Oregon grape, and ferns.

The Smith River provides good salmon, steelhead, and trout fishing in season and sandy beaches for sunbathing. There are numerous campsites and trails. Crescent City, at the northern gateway to the park, sits alongside a captivating harbor. Information on the area is available from the Crescent City Chamber of Commerce and the national park's headquarters and information center. For more information write to Redwood National Park, P.O. Drawer N, Crescent City, CA 95531.

Battery Point Lighthouse, built in 1856, stands on a small island approximately 20 yards from shore. Visitors may walk to it at low tide. Though your goal is the museum inside the lighthouse, most of the fun lies in getting there.

The small museum is open Wednesdays through Sundays.

INNS ARE IN—UP NORTH

Mellow old inns offer a warm welcome to North Coast visitors. Most hug the Mendocino area and serve as bases for exploring the countryside. Varying from the intimate home to the sprawling lodge with cottages, each hostelry has charm. Most operate on American (full meals) or modified (breakfast and dinner) plans.

A sampling of inns appears below. Plan to make reservations well in advance and note closed periods. Some of the well-known inns are booked completely for weekends a year in advance. For rates and additional information, write or call the inn directly.

Benbow Inn, Garberville, CA 95440; (707) 923-2124: Tudor inn in redwoods; Eel River forms lake and beach; 9-hole regulation golf course; large living room, restaurant, and lounge; open late March through November, Christmas.

Dehaven Valley Farm, Westport, CA 95488; (707) 964-2931: Restored Victorian (7 guest rooms) in rural setting next to beach; ample continental breakfast included; larger breakfast menu and six-course Saturday dinners by reservation; closed Mondays; might be closed January and February.

Elk Cove Inn, Elk, CA 95432; (707) 877-3321: Small Victorian home built in early 1880s sits in bluff hiding its private beaches; attractive annex up the street brings guest capacity to 14; breakfast and dinner served Thursday through Sunday; advance reservations only.

Harbor House, Elk, CA 95432; (707) 877-3203: Lovely redwood home in Bernard Maybeck style and cottages (7 rooms total) on the ocean side with path to the beach; open all year; reservations only.

Heritage House, Little River, CA 95456; (707) 937-5885: Original farmhouse built on the cove in 1877 by relatives of present owner; interesting names and architecture for all 46 units; beautiful living room, lounge, and dining room; notice plantings on sod roofs; closed December and January.

Joshua Grindle Inn, Mendocino, CA 95460; (707)937-4143: Vintage 1879 home, now refurbished as most attractive inn; 5 rooms, each with private bath and distinctive decor; full breakfast in cheerful dining room; children discouraged.

Little River Inn, Little River, CA 95456; (707) 937-5942: Maine-style mansion, vintage 1853, forms heart of complex offering "attic rooms," casual cottages, or contemporary hilltop rooms; 9-hole regulation golf course; open all year (lounge and dining room closed for a few weeks before Christmas).

MacCallum House, 740 Albion St., Mendocino, CA 95460; (707) 937-0289: Landmark house sold with treasure of contents is now enticing new inn; fruit bowls highlight breakfast in your room; dining room on premises.

Mendocino Hotel, Mendocino, CA 95460; (707) 937-0511: Lone survivor of hotels once lining Main Street; extensive renovation lends air of opulence; costumed staff; public restaurant.

Hill House, Mendocino, CA 95460; (707) 937-0554: New inn with deliberate patina of age; ocean view from some units; 21 rooms with private baths; beautiful appointments; continental breakfast; open all year.

Schoolhouse Creek Inn, Little River, CA 95456; (707)937-5525: Rustic cottages and modern rooms with Franklin stoves have ocean view; stroll to secluded ocean cove, fern canyon, or through apple orchard; adjoining restaurant offers dinners built from scratch.

The growing appreciation of wines in the United States has uncorked a new flow of visitors to California's vineyards and tasting rooms. Between 1½ and 3 million people visit the Napa and Sonoma wineries (backbone of the North Coast wine district) each year. Here you see vinous works of art created and sample the results of the creativity—a delicious way to increase your knowledge of wine.

Winery architecture is unexpectedly diverse. Handsome traditional buildings from the late 1800s show their European heritage; California ingenuity adds a variety of touches, ranging from mission to modern.

You could visit as many as 20 cellars in a day, if you planned your route with care. But you would miss the details—and details are what make wine. Don't try to visit more than three or four wineries in one day. Do plan to stop and visit other attractions in the area. The wine country lends itself to lazing; bring a picnic basket along or stop at bakeries, delis, or cheese shops along the way.

When to go? The best time to visit the wine country is the most active period—late September and early October—when the crush (the first step toward the new year's wines) takes place. The heady aroma of newly fermenting wine charges the warm afternoon air. Vines, stripped of their clusters of grapes, are tinged with gold and scarlet. Inside the wineries, in spite of hurried labor over the new wines, amiable guides welcome visitors as nonchalantly as they might in the still days of winter when the wines take care of themselves.

Divided into regions, this chapter points out typical wineries, lists main attractions, and offers a cool look at water sports, hiking and camping locations. Students of wine seeking a complete list of visitable wineries may write Wine Institute (165 Post Street, San Francisco, CA 94105) for a free copy of *Wine Wonderland*. A complete tour book of all wineries in the state is *Sunset's Guide to California's Wine Country*.

Napa Valley: For touring and tasting

Many people consider the Napa Valley synonymous with "The Wine Country"—and with good reason. The vine-covered floor of the valley, flanked with tall hills and dotted with evocative wineries, may have its peers, but it has few superiors.

Easy to get to, Napa Valley is most accessible from Sacramento, San Francisco, and Oakland on a combination of Interstate Highway 80 and State Highway 29 from Vallejo. Another slower, hillier, and prettier route

REDS, YELLOWS, AND ORANGES light up Napa Valley vineyards when fall comes to the wine country. During harvest season, crushed grapes' piquant bouquet fills the air.

North of San Francisco lie the valleys and hills synonymous with California wine. Large and small wineries dot the countryside with architecture ranging from traditional European to refreshingly contemporary design. Leisurely savor the delights of winemaking by visiting three or four wineries a day. Autumn crush is the most picturesque and exciting season; hills blaze hues of red, orange, and gold, and fermentation sweetens the cool fall air. Sample other wine country highlights—walk around a small town, tour a museum or mission, raft down a river, or slither into a steaming bath of mud at a spa.

Wine Country

from San Francisco goes across the Golden Gate and then north on U.S. Highway 101, State highways 37 and 121. From the north, take U.S. 101 and State Highway 128 for a pleasant drive.

The greatest concentration of wineries open to visitors flanks State 29 north and south of the unhurried town of St. Helena. A parallel road, the Silverado Trail, has more wineries sprinkled on the slopes of the east hills. Elevated enough to afford panoramic vineyard views, most of the old stagecoach route has been widened and straightened to suit the modern automobile. Crossroads among the vines tie the two arteries together, making easy access to the entire valley.

Though the city of Napa is by far the largest in the valley, its occupation with wine is minimal. The city has an impressive quarter of fine Victorian houses southwest of an agreeable shopping district, but most of the romantic traditions of the Napa Valley are to be found farther north.

St. Helena—the wine center

The 1890s look of Main Street, St. Helena, is proudly maintained, and so is the century-old emphasis on wine. Oddly enough, the single sharpest focal point is the town's new-in-1979 library building, which houses both a major collection of wine literature and an independent museum celebrating the life and works of the author of *Kidnapped* and *Treasure Island,* Robert Louis Stevenson.

Napa Valley Wine Library Association assembled this collection of wine literature, and continues to expand it. The association also conducts several weekend courses in wine appreciation for its members each summer. (There is a waiting list; for details, write NVWLA, PO Box 328, St. Helena, CA 94574.)

The Silverado Museum occupies a separate wing of the library building. Based on the collections of Norman Strouse, the museum houses a large display of Robert Louis Stevenson memorabilia including original manuscripts and letters, portraits and photographs of the writer, and a desk he used in Samoa. To find this museum here is historically fitting because the peripatetic author honeymooned in an abandoned bunkhouse of the defunct Silverado Mine on Mount St. Helena in 1880-81. In 1883 he recounted that experience in his book *Silverado Squatters*.

The buildings are two blocks east of Main Street via Adams.

The Napa Valley Olive Oil Manufactory, on Charter Oak Avenue, is a grand place to pick up picnic fixings to go along with your wine tour. You'll find fragrant olive oil, cheeses, patés, dried mushrooms, and breadsticks.

The Hurd Candle Factory, in Freemark Abbey, is the center of a complex of shops offering foods, cookware, and wine accessories. Beeswax candles hang near good wine sleeping in cellars below.

To Calistoga for mud baths and geysers

St. Helena's life centers around grapes, Calistoga's around health. Situated at the foot of Mount St. Helena,
Calistoga is famous throughout the country as a spa.

Mud baths bring thousands of tourists to this year-round resort. Visitors have been arriving ever since Samuel Brannan built his opulent spa in 1859. In addition to bath houses—where swimming pools may be mineral or hot spring water—motels, hotels, and resorts abound. Calistoga is a mecca for glider pilots. And you can take the scenic drive to the Petrified Forest, west of the city.

Napa County Historical Society Museum is located in town. History buffs will find some fascinating facts on the life of the wealthy of the late 1800s.

California's "Old Faithful" geyser, impressive spectacle in a region of hot springs and fumaroles, spews a 60-foot shower of steam and vapor at 50-minute intervals. The eruption continues for about 3 minutes, after which the geyser retreats until its next performance. Visitors learn about the origins of geothermal steam. Located just north of town on Tubbs Road (turn east from State 128), the grounds are open from 8 A.M. to dusk; there's a slight admission charge.

Yountville—for food and lodging

Named for Napa County's first white settler, George Yount, this once-sleepy town has experienced a renaissance. After years of being geared to the pace of the nearby veterans' home, it is now enlivened by a rural counterpart to Ghirardelli Square and by several elegant inns and restaurants.

In 1870, G. Grozinger built a large brick winery here. His old cellar now stocks a collection of shops, galleries, and eating spots under the collective banner of Vintage 1870. Even a theater is tucked away in one cavernous corner of the place. Other shops and restaurants flank Vintage 1870.

Not far away, Yount's final resting place is in the local cemetery, hard by the land in which he planted the valley's first vines in the 1850s.

Hiking and camping spots

Beautiful weather, along with a variety of attractions, makes the Napa Valley an ideal place to spend more than a day. Fortunately you'll find a number of areas where you can pitch a tent, park a trailer, or unroll a sleeping bag. Hiking and biking are good ways to get around on the valley floor; heading up into the surrounding hills provides plenty of exercise. Swimmers, boaters, and fishermen will find natural and manmade lakes appealing.

Bothe-Napa Valley State Park, more than 1,000 acres of broad-leafed trees and conifers and second-growth redwoods, extends west into the hills. Facilities include camping and picnicking sites, hiking trails, and a swimming pool. The park is on the west side of State 29 about 4 miles north of St. Helena.

The Old Bale Mill, a short distance south of Bothe-Napa, was added to the park. Set in motion in 1846 for the convenience of nearby residents who needed their grain ground into meal, the grinding stones were active for more than 35 years.

Robert Louis Stevenson State Park, between Calistoga and Middletown, encompasses about 3,000 acres of wild area on the eastern slopes and around the summit of Mount St. Helena. A monument testifies that the author spent his honeymoon here. The site is undeveloped except for a fire trail leading to the remnants of his cabin and the old Silverado Mine. You can continue up to the lookout (about 4 miles) on top of this 4,344-foot peak that Stevenson called the "Mont Blanc of the Coast Range." Picnicking is permitted, but no fires.

Conn Dam Recreation Area, up off the valley floor in the east hills, is a stopping-off spot offering cool Lake Hennessey for bank fishing and picnicking. The turnoff from the Silverado Trail is marked State 128-Conn Dam.

Lake Berryessa, isolated in the dry, grassy hills that separate the Napa Valley from the Sacramento Valley, is principally a summer haunt of water-skiers and speed-minded boaters. But this popular, year-round fishing hole also has many quiet coves for hot-weather anglers.

All of the modest development is along 12 miles of the west shore, which falls into shadow while the east margin still bakes in the summer sun. A string of camper resorts can be reached by plainly marked stub roads leading away from State 128. Easiest access, especially for anyone trailering a boat or camper, is from Interstate 80. Accommodations range from campsites to motels. Fairly extensive stretches of shoreline are open to bank fishing and rough picnicking. The east shore is closed to all use because fire hazard is extreme.

Boating is the best way to explore the lake. Launches are spaced at close intervals from Markley Canyon near the dam up to Putah Creek. (All are operated by resorts and charge fees, with the exception of one unimproved ramp east of the bridge across a narrow arm just south of Putah.)

Fishing is principally for trophy trout and bass in this sun-warmed lake. Shore fishing is best on points jutting into the lake. Anglers working from boats try for blue gill, crappie, catfish, Kokanee salmon, and trout.

Clear Lake is the largest lake entirely within California. (Tahoe is bigger, but not wholly within the state.) A natural, fairly shallow lake, it's about 19 miles long and up to 7½ miles wide, with a shore amply developed for recreation. In summer the water temperature reaches as high as 76°F/24°C, ideal for water sports.

The direct route from the Bay Area to the southern tip of the lake (about 120 miles from San Francisco) is on State 29 through the Napa Valley. From the west, turn off from U.S. 101 at Hopland and follow State Highway 175 to the lake and south to the Cobb Mountain area.

Anglers flock to Clear Lake for some good bass fishing in spring and early summer. But October, with its balmy fall weather and scarcity of swimmers, speedboats, and water-skiers, offers the best fishing.

On the west side of the lake, resorts are concentrated from the junction of State 29 with State Highway 175 north to the boater's capital at Lakeport. On the east side, one center of activity is in the district of Lucerne and Nice while another is south at Clearlake Oaks.

Clear Lake State Park covers two miles of shoreline at Soda Bay, on the west side.

In the Valley of the Moon

Historically, Sonoma is one of the most interesting towns in California. It's the site of Mission San Francisco Solano, last and northernmost of the 21 missions founded by the Franciscan fellows of Fra Junipero Serra. The Sonoma pueblo was headquarters for General Mariano Vallejo, the Mexican administrator at the time of the Bear Flag Revolt. It's where the Hungarian Agoston Haraszthy laid the groundwork for some premium California wines at his Buena Vista winery. And Sonoma was the last home of author Jack London, who so romantically named the valley.

Sonoma lies 45 miles north of San Francisco. U.S. 101 across the Golden Gate is the main northward artery; then take State 37 east to an intersection with State 121, which heads north toward the town of Sonoma. One more turn, clearly marked, onto State Highway 12 leads you right to the plaza.

The main approach from the north is State 12, cutting inland from U.S. 101 at Santa Rosa. Take the State 12 exit from the freeway. Coming from the east on Interstate 80, turn off onto State 37 at Vallejo and follow it along the north margin of the bay to its intersection with State 121.

Two separate clusters of wineries are open to visitors in the Valley of the Moon. One begins in Sonoma town and stretches a mile or two east. The other group is toward the head of the valley, north of Sonoma town along State Highway 12. In or near Sonoma: Sebastiani (sizable, with tours of a large cellar and tasting), Buena Vista (tours and tasting in the old cellar where Agoston Haraszthy did much to set north coast wine on its present road), Gundlach-Bundschu (tasting mostly on weekends), and Hacienda (tasting and a handsome picnic ground). To the north, from Glen Ellen to Kenwood: Chateau St. Jean, Kenwood, and Grand Cru all offer tasting regularly, but tours only by appointment. Between the two groups is the old-line family cellar called Val-Moon.

In and around Sonoma

The town of Sonoma embraces a spacious central plaza. Across from the northeast corner of the plaza stands the mission, founded July 4, 1823. Now a state historic monument and museum, it contains historic church vestments, early photographs and documents, and 62 oil paintings of the missions. The chapel is preserved, although it is no longer used for religious services. Museum hours are 9 A.M. to 5 P.M. Of several annual events staged on the plaza, the Vintage Festival in September is the most famous.

Sonoma State Historic Park includes a number of buildings in addition to the mission. The long, low adobe structure across Spain Street is the Blue Wing Inn, gambling room and saloon of the Gold Rush era. West on Spain from the mission, you pass Bear Flag National Historic Monument (in the northeast corner of the plaza park), Sonoma Barracks, Toscano Hotel, the servants' wing of Casa Grande (Vallejo's first home, most of which was destroyed by fire in 1867), Swiss Hotel (still in use as a restaurant), and the home of Salvador Vallejo.

For gastronomical rather than historical stops, try the French Bakery on the east side of the plaza or the Sonoma Cheese Factory on the north side.

General Mariano Vallejo's home is two blocks west and then north on Third Street West. Its name, Lachryma Montis ("mountain tear"), was suggested by the natural spring in the area. Adobe brick walls were covered by wood, so what looks like a conventional Victorian Gothic house is surprisingly cool inside on a hot day. Also on the site is a handsome old warehouse built in 1852 of timber and bricks shipped around Cape Horn. Eventually converted to residential use, it became known as the Swiss Chalet. Today it serves as a museum and interpretive center for the Vallejo Home Historic Monument (open from 10 A.M. to 5 P.M.).

Train Town is a private 10-acre park on State 12, about a mile south of the plaza. For a small fee, you can ride the reproductions of classic trains into a miniature mining village. The road is known as the Sonoma Gaslight & Western RR. The park is open daily in summer, on weekends from Labor Day until June.

Jack London State Historic Park is situated in the hills above the tiny community of Glen Ellen. The House of Happy Walls, built by London's wife, Charmain, after his death, is now a museum of the author's personal and professional life. The great rock walls and chimneys of Wolf House, which London planned but never occupied, are also in the park at the end of a ¾-mile trail beginning at the museum. London's grave, marked by a simple engraved lava boulder, is nearby.

To reach the park, turn off State 12 from Sonoma to Glen Ellen and continue uphill about a mile, following park signs. Hours are 10 A.M. to 5 P.M. except for major holidays.

Touring the wineries

Wineries on or near U.S. 101 between Santa Rosa and Healdsburg include Sonoma Vineyards (in a dramatic cross between a cross and pyramid), Landmark, and Foppiano. From Healdsburg north to Cloverdale, the roster includes Simi, Souverain (with a major restaurant on the premises), Trentadue, Geyser Peak, and Italian Swiss Colony. West of U.S. 101 near Healdsburg are Dry Creek Vineyards and Pedroncelli. East of Healdsburg on State 128 are Alexander Valley Vineyards, Field Stone, and Johnson's of Alexander Valley. Out in the plain west of Santa Rosa, the venerable sparkling wine firm of F. Korbel & Bros. is at Rio Nido. Also in the region are Davis Bynum and Hop Kiln. All offer tasting; most offer tours, although some of the smaller cellars require appointments for the latter.

Hiking and camping spots

Visitors to the upper end of the Valley of the Moon are near two fairly new parks that are inviting camping and picnicking sites. Equestrians will find the parks particularly attractive because they can stay overnight in one and ride extensively in the other.

Sugarloaf Ridge State Park is a 2,000-acre preserve of forest, field, and stream that reaches up oak-covered hills to edge over the Sonoma-Napa county line. Warm in summer, pleasant in spring and fall, it's likely to be wet in winter. A group campground invites equestrians to spend the night, ride over the meadowland, and view sites of old farm buildings. Stream fishing for trout is a good spring pastime.

You enter the park on Adobe Canyon Road, off State 12. The park gate is 2½ miles farther; the access road is not recommended for trailers.

Annadel State Park is for hikers, bikers, and riders—not auto explorers or campers. Keeping this in mind, you'll find plenty to enjoy in this almost 5,000-acre retreat of forest, lake, and meadow. Originally Pomo Indian land, it became part of a sprawling Spanish rancho and later a ranch called Annadel Farms. Rocky ledges around Lake Ilsanjo make welcoming picnic sites (bring your own water); no swimming, boating, or rafting allowed. Stocked in 1957, the lake still yields largemouth black bass and bluegill. Below Bennett Ridge, in the southeastern part of the park, is Ledsen Marsh—an ecological community of waterfowl and wildlife.

To reach the park from Oakmont, take State 12 toward downtown Santa Rosa; turn south on Los Alamos Road, which becomes Montgomery Drive. At Channel Drive turn left and follow signs to the parking lot. Here you can pick up a park folder and trail map.

Russian River's valleys

Early in the 1970s, the Russian River valleys began to emerge as a tourable wine district. The transformation from a region of bulk producers into one of bottled varietal wineries has been accompanied by an architectural flowering.

The most impressive wineries in the region are near Healdsburg, most of them along U.S. 101, but many lie to the west in Dry Creek Valley, and to the east in Alexander Valley. Still others are scattered across the plain west of Santa Rosa. Healdsburg is about 1½ hours driving time north of San Francisco on U.S. 101.

In and around Santa Rosa

Sonoma County's largest city and the county seat, Santa Rosa was founded in 1833 by General Vallejo. Its Spanish, Mexican, and early American periods are still reflected in its architecture. The Marshall House, 835 Second Street (near the center of town), is a charming and accessible example. Lunch is served daily (except Sunday) from 11:30 A.M. to 2:30 P.M. in elegant, spacious, high-ceilinged rooms with crystal chandeliers and other Victorian appointments. A second floor gift shop is open from 11 A.M. to 4 P.M.

Good picnic spots include Spring Lake County Park (swimming, camping) on the east edge of town and Mount Hood County Park (day use only) 5 miles northeast of Santa Rosa.

*SUN-DAPPLED tasting room at
Sterling Vineyards (above)
provides relaxing atmosphere to sample
winery's wares—perfect finale
for a tour-filled day.*

*MISSION'S RUGGED FACADE
(right) brilliantly stands out against
azure sky. San Francisco Solano,
located in Sonoma on State Highway
12, is last and northernmost of 21
Franciscan missions.*

Howarth Memorial Park is Santa Rosa's biggest and most attractive. A 152-acre, tree-shaded retreat, it sits at the foot of the Coast Range. An imaginative, 20-acre children's area includes a pony ride, animal farm, merry-go-round, miniature train, and playground. Rides cost a minimal fee; other attractions are free.

A feature of the main park is a lovely 32-acre lake. Motorboats are prohibited, but you can rent sailboats, canoes, and rowboats for a modest hourly charge. The park also has picnic areas, several miles of hiking trails, tennis courts, and a softball field.

You enter on Summerfield Road between Sonoma Avenue and Montgomery Drive, about 5 minutes from the freeway. Howarth Park is open daily the year-round; however, amusement rides and boat rentals are open daily in the summer but weekends only during spring and fall.

The Luther Burbank Memorial Gardens, now a city park, is a living testament to a great naturalist. Searching for the perfect climate and soil to start experimenting with plants, Burbank chose the Santa Rosa Valley. And it is here that he is buried, under a Cedar of Lebanon that he planted. Examples of his work are shown in the gardens.

One block west is "The Church From One Tree," a chapel (complete with steeple) built from a single redwood; it's now the interesting Robert Ripley Museum.

Highways and byways lead north from Santa Rosa on U.S. 101, passing through Healdsburg, one of the few areas still holding a spring blossom tour. As a wine center, it also hosts a wine festival each May. At Geyserville, 7 miles north, is the turnoff for Devil's Canyon Geysers, 22 miles east. (This is the site of Pacific Gas & Electric Company's geothermal electric generating plant; there is no tour, and the sulfur fumes may keep you in your car, but the plant is spectacular for its roaring plumes of steam.) Cloverdale, once the northernmost of the country's commercial citrus growing areas, has the state's oldest fair, dating back to 1892.

South of Santa Rosa is Petaluma, a dairy center now, but in an earlier era a challenger to Detroit as one of the country's foremost carriage building centers. That and other prosperous times left an architecturally wealthy downtown, four blocks of it preserved as a historic site. Petaluma is also home to the world championships of wrist wrestling. Four miles east of town is Petaluma Adobe State Historic Park. Once General Vallejo's house and fort, it is now a museum furnished with period pieces and is one of the largest adobes still standing in California. Nine miles west of Petaluma on Red Hill Road is the over-century-old Rouge et Noir Cheese Factory. You can take a guided tour between 10 A.M. and 4 P.M., buy cheeses and other snacks, and have a picnic on the lawn overlooking the lake.

Sonoma County's back roads are good sources for fresh farm produce and handcrafts. For a free map and guide, write to Sonoma County Farm Trails, P.O. Box 6043, Santa Rosa, CA 95406.

Along the Russian River

To summer visitors who have swarmed there since the early days of San Francisco, "The River" is the 12-mile cluster of resorts from Mirabel Park to Monte Rio. The most direct approach from the south is U.S. 101 to Cotati (48 miles from San Francisco) and then left on State 116 to Sebastopol and the river.

For a more leisurely approach, take either Guerneville Road from Santa Rosa, Fulton-Trenton Road (3½ miles north of Santa Rosa), Eastside Road (3½ miles south of Healdsburg), or Westside Road from Healdsburg to Hacienda. Other minor roads crisscross the area.

West and north on the river's great semicircle, the mountains rise to a seemingly inaccessible steepness.

Wine Country

Scale in Miles
0 10 20

Scale in Kilometers
0 10 20

101 Redwood Valley
Ukiah
Lake Mendocino
20
Russian River
Nice
Lakeport
Lucerne
Hopland
175
Clear Lake
CLEAR LAKE STATE PARK
Clearlake Oaks
Kelseyville
Mt. Konocti
Cloverdale
29
53
The Geysers
Clearlake Highlands
Asti
Lower Lake
20
Williams
Armstrong Redwoods State Reserve
Geyserville
175
Healdsburg
Middletown
Rio Nido
128
Mt. St. Helena
5
Guerneville
Windsor
29
Monte Rio
101
Petrified Forest
Robert Louis Stevenson Memorial State Park
Sebastopol
Calistoga
Burbank Gardens
BOTHE-NAPA VALLEY STATE PARK
Santa Rosa
Oakmont
Silverado Museum
ANNADEL STATE PARK
St. Helena
Lake Berryessa
Cotati
SUGAR-LOAF RIDGE ST. PARK
Lake Hennessey
505
Rutherford
Jack London State Historic Park
Glen Ellen
Oakville
128
Petaluma
12
Yountville
Winters
Sonoma State Historic Park
Sonoma
Vallejo Home
121
Petaluma Adobe State Historic Park
116
Mission San Francisco Solano
Napa
To Sacramento
Novato
121
37
29
80
Vacaville
San Pablo Bay
101
Vallejo
To San Francisco

You can explore them on a drive up narrow Mill Creek Road that starts 1½ miles from Healdsburg on Westside Road. Its 4 miles of pavement take you up into the tangy air and forest stillness of Mill Creek Canyon.

Guerneville is the center of the river resort area that extends as far east as Mirabel Park and west to Jenner, at the river's Pacific mouth. You will find restaurants and places to stay overnight in Guerneville. During the summer season, this is the scene of bustling activity, with thousands of vacationers seeking a variety of ways to relax. (Make reservations well ahead of time if you plan to stay overnight.) The Pageant of Fire Mountain, an annual spectacular event, takes place Labor Day weekend.

Farther upstream is good canoeing, where the Russian River flows through Alexander Valley. With a durable canoe or kayak, you can float between Asti and Healdsburg (where canoes can be rented) and Guerneville. River trips can last from 4 hours to 2 days. Be sure to include drinking water and a picnic, and wear protective clothing against the hot summer sun.

Touring the wineries

For years Mendocino County's vineyards were quite anonymous, an appendage to Sonoma County's. But in the early 1970s, vast new plantings brought new wineries and more tourists.

The Ukiah Valley is the smallest of this quartet, with the fewest of wineries to visit. At Ukiah: Parducci (tours and tasting at the patriarch of Mendocino cellars), Cresta Blanca (also tours and tasting), and Weibel (tasting only). A few miles south at Hopland are Fetzer (tasting only) and Milano (tours of a dramatic cellar housed in a one-time hop kiln as well as tasting).

Camping in the redwoods, away from the river, is easy if you visit either of two nearby parks. Choose between cool, dark, dense redwood groves or rolling coastal mountain country.

Armstrong Redwoods State Reserve, 2 miles north of Guerneville, has a driving loop through dimly lit aisles of giant trees or hiking trails leading to park limits. Day-use picnic sites are among the trees or at the edge of a meadow. The large Redwood Forest Theater has stage and musical productions during the summer and outdoor weddings the year around.

Austin Creek State Recreation Area, really an extension of Armstrong Redwoods, has more than 4,000 acres (compared to Armstrong's 700) and a complete change of terrain. Much of it is meadowland with madrone, Douglas fir, and alder in the canyons. Three creeks and about 100 springs run all year. Unlike Armstong, it is warm in the winter. Equestrians use Horse Haven, a small primitive camping area.

To reach Austin Creek, stay to the right after entering Armstrong until you see the sign reading Redwood Lake Campground. From here, a narrow, steep, winding road (not recommended for trailers) runs 2½ miles to the top of a ridge, 2,000 feet above.

In and around Ukiah

Although wine touring is relatively new, Ukiah has ample history. A useful walker's guide to the town's old homes costs $4 at the gift shop at Sun House, 431 S. Main Street. The shop is open Wednesday through Friday from 10 A.M. to 3 P.M. Sun House itself is the historic residence of painter Grace Carpenter Hudson; on the fourth Saturday of each month it is open from 1 to 4 P.M. for visitors to see her paintings and Indian artifacts.

The recently restored Palace Hotel at 272 N. State Street offers food and lodging in elegant surroundings. Most of the refurbished, turn-of-the-century rooms have baths. The lobby is a gallery for artifacts of bygone days.

HOW TO BECOME A WINE SNOB

Though wine tasting is fun, there's no short course in becoming a "pro." The complexities of enology take years to learn. Most wineries run tasting room with wines organized in a sequence so each sample shows off to advantage: dry whites first, followed by rosés, reds, appetizers, then desserts; sparkling wines come last.

Here are a few basic tests that may help make you more knowledgeable:

Sight—Look for color and clarity. The liquid should be clear. Table wines should not have brownish tints (whites range from pale gold to straw yellow, reds from crimson to ruby or slightly purplish, rosés from pink orange to pink). Most dessert wines will have a brownish or even deep amber tint, depending on type.

Smell—Is it fresh and fruity? Don't confuse *aroma*, the smell of the grapes, with *bouquet*, the smell of fermentation and aging. New wines seldom have bouquet; appetizer and dessert wines have little aroma and substantial bouquet.

Taste—It can range from sweet to sour, bitter, and salty. Most "taste" is an extension of smell. Some qualities can be perceived only after the wine is on the taster's palate; these qualities are acidity (liveliness versus flatness), astringency (young red wines will have a tannic puckeriness in all but the most mellow), and weight or body (light versus rich).

A last note. "Dry" simply describes the absence of sugar. Dry wines are sometimes considered sour because acidity and tannin are more evident.

Described as a "range of light" by the great naturalist John Muir, the Sierra Nevada is the largest single mountain range in the country. Rising gradually from the floor of the Central Valley, these mighty mountains ascend to jagged crests 7,000 to more than 14,000 feet high and then plunge almost vertically to desertlike Owens Valley to the east.

Glacial sculpturing is visible in many areas. Nearly every deep-cut valley owes its present configuration to glacial abrasion. The best-known evidence of glacial power is Yosemite Valley, formed by the cutting action of slow-moving ice during the Ice Age.

Higher elevations of the Sierra offer fishing in clear mountain lakes and streams, boating and water-skiing on large and lovely Lake Tahoe, and hiking trails into wilderness areas. In winter, skiers flock to its many snow-clad slopes. Awe-inspiring scenery attracts many visitors to Yosemite National Park, at its most dramatic in spring when waterfalls plunge over valley walls to splash rocks 1,400 feet below.

Along the Sierra foothills between Yosemite and Tahoe are reminders of bustling Gold Rush days. Small mining operations continue—every spring gold-seekers patiently pan for "color" alongside rushing streams. The old towns are well worth visiting. Many verge on ghost town status; some are covered by a façade of modernity. A few have been preserved in a state of arrested decay as state historic parks. One (Columbia State Historic Park) is being restored as a model of early days in California history when every would-be prospector's dream was "going to see the elephant" (anticipating experiences in the gold fields).

Largest single mountain range in the country, the Sierra Nevada boasts peaks of 14,000 feet. Stark and brooding from a distance, the Sierra unlocks a magical outdoor world. Stunningly blue Lake Tahoe provides a summer boating and hiking playground; in winter, skiers delight in its snow-covered slopes. Glacier-carved Yosemite National Park's massive cliffs, cascading waterfalls, and pristine high country make it the highlight of the central range. Snuggled into the Sierra foothills lie treasures of the Gold Rush country—historic towns, and clear rushing streams where visitors can pan for gold.

The Sierra

YOSEMITE

By any standard one of the most spectacular national parks, Yosemite has beauty of form in graceful domes and towering cliffs, beauty of motion in plunging waterfalls and rippling rivers, and beauty of color—from the red snow plant to the purple glow of sunset on canyon walls.

Only 7 of Yosemite's approximately 1,200 square miles are occupied by its famous valley. But here most visitors concentrate, missing other beauties and wonders—glaciers, giant sequoias, alpine meadows, and 13,000-foot Sierra Nevada peaks. Though the valley is a logical place to begin a visit, one should go to Yosemite with the knowledge that not all is found there.

A very popular vacation destination, Yosemite National Park offers an exceptionally wide variety of things to do and places to stay.

VERNAL FALLS' STUNNING BEAUTY veils sheer granite cliffs in Yosemite National Park. Hikers get close view along nearby Mist Trail.

If you drive to Yosemite, take State Highway 120 from Manteca or Modesto or State Highway 140 from Merced. From Southern California, take State Highway 41 from Fresno. During the summer when the road is clear of snow, you can enter from the east side of the park (via U.S. Highway 395) over Tioga Pass on State 120. U.S. 395, State 120, and State Highway 89 provide a scenic back road link between Yosemite and Lake Tahoe—particularly lovely in autumn.

Yosemite Transportation Service provides connecting bus service to Yosemite from Merced (the year around) and Fresno (summer). For information and reservations, write Yosemite Park and Curry Co., Yosemite National Park, CA 95389, or call (209) 373-4171.

Timing your visit

June, July, August, and September are Yosemite's busiest months—especially in the valley. Though an experimental valley campsite reservation system (summers) helps relieve some park congestion, campsites are usually filled to capacity throughout the summer. Reservations for indoor valley accommodations are recommended weeks in advance and as much as 6 months in advance for the Wawona and Ahwahnee hotels. Make reservations through Yosemite Park and Curry Co.

If you're seeking a more isolated wilderness experience, escape the crowds and visit the high country. Yosemite offers miles of back country trails. Or visit the park during the off season (before Memorial Day and after October 1).

In the fall the valley quiets down and autumn reflections subtly color the Merced River. Winter gives Yosemite a fragile, fairyland look. Frosty weather makes difficult hiking but signals the beginning of snow fun. Major valley roads from the west are kept open (State 140 has first priority for snow removal); be sure to carry chains. A Yosemite spring is beautiful. Waterfalls splash through misty rainbows to the valley floor.

Lodging—luxury hotel to canvas tent

Yosemite offers a wide range of accommodations. Besides the valley, in summer months you may stay at Wawona (through October—you'll need reservations), Tuolumne Meadows, and White Wolf, which are often less crowded than valley lodgings.

In Yosemite Valley the Ahwahnee Hotel offers luxurious accommodations. Open the year around, except for a short time in December, the Ahwahnee has a gift shop, lounge, and spectacular dining room.

Popular Yosemite Lodge, with Yosemite Falls as a backdrop, is within walking distance of the village. Open all year, the lodge offers sleeping accommodations that range from attractive hotel rooms to redwood cabins with or without bath. Lodge buildings contain a lounge, shops, cafeteria, restaurants, and snack stand.

Curry Village, rustic and informal, has cabins, tent cabins, and some hotel-type rooms. Cabins come with or without bath and are available the year around.

At Wawona the hotel is informal but gracious. It has a dining room, swimming pool, tennis court, 9-hole golf course, and it is near stables. This area is popular partly because of its tree-fringed setting and relative isolation.

Above the valley floor, Tuolumne Meadows Lodge has simple tent cabins and a central dining hall where meals are served family style. White Wolf Lodge has both cabins and tents. Both Tuolumne Meadows and White Wolf are reached along the Tioga Road; Tuolumne, near the park's east entrance, is 55 miles from the valley, and White Wolf, near the Middle Fork of the Tuolumne River, is 31 miles away. Both lodges are open in summer only.

Campgrounds throughout the valley are open from Memorial Day through the end of September. At least two valley campgrounds and the one at Wawona are now open the year around. In the high country, campgrounds have a shorter season, and stay open as weather conditions allow.

During summer camping season, valley campgrounds are on a reservation basis. You may reserve campsites in person at Ticketron sales offices. You may also reserve campsites at the National Park Service Western Regional Office in San Francisco (see page 8 for address) or the field office at 300 N. Los Angeles Street, Room 1013, Los Angeles, CA 90012. A 7-day camping limit is enforced for all valley campgrounds; a 14-day limit for other park campsites. Trailers are accommodated in most campgrounds, but no utility hookups are provided except at a private camp at Wawona. Some campgrounds have sanitary stations. Pets are allowed only in specified campgrounds and must be kept on leashes and off trails.

Getting to know the park

Yosemite's wonders range wide over its 1,200 acres, from the majestic sequoias in Mariposa to the pristine Tuolumne high country. Yet, it's to the valley—less than 1 percent of the total park—that most of Yosemite's annual 2 million visitors flock. They come to relax in the valley's tranquillity, but they're sometimes met with the citylike hustle and bustle they sought to escape. In the past, horror stories were not of the bear that got away, but of accommodations impossible to secure, traffic jams, overnight vigils for a campsite, and lines at the village store that would rival any at a thriving supermarket.

If you haven't been to Yosemite recently, you'll be pleased to discover the park service has made changes. Foremost among them is a valley campsite reservation system designed to alleviate problems accompanying heavy park use, thus protecting the park's unique natural resources.

Protecting Yosemite against manmade intrusion is not a new idea. As early as the 1860s, President Lincoln set aside Mariposa and the Big Trees Grove from development. Scheduled for publication this year is a general plan describing the direction the park service hopes to take in Yosemite over the next 15 years. These are major points: Visitors will be encouraged to use public transit when touring the valley and to try to see Yosemite during the off season. An effort will be made to remove nonessential services from the valley, returning it as much as possible to a more natural state. Finally, new interpretive programs will expand visitor awareness of cultural, historic, and environmental aspects of the park.

Touring the park

Once you're in the park, make the visitor center at Yosemite Village your first stop. Here (as well as at the park entrances) you can pick up the free park newspaper, *The Yosemite Guide,* that lists monthly happenings. They include year-round programs by naturalists offering campfire talks, nature walks, and lectures.

Getting around the park is easy. Park your car and ride the free shuttle buses that run along the eastern half of the valley floor. Guided bus tours, full and half-day, jaunt to valley and other park highlights, such as Mariposa Grove and Glacier Point. Backpackers can take buses to major high-country trailheads.

An increasingly popular way to see the valley is by bicycle—roads are mostly level and easily pedaled. · From Easter through Thanksgiving, bikes can be rented at Yosemite Lodge and Curry Village.

Saddle and pack animals are available at Yosemite Valley stables and outside the valley at Tuolumne Meadows, Wawona, and White Wolf.

For more information on bus and tour schedules, prices, and trail maps, contact the visitor information center or call (209) 372-4611.

Highlights of the valley

The 7-square-mile Yosemite Valley is neither the deepest nor the longest phenomenon of its kind in the Sierra, but of all the glacial gorges it exhibits the sheerest walls, the most distinctive monoliths, the flattest floor, the widest meadows, and the finest array of waterfalls.

The floor of the valley is a level meadow threaded by a dashing mountain river (the Merced) and diversified with groves of pines and oaks, thickets of shrubbery, and beautiful varieties of flowers, ferns, and grasses.

The valley walls rise, almost vertically, to a height of 2,000 to 4,000 feet above the meadow. Great domes and pinnacles stand out against the sky. Most conspicuous are El Capitan, Cathedral Rocks, Three Brothers, Sentinel Rock, and Half Dome.

Rushing waterfalls tumble from the cliffs, each with its own particular beauty. A ¼-mile walk to the rustic bridge over Yosemite Creek gives you an idea of Yosemite Falls' awesome power and volume. Bridalveil impresses, not because of its size but because of its sheer, lacy beauty.

The Indian Cultural Museum, located in the valley district building adjoining the center, displays exhibits of native American artifacts.

Happy Isles Nature Center is another valley museum. Ranger naturalists interpret park features and satisfy visitor curiosity. Happy Isles is also a trailhead for the John Muir Trail, Vernal and Nevada Falls (the Mist Trail), and the high country. Happy Isles itself is delightful, especially in early morning and evening—here, the Merced River breaks up into fingers and flows around several tiny islands. Nearby are the Indian Caves and natural Mirror Lake, worthy attractions in the upper valley.

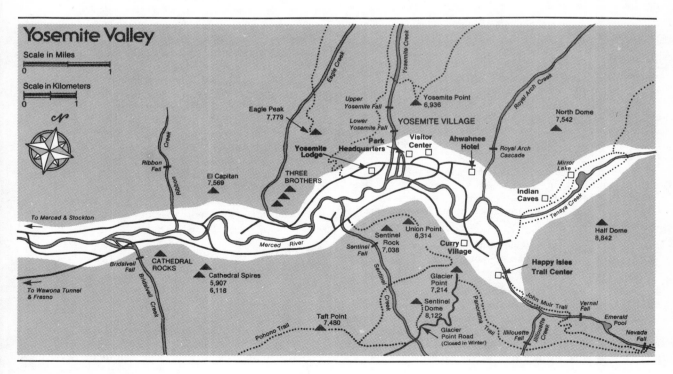

Wawona—home of big trees

Known for its grove of giant sequoias, the Wawona region, near the south entrance (State 41) at about the same altitude as the valley (4,000 feet), is a popular place to stay.

The Mariposa Grove, part of President Lincoln's original grant for preservation in 1864, is an outstanding feature. You may have heard about this grove because of its famous "tree you can drive through." A tunnel was cut in 1881 to permit passage of horse-drawn stagecoaches. Though the tree fell in the winter of 1969, you can still view the shattered trunk.

In the Mariposa Grove are over 200 trees that measure 10 feet or more in diameter, and thousands of smaller ones. The largest tree in Yosemite, and probably the oldest, is the Grizzly Giant, which approaches the size of the largest tree in the world (the General Sherman in Sequoia National Park).

Park private vehicles in the parking lot at the edge of the grove; free trams transport visitors through the trees, where the sequoia story is presented by park interpreters. Trams leave every 15 minutes in summer, hourly in spring and fall. Twice a day during summer rangers lead 2½-hour tram and walking tours through the big trees.

Wandering through the groves gives one a serene feeling and a sense of reverence for these long-living giants of nature. At Wawona Point beautiful panoramas unfold.

Pioneer Yosemite History Center, at Wawona, tells of man's role in the development of Yosemite as a national park. You'll see some of the first buildings, horse-drawn vehicles, and "living history" demonstrations during summer. To get to the history center, you cross a covered bridge, built in 1858.

Panorama from Glacier Point

The view is the thing at Glacier Point—a tremendous sweep of the length of the valley in both directions. Half Dome is at your front door; Vernal Fall is prominent; Nevada Fall's roar deafens; and beyond rise the snow-clad peaks of Yosemite's back country. You look down into a world of miniature people, cars, and buildings; the Merced River is like a tiny creek, and the roads are a network of dark ribbons.

The road to Glacier Point (closed in winter about a mile beyond Badger Pass Ski Area) winds through the forest and around lush meadow. After getting a ride to Glacier Point, you can hike down along one of several fine trails to the valley floor.

Four-mile Trail zigzags down the canyon wall to the valley floor about 2.2 miles west of Curry Village. Short and steep, it's about 4.6 miles.

Panorama Trail drops down into Illilouette Canyon and beyond, ending eventually at Happy Isles. Varied terrain makes all of this 8-mile route interesting—from infrequently seen Illilouette Fall across thundering Nevada Fall (a great picnic spot) and down the stone steps of the Mist Trail, wet from Vernal Fall.

Pohono Trail follows the rim for almost the full length of the valley, descending near the Wawona Tunnel (13 miles). It's particularly lovely when the wildflowers bloom in June and early July.

The high country—Yosemite's back door

If you leave Yosemite without a visit to the back country you're missing a large part of the park. Here miles of primitive wilderness offer a place for solitude and reflection, plus a hearty hiking challenge. With almost 800 miles of trails, almost any kind of hiking experience is possible—from short day hikes to trips of a week or longer. But 10 percent of the trails get 75 percent of the total use, with most hikers arriving on weekends. Crowded trails are the High Sierra Loop Trail, the John Muir Trail, the Cathedral Lakes area, Sunrise Meadows, Glen Aulin, and the top of Yosemite Falls. The less-used areas are generally in the northwest section and the southernmost area of the park.

To prevent overcrowding, wilderness permits are now required for all overnight back country trips. Permits are not required for day hikes. Free permits may be obtained by applying in person at any of the park's five issuing stations (Visitor Center, Tuolumne Meadows, Wawona, Big Oak Flat, and White Wolf). Dogs and other pets are not permitted in the back country, and groups of more than 15 should ask for the park's Backcountry Office. Call at least 2 weeks in advance.

Five High Sierra camps not accessible by road are maintained by the Yosemite Park and Curry Co. for hikers and saddle parties wishing to enjoy this country with maximum convenience. Camps at Merced Lake, Voglesang, Sunrise, Glen Aulin, and May Lake are about 10 miles apart. Dormitory tents cluster near a large central dining tent in which family-style meals are served. Reservations are always required.

Tuolumne Meadows Lodge is the gateway to the camps and to the high country. Fees at the camps include breakfast and dinner; box lunches may be purchased separately.

Several days a week during the summer, a 6-day guided saddle trip leaves Yosemite Valley and makes a circuit of the High Sierra camps, stopping one night in each camp. A 4-day saddle trip leaves Tuolumne Meadows with overnight stops at Glen Aulin, May Lake, and Sunrise camps.

For those who prefer to hike, there are guided 7-day trips leaving Tuolumne Meadows each Monday during the summer. Reservations must be made at least 6 months in advance for saddle or hiking trips. For rates and information, write to Yosemite Park and Curry Co.

Yosemite in winter

Yosemite Valley is especially splendid when snow fills the meadows and drapes the surrounding cliffs and sentinel peaks. In this picture-book setting, you can enjoy sledding, ski touring, and other winter activities against a backdrop of white-etched canyon walls and waterfall courses whitened by frozen mist.

Badger Pass, the ski area, is a 20-mile drive from the

BRILLIANT ALPINE DAY *greets backpackers in Tuolumne Meadows (above). Dense pine forests and spired peaks pierce horizon in Yosemite's high country.*

THUNDERING YOSEMITE FALLS *cascade 2,430 feet down to verdant valley floor (right). Falls are most spectacular in late spring after snowmelt.*

AUTUMN LEAVES GRACEFULLY FRAME *majestic Half Dome (above) in Yosemite Valley. Season's first snow dusts peak's famous face high above valley floor.*

valley floor. Facilities include three double chair lifts, two T-bars, day lodge, snack bar, and child care center at the Ski Tots Playhouse.

More than 90 miles of cross-country ski touring trails are now open in the park—at Tuolumne Meadows, Glacier Point, Crane Flat, Mariposa Grove, and the valley floor. Cross-country skiing lessons are given by personnel of the Yosemite Mountaineering School in the valley.

Ski season usually lasts from Thanksgiving to mid-April. From the valley, you can get a bus to the Badger Pass Ski Area.

Wilderness north & south of Yosemite

Massive granite peaks along the Sierra's backbone tower above the pine forests, green meadows, and alpine lakes of the wild areas on both sides of the national park. Isolated in winter, except for skiing on the eastern side near June and Mammoth lakes, the peaks are penetrated during the summer by hikers, backpackers, and mountain climbers following well-marked trails.

Emigrant Wilderness

Emigrant Basin Primitive Area became Emigrant Wilderness in early 1975. Located just north of Yosemite National Park, it covers 105,000 acres—all within the Stanislaus National Forest. Elevations range from 5,200 feet near Cherry Lake at the south to 11,570 feet at Leavitt Peak at the northeast corner. Snow blankets the area from mid-October until June, covering some sections the year around. Summer temperatures fluctuate—from 90°F/32°C during the day to below freezing at night.

The basin was named for a party of emigrants seeking a short cut over the Sierra Nevada; a headstone marks the grave of one pioneer who died in 1853 near Summit Creek.

About 100 lakes in Emigrant Basin offer trout fishing; some of the larger lakes (Huckleberry, Emigrant, and Long) stretch over more than 100 acres. Nearest main highway is State 108, from which short stub roads lead to trailheads. Lakes, streams, and campsites are connected by 142 miles of trails. Though there are no improved campgrounds, some of the heavily used sites, such as Emigrant Lake, Cow Meadow, and Bucks Lake, have log tables and sanitation facilities. In most of the basin, you'll find plenty of wood and water.

Minarets Wilderness

From Yosemite the John Muir Trail enters the Minarets Wilderness at Donohue Pass (11,100 feet). The trail leaves the wilderness 4 miles northwest of the Devil's Post Pile National Monument. Elevations vary from 7,600 to 13,157 feet. Mount Dana, jewel of the north corner, stands over 13,000 feet, towering above its sister peaks—Mount Gibbs, Mount Lewis, and nearly a dozen more—all over 12,000 feet. Glaciers and barren peaks

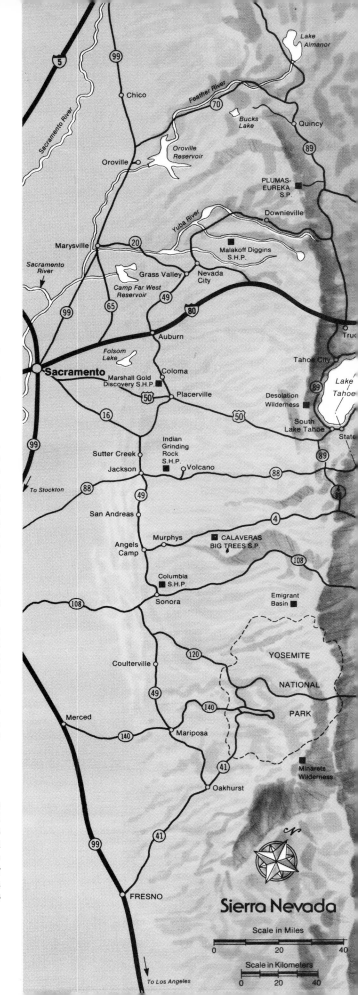

Sierra Nevada

Scale in Miles

0   20   40

Scale in Kilometers

0   20   40

offer excellent opportunities for mountaineers.

Backpacking and camping traffic is heavy during the summer; along the more heavily traveled trails, it's a little hard to find the wilderness experience.

Garnet Lake, Thousand Island Lake, and Shadow Lake are among the numerous lakes and large streams forming the headwaters of the Middle and North Forks of the San Joaquin River. Trout fishing is excellent in these 109,500 acres.

Access to the Minarets is from State 120 on the north, from State 203 through Mammoth Lakes on the east, and from Clover Meadow from the town of North Fork on the west. Commercial packers operate from Agnew Meadow and Reds Meadow on the east and from Clover Meadow on the west.

GOLD COUNTRY

James Marshall changed the course of California history in January 1848 when he discovered gold in the millrace of Sutter's sawmill in Coloma. Within a year, California was known worldwide, and fortune seekers started the migration that would open the West.

Remnants of these tumultuous times still exist in the Gold Rush Country of the Sierra Nevada foothills. Appropriately numbered State Highway 49 runs through the heart of this rolling grassland and fir-clad hills, its elevation around 2,000 feet except where it dips into deep river canyons and climbs mountains above Downieville.

The Gold Country has comfortable, up-to-date hotels and motels and a few charming old inns. Camping is impractical in summer at lower elevations unless you're around a lake to cool off. But heading east from State 49 you can reach campgrounds at higher, cooler levels.

For a more detailed description of the Gold Country and for some of its rich history and lore, refer to the *Sunset* book *Gold Rush Country*.

Scouting the Southern Mines

The placer and quartz veins in the Southern Mines never rivaled those to the north. At the southern tip near Yosemite, the country was better known to Mexican ranchers and Indian traders than to gold seekers. Tourists arrived almost as soon as the prospectors did.

This section contains a large, active town, a few smaller communities, and isolated hamlets almost qualifying as ghost towns. Lively Oakhurst, Mariposa, and Sonora make good bases for exploring the surrounding countryside; elsewhere, facilities are limited.

Back roads from Oakhurst

The southern terminus of the Mother Lode Highway (State 49), Oakhurst—called Fresno Flats in its hey-day—today shows little evidence of once-hectic mining activity. The original jail (now a shop at the Holiday Village center), the church down the street, and the developing Fresno Flats Historical Park at 427 High School Road are remnants of its more romantic past.

During the summer, Oakhurst presents melodramas Friday and Saturday evenings in a 19th century theater.

Coarsegold—8 miles south of Oakhurst on State Highway 41—survives. A single nugget worth $15,000 started the mining claim called Texas Flats—one of the oldest, deepest, and most extensively worked mines in this area. Rubble remains. One reminder of the past is a pump, dated 1852, that served a well dug in the middle of the main street.

A series of back roads northeast of Coarsegold leads through Knowles, with its landscape of granite, and Raymond, an early stage stop for Yosemite-bound travelers. Along Ben Hur Road, you'll pass crumbling remains of an early Chinese "stone wall"; workers received 25 cents for laying 25 feet of this wall daily.

Mariposa—a key to the past

Far from being a ghost town, Mariposa gets a sizable amount of traffic because of its convenient location halfway between Merced and Yosemite. Scattered along the sides of the valley enfolding Mariposa Creek, buildings are a blend of old and new. One of the Gold Country's choicest bits of architecture, the two-story courthouse at the north end of town has been in use continuously since it was erected in 1854; its tower clock has dutifully rung the hours since its installation in 1866. An excellent historical center and museum on Jessie Street depicts life over a century ago. Open daily May through October, it's closed in January, open weekends the rest of the year.

North of Mariposa, watch for Mount Bullion, where more than $4 million in gold came from the now-vanished Princeton Mine. Mount Ophir, up the road, had California's first private mint, which supposedly produced $50 hexagonal gold slugs; none have been found.

A side trip to Hornitos can be made from Mount Bullion (13 miles) or from Bear Valley (11 miles). A small, lazy town, Hornitos has many charming old buildings framing its Mexican-style plaza. At High Street and Bear Valley Road is the outlet to an escape tunnel through which the Mother Lode's most famous badman, Joaquin Murieta, retreated from the fandango hall when things got too hot upstairs. Interesting remains include a grim little jail, now a museum; ruins of the Ghirardelli Store operated by San Francisco's chocolate king; St. Catherine's Church and the boot hill below; and the school, built in the early 1860s.

At Bear Valley, ruins strung along the highway include the Bon Ton Saloon (a café), a boarding house, Trabucco's store, and the Odd Fellows Hall which houses the Oso Museum. Nothing remains of John C. Fremont's "White House," from which he conducted his vast grant.

About 2 miles north of Bear Valley, a turnout off State 49 affords excellent views of the Merced River gorge below and the sinuous, 1,000-foot descent into Hell's Hollow. At the bottom are Lake McClure and the Bagby Recreation Area.

BUXOM BLONDE (below) belts out song and dance in Drytown melodrama. Claypipers, one of Mother Lode's oldest troupes, offer saucy Saturday night olios.

GINGERBREAD ICING, open balconies, and gothic windows make historic Red Castle hotel (above) a favorite with visitors to Nevada City.

ABANDONED STRUCTURES (below) peek through sun-bleached fields along rambling Gold Country back roads.

Coulterville is enriched by the presence of the old Jeffrey Hotel, built in 1851 of rock and adobe; the walls are 3 feet thick. Adjoining it is the Magnolia Saloon, displaying a fine collection of firearms, minerals, coins, and other memorabilia. Across the street are the remains of the Coulter Hotel and the Wells Fargo building, once operated by Buffalo Bill's brother. In front of these buildings in the small plaza are the local "hangin' tree" and a small steam engine once used to haul ore from the Mary Harrison Mine north of town. One Chinese adobe, the Sun Sun Wo store, is all that remains of a sizable Chinese population.

Chinese Camp lies 21 miles north of Coulterville along State 49. Driving north, watch for the Moccasin Creek Power Plant where State 120 intersects State 49. A marker near the bridge tells of Jacksonville, a once-important gold town now inundated by the Don Pedro Reservoir.

Notice the "trees of heaven" in picturesque Chinese Camp. No one knows where the Chinese who settled here came from, but there were at least 5,000 mining the area in the early 1850s, and a full scale war once took place between two tongs. It's a popular place to explore; you'll find good ruins and a few homes along the tranquil streets.

History lives around Sonora

Sonora is as bustling today as it was a century ago. The county seat of Tuolumne and a trading center for the surrounding cattle and lumber country, Sonora has layered modern façades over the aged buildings lining Washington Street. Traffic moves slowly along the crowded thoroughfare, but a half-block drive off the main street takes you back to Gold Rush days. Sonora's outstanding landmark is St. James Episcopal Church—on Washington Street at the north end of town. Built in 1860, the graceful structure is said to be the Gold Country's most beautiful frame building. At the century-old jail on West Bradford Street, you can pick up a walking map of heritage homes, including the Gunn House, now an inn.

Jamestown, south of Sonora, tries valiantly to retain its antiquity. Some of the best wood-frame structures were destroyed by a fire in the 1960s, but a few proud buildings remain, among them a fancy gingerbread and brick emporium on Main Street and the Community Methodist Church. The Sierra Railway depot and yards were restored in 1971 and were open to visitors until early 1980. This narrow-gauge line formerly connected the Gold Country mines with shipping centers in the San Joaquin Valley; it still carries freight but no passengers.

A few miles away, another narrow gauge railroad offers a chance to ride into the past. For information on operating schedules, write Westside & Cherry Valley Railway, P.O. Box 1017, Tuolumne, CA 95379.

Columbia State Historic Park is an ideal starting point for any Gold Country touring. Columbia will provide you with a sizable fund of knowledge about mining and miners' habits that will help you understand other, more confusing ruins and deserted mining camps.

Everything in Columbia is clearly labeled, and an abundance of maps and guidebooks explain attractions in detail. For best use of your time, stop by the park headquarters for a brochure that outlines an 1½-hour stroll. Children enjoy panning for "color," riding the jouncing stagecoach, sipping sarsaparilla at a saloon, or even getting a haircut at the state's oldest barbershop. Summer theatrical performances have taken place at Fallon House for 30 years; the Fandango Hall houses melodrama; and the City Hotel is back in business.

Once called the "Gem of the Southern Mines" for its gold output, Columbia (4 miles north of Sonora) glitters today in its unparalleled collection of reconstructed buildings and mining artifacts.

Jackass Hill and Tuttletown, north of Columbia, acquired most of their fame from early residents. Mark Twain's cabin is reconstructed on its original site on Jackass Hill. Ruins remain of Swerer's store in Tuttletown, where Bret Harte was once a clerk and Twain a customer.

Central Mother Lode— heart of the Gold Country

Much of California's Gold Country was called the Mother Lode, but the section between Melones to the south and Auburn to the north contained the primary gold vein that gave the area its name. The most-visited part of the Gold Country, the Mother Lode contains most of the interesting, attractive historical towns that are relatively intact. Colorful annual events include the crowd-drawing Jumping Frog Contest. Family recreational activities, such as fishing, boating, swimming, and skiing, abound.

Angels Camp to San Andreas: From frogs to fandangos

Thanks to Mark Twain, Angels Camp is probably better noted for its frog-jumping contest in May than for its important Gold Rush background. In Angels Camp you'll find a few remembrances of the past—the Angels Hotel and jailhouse behind, foundations of the Angels mine (one of the best in the area), and a museum with a good collection of minerals and early-day artifacts scattered inside and outside a building at the north end of town.

At Carson Hill, south of town, a nugget weighing 195 pounds came from this richest of all Mother Lode camps. Fifteen miles of tunnels honeycomb the hill; they extend down as far as 5,000 feet.

Detour to Murphys (on State Highway 4), and you'll feel as if the clock stopped almost a half-century ago. Gingerbread Victorians peek shyly from behind white picket fences and the tall locust trees that line the main streets. It's a good town for strolling; tourists are treated like guests. Settled in 1848 by the Murphy brothers, Murphys claimed a population of 5,000 at its rollicking peak. The Murphys Hotel, opened in 1856 by James Sperry and John Perry, has an illustrious register of temporary residents—U. S. Grant, Thomas Lipton, Horatio Alger, "Charles Bolton" (better known as Black Bart, the notorious stagecoach robber), and many more.

Other buildings of interest include the Peter Traver building, housing the Old Timers Museum; the ever-present I.O.O.F. Hall; St. Patrick's Catholic Church; and the one-room jail.

Many caverns are found around Murphys. Mercer Caves (1 mile north) and Moaning Cave (on the Murphys-Vallecito Road) welcome amateur underground spelunkers for a modest fee.

Calaveras Big Trees State Park, about 15 miles northeast of Murphys on State 4, has the only groves of *Sequoiadendron giganteum* (the huge cousin of the coast redwoods) in a state park. By following the nature trail, you can climb a stairway to the top of a 24-foot-wide stump for a special look at these giants. Year-round camping allows for snow fun in winter and water play in summer on the North Fork of the Stanislaus River, which runs through the park. Both the river and Beaver Creek offer trout fishing. Two campgrounds provide 129 improved campsites; reservations are required during busy months.

Bear Valley, farther up the road, is not to be confused with the ghost town to the south. This is an all-year recreation area where you can ski Mount Reba's trails in winter or enjoy riding, swimming, and tennis when the snow melts. Lodging ranges from a hotel room to a mountain cabin. In August, Bear Valley presents a weekend concert series ranging from chamber music to light opera. For information, write Music from Bear Valley, P.O. Box 68, Bear Valley, CA 95223.

San Andreas, 12 miles from Angels Camp on State 49, can be reached by a series of interesting side roads east of the main highway. One leads through the little mountain towns of Sheepranch (where George Hearst, father of William Randolph, ran the profitable Sheepranch Mine, which helped enhance the great family fortune) and Mountain Ranch, where a former dance hall now respectably houses memorabilia.

Another interesting approach is the road paralleling State 49 between Altaville and San Andreas. You pass through sites of former mining camps of Dogtown, Scratch Gulch, and Brandy Flat. At Calaveritas you'll see the only tangible evidence of a once-flourishing gold area. Supposedly, Joaquin Murieta was a frequent visitor to the fandango halls; the old Costa store stands as mute testimony to these turbulent times.

Little of San Andreas shows its past. But the county museum, housed in the courthouse one block off Main Street, is worth a stop. Behind it is the old jail where Black Bart was held for trial. West of town is the Pioneer Cemetery, dating back at least to 1851. You'll find some intriguing inscriptions on the headstones still standing.

Cuisine & culture around Jackson

Jackson, a town that has kept up with progress, is also trying to preserve its 19th century heritage. Modern façades have transformed many of the old buildings along the main street, but a walk along side streets reveals some of the flavor of the past.

One of the most interesting buildings in town is the Brown House, built in the 1860s on a hill about 2 blocks east of the main part of town. Today it serves as the county museum. On the narrow main street are the Odd Fellows Hall and the restored National Hotel. St. Sava's Serbian Orthodox Church may be tiny—but it's the mother church of the entire western hemisphere. Built in 1894, it's a few blocks off the main street.

For many decades two great hard-rock mines—the Kennedy and the Argonaut—were very important to Jackson's economy, but neither has been worked in many years. The huge tailing wheels built to carry waste from the mines to a settling pond on the other side of the hills are still there (two in pieces); they can be seen from State 49. For a closer view, drive the Jackson Gate road northeast from town and hike the well-marked trails. Along this road you'll find some good Italian restaurants.

At the Chamber of Commerce office (junction of State highways 88 and 49), you can pick up walking tours of Amador County towns, as well as a well-done area map. Bikers will want a copy of a 27-mile bike route. Though the chamber office is closed weekends, printed material is also available at the museum.

State 88 (open all year) heads east from Jackson over Carson Pass past several good summer trout lakes (Bear Reservoir, Silver Lake, and Caples Lake) and a couple of winter ski areas—the newest and largest is Kirkwood at 7,800 feet.

Mokelumne Hill, 7 miles south of Jackson on State 49, has many buildings constructed of light brown stone (rhyolite tuff), a material common to much of the Mother Lode. The I.O.O.F. Hall was the first three-story building in the Gold Country. Once a tough, wild town, "Mok Hill" has had two racial strifes—the Chilean War, at nearby Chili Gulch, and the French War, on a hill overlooking town. A murder a week was not uncommon during the early days—hard to believe when you stroll through this most peaceful community.

Interesting buildings include the remains of the Mayer store, the beautiful wooden Congregational Church (oldest in California), and famous old Hotel Leger (still operating as an inn), which incorporates the building that was once the county courthouse.

Volcano, a side trip of about 12 miles east from Jackson off State 88 on Volcano Road, has many remains of the early town—the St. George Hotel, the old jail, a brewery built in 1856, the Odd Fellows-Masonic Hall, the Adams Express Office, and the assay office. Don't miss Old Abe, a Civil War cannon. On summer weekends in the Cobblestone Gallery, the Volcano Pioneer Players perform.

Near Volcano are Indian Grinding Rock State Historic Park (camping, huge limestone outcropping, reconstructed Miwok village, and visitor center); Masonic Cave, where meetings were held in 1854; and Daffodil Hill, where you'll see a springtime explosion of color.

Sutter Creek, Amador City, and Drytown (north of Jackson) are meccas for antiquers. In addition to shops on tiny main streets, you'll usually find a flea market somewhere. Craft stores sell everything from hand-loomed skirts to nugget jewelry. Sutter Creek and Amador City were important quartz mining centers; headframes attest to one-time mining activities. Both towns have interesting inns, and Drytown offers the famed Claypipers, performing summertime melodramas.

Poking around Placerville

Placerville, county seat of El Dorado County, was one of the great camps of the Gold Country. Founded in 1848, it was originally called Dry Diggin's because the miners had to cart the dry soil down to running water to wash out the gold. The next year some grisly lynchings gave the town a new name—Hangtown. In 1854 it became Placerville, a bow to self-conscious pride, but movement is afoot by some citizens to revive its previous foreboding name, even though today Hangman's Tree is marked only by a plaque.

The Old City Hall (built in 1857) and its next-door neighbor have been refurbished in 49er style and still serve as city offices. The Odd Fellows have been using their hall since 1859. The County Museum in the fairgrounds houses memorabilia of some of the men who began their careers here—Studebaker, Armour, and Stanford.

In Bedford Park, 1 mile north of town, you can don a hard hat and visit the old Gold Bug Mine, check out a gold pan and sift the sands of Little Big Creek, and drive up the hill to view the stamp press mill. The park is a good spot for hiking or picnicking.

Coloma, north of Placerville on State 49, is the birthplace of California's golden history. Now a state park, Coloma is one of the most important stops in the Mother Lode. Here James Marshall first discovered gold on John Sutter's land; here you will see Sutter's Mill reconstructed exactly to match the original. On the hill behind town is a bronze statue of Marshall, and down the road from the statue is the cabin he lived in after the gold discovery.

About 70 percent of the town of Coloma is within the park. Buildings are marked for easy identification, and rangers in the museum provide detailed maps showing the points of interest. The Coloma Crescent Players present melodrama during the summer.

Private campgrounds are scattered around the area of the American River, and you'll find two hotels: the Sierra Nevada House III (well-appointed replica of an old-timer) and the restored Victorian Vineyard House in Coloma.

Auburn, farther north at the junction of State 49 and Interstate Highway 80, is modern at the top of the hill and traditional below and west of the imposing county courthouse. To see the brick and stone structures built in the 1850s and 1860s, walk along Lincoln Way and Court and Commercial streets. You can pick up a complimentary "Guide to Auburn's Old Town" from the Chamber of Commerce at 1101 High Street. Look for the round-fronted brick Union Bar; the little frame Joss House, distinguished only by the plank with foot-high, incised Chinese characters above the door; the square, four-story firehouse; the Wells Fargo Office, now a gift shop; and the post office.

The Northern Mines

Deep-quartz mining was first developed in the Northern Mines. The area is also the birthplace of hydraulic mining, a highly destructive process in which entire mountain ridges are washed away. Summer is the time to visit this area because the best wanderings are on side roads, often impassable because of winter snows and spring runoff. Accommodations are primarily limited to the Grass Valley-Nevada City area. Make sure you have enough fuel and supplies for a day's outing; services are sparse. Plan a picnic beside a waterfall on a back road to Alleghany, or sift sands along a rushing river near Downieville.

Grass Valley & west

A disastrous fire in 1855 destroyed the early community of Grass Valley, leaving little to recall the town's mining camp days. But it still has narrow streets, scattered headframes, and the Empire Mine, now a state historic park. Today's visitors get a good look at what was once the state's oldest, largest, and richest gold mine.

Plan a stop at the best mining museum in the Gold Country—the Nevada County Historical Mining Museum in Boston Ravine (Lower Mill Street), open daily in summer. Even the most sophisticated tourist is impressed by the vast display of mining equipment.

West of Grass Valley on State Highway 20 are a few hamlets worth a slight detour. Rough and Ready seceded from the Union in 1850 and did not legally return until 1948. Three of the oldest landmarks are the schoolhouse, the I.O.O.F. Hall, and the blacksmith shop. The Old Toll House now extracts revenues from the sale of antiques. Smartville, Timbuctoo, and Browns Valley were once properous mining towns, but only a few structures and some ruins remain. Two miles southwest of French Corral, across the South Fork of the Yuba River, stretches the Bridgeport Bridge, longest (230 feet) remaining single-span covered bridge in the entire West.

Nevada City through Sierra City

Nevada City has a well-deserved reputation for beautiful homes, interesting shops, and carefully preserved antiquity. It's a good base from which to explore side roads east of State 49, and it's only a few miles to Malakoff Diggins State Historic Park, an impressive example of hydraulic mining.

Residential sections of town have many gabled frame houses; downtown are the Ott Assay Office, where ore from the Comstock Lode was first analyzed and found rich in silver; the National Hotel, whose balconies and balustrades reach out over the sidewalk; and the red brick Firehouse No. 2, now a museum with a collection of Gold Rush remnants.

For further exploration follow some of the side roads. You can reach the old high-country camps of Goodyears Bar, Forest, and Alleghany by turning south off State 49 on the Mountain House Road 3 miles west of Downieville.

Fire and flood have done their best to destroy the mountain settlement of Downieville, but it is still one of the most entrancing of the remaining gold towns. The old stone, brick, and frame buildings—many built in the 1860s or earlier—face on quiet, crooked streets and cling to the mountainsides above the Yuba River.

The towering, jagged Sierra Buttes, visible for many miles in all directions, overshadow the half-ghost town of Sierra City. Between 1850 and 1852, Sierra City miners tunneled through these dramatic granite peaks in their search for gold-bearing rock. In Sierra City are several structures of an early vintage—the largest is Busch Building, two stories of brick and a third of lumber, built in 1871.

FEATHER RIVER COUNTRY

Rich in scenery and history, the Feather River country presents a varied topography—rocky canyons, fern-filled ravines, high mountains, leaf-covered foothills, chaparral-swathed slopes, and second-growth forests of pine and fir. Through all this flows the Feather River.

Three major waterways form the Feather River: North Fork, Middle Fork, and South Fork. A lesser one flowing into the North Fork is the West Branch. State 70 follows the North Fork of the Feather and affords panoramic views of canyon country. The Middle Fork, the most rugged, offers some of the finest trout fishing in California. The site of early placer mining locations, the South Fork has many swimming holes and hiking trails. Along its stretches are seven reservoirs—the highest (5,000 feet) is 500-acre Grass Valley Lake.

Spanish explorer Don Luis Arguello named the river in 1820. He reached its lower end during the band-tailed pigeon migration and dubbed it "El Rio de las Plumas" for the feathers floating in it.

The Maidu Indians inhabited the area, hunting deer with bow and arrow, spearing salmon and steelhead, and searching the hillsides for acorns, roots, and herbs. These higher Sierra Nevada regions were the last to be prospected during the early days of the Gold Rush. One argonaut told the tale of discovering a lake whose shores were covered by gold. Though the lake was never discovered, the tale brought prospectors into the region. Because the Feather River was the site of major gold strikes, by 1860 the Indian way of life was destroyed by the hordes of gold seekers.

The Feather River Highway, State 70, connects the Central Valley and the Sierra. Following the deep canyon of the North Fork, it touches the edges of the upper Middle Fork, crosses nine bridges, and tunnels through three outcroppings of solid granite.

Along most of this route are a number of U.S. Forest Service campgrounds, major resorts, and cabin settlements. Most stretches along the way are heavily fished. Stub roads lead to old mining settlements, to pocket valleys that have been cultivated since 1850, and to trout-filled lakes beneath granite domes. Trails take off where roads end. You'll find a backpack handy for spur-of-the-moment hikes.

Sights around Oroville

Oroville, 70 miles north of Sacramento on State Highway 70, is the gateway to the Feather River ·country. Today a lumber processing center and olive-growing area, Oroville first sprang up as Ophir City—a boisterous tent town of Gold Rush days. In the 1870s, when thousands of Chinese worked the diggings in the area, Oroville's Chinatown was the largest in California.

Temple, frame house & diamonds

The richest reminder of Oroville's past is the Chinese Temple, built in 1863. Now a museum of Oriental artifacts, it's at Broderick Street behind the levee of the Feather River. A more recent addition, Tapestry Hall, is connected to the temple by an open courtyard and garden with a graceful copper pagoda and small reflecting pool surrounded by Chinese plantings. At the entrance to the temple is a 2-ton brass incense burner said to have been the gift of Emperor Quong She of the Ching Dynasty. You can visit the temple from 10 A.M. to 4:30 P.M., Friday through Tuesday plus Wednesday and Thursday afternoons.

Another Oroville landmark is the Judge C. F. Lott Memorial Home in Sank Park. Completed in 1856, the white frame dwelling is furnished with period pieces and sits among landscaped gardens. The house is open 10 A.M. to 4:30 P.M., Friday through Tuesday; 1 to 4:30 P.M. Wednesday and Thursday. A broad patio, added more recently, is the site of afternoon programs during spring and summer months.

North of Oroville, in the tiny town of Cherokee, you'll see a few more remnants of gold mining days—ruins of the Spring Valley Assay Office and an old hotel converted to a museum. The first diamonds discovered in the United States were picked out of a sluice box here in 1866, but no extensive diamond mining was ever done.

Superlatives apply to Lake Oroville

With a surface area of about 15,800 acres and about 167 miles of shoreline, Lake Oroville was created by the Oroville Dam, 5½ miles northeast of Oroville. Towering 770 feet above metropolitan Oroville, it is the highest dam in the United States and the highest earth fill dam in the world.

Much of the water stored in the lake is diverted into a system of aqueducts, tunnels, and basins extending the length of California. Adjoining the dam in the Feather River Canyon wall is a powerhouse that can generate enough electricity to supply a city of a million people. The dam offers a large measure of protection against river floods.

The lake, now designated a state recreation area, affords a variety of outdoor activities. Most popular are boating, water-skiing, swimming, fishing, and sailing. Picnicking and camping facilities are available, and there are reserved areas for boat-in camping and houseboat mooring.

TIME SOFTENS SCARS at Malakoff Diggins (above), former site of hydraulic mining. Once-barren cliffs and colorfully streaked slopes are reflected in rain-fed lake.

SIERRA STREAMS attract white water rafting enthusiasts in the summer. Some accessible rivers to run include the Stanislaus (shown at right), the American, the Mokelumne, and the Tuolumne.

GOLD COUNTRY HOSTELRIES

California's Gold Country has several mellow old inns scattered throughout a once-feverish mining area. These inns warmly welcome travelers and serve as bases for exploring the countryside.

All the inns listed (from north to south) are in towns on State Highway 49 or a few miles east or west. Reservations are always advisable; some hotels close for brief periods during the year.

Some of the hostelries have been in operation for more than a century and are members of the 100-Year Club. Others are historic buildings more recently converted to accommodate guests; one is a replica of a hotel active in Gold Rush times. Accommodations range from rustic to Victorian opulence, but all the innkeepers work hard to preserve the feeling of old-fashioned hospitality.

Nevada City. National Hotel, Nevada City, California 95959; (916) 265-4551: Gold Rush exterior remains intact, and the interior furnishings are Victorian; private baths; dining room; pool.

Red Castle, 109 Prospect Street, Nevada City, California 95959; (916) 265-5135: Restored, 1860-era, private residence overlooks city; lovely antiques; suites have private baths; continental breakfast included; no children.

Coloma. Sierra Nevada House III, Box 268, Coloma, California 95613; (916) 622-5856. Well-appointed replica of an old-timer; private baths; old soda parlor serves meals; dining is also available (with reservations) in Gold Rush and Victorian rooms; price of room includes breakfast.

Vineyard House, Box 176, Coloma, California 95613; (916) 622-2217: Restored Victorian private residence and inn; 7 rooms, bath down the hall; continental breakfast included; no children; restaurant open Wednesday through Sunday for dinner.

Amador City. The Mine House, Box 226, Amador City, California 95601; (209) 267-5900: Formerly Keystone Mine offices; each of 8 rooms (with baths) named for original use—Vault, Retort, Assay, Stores, Grinding, Directors, Bookkeeping, and Keystone; morning coffee and juice brought to room; pool.

Sutter Creek. Nine Eureka Street, Sutter Creek, California 95685; (209) 267-0342: Private home turned inn provides 5 well-decorated rooms with baths; continental breakfast; sitting room for evening reading; no children.

Sutter Creek Inn, 75 Main Street, Sutter Creek, California 95685; (209) 267-5606: Eighteen rooms in this converted old home and outbuildings; intimate comfort is keynote; some rooms with fireplaces, some have private baths, others share bath; for fun, try the swinging beds; breakfast in kitchen included in price; no children.

Bellotti Inn, 53 Main Street, Sutter Creek, California 95685; (209) 267-5211: Three-story, unpretentious hostelry over a century old; 28 rooms, 15 with private baths; restaurant open daily for lunch and dinner.

Volcano. St. George Hotel, Volcano, California 95685; (209) 296-4458: Venerable, three-story building; simple comfortable furnishings in rooms, with nearby bathrooms; dining room serves meals to those with advance reservations.

Jackson. National Hotel, 2 Water Street, Jackson, California; (209) 223-0500: Old-fashioned saloon entrance, 50 rooms upstairs, over half with private baths; Louisiana House, on lower level, serves dinner Wednesday through Sunday, breakfast on Sunday.

The Court Street Inn, 215 Court Street, Jackson, California 95642; (209) 223-1416: Five rooms furnished with antiques, three with private baths; breakfast included in price; no children; listed on National Register of Historic Places.

Mokelumne Hill. Hotel Leger, Mokelumne Hill, California 95245; (209) 286-1312: Handsome Victorian hotel; spacious rooms, 7 with private baths; pool; dining room open daily.

Murphys. Murphys Hotel, Box 329, Murphys, California 95247; (209) 728-3454: Two-story, 1860-era hotel; 12 rooms upstairs with 2 modern baths; 20 motel units with private baths; dining room open daily; historic guest ledger.

Columbia. The City Hotel was operating in the late 1800s. Nine rooms, furnished in that period, have wash basins and stools; showers are down the hall; dining room serves meals (closed Monday). For reservations, write City Hotel, P.O. Box 1870, Columbia, California 95310, or call (209) 532-1479.

Sonora. Gunn House, Sonora, California 95370; (209) 532-3421: Priceless antiques combine with modern conveniences in 1851 adobe hotel, once a private residence; 28 large, well-furnished rooms with private baths.

The park's visitor center has interpretive displays and information on the dam and lake. An observation area affords a panoramic view of Lake Oroville on one side and Oroville and the remainder of the vast water project on the other side.

Across the Middle Fork arm of Lake Oroville is the Bidwell Bar Bridge. The suspension bridge, 627 feet above the river bed before the lake was full, is now only 47 feet above water.

If forest recreation attracts you...

Thousands of acres of forested land in the Plumas and Tahoe national forests offer trout fishing or swimming in mountain streams, camping in secluded spots, hiking or horseback riding, and skiing. Interstate highways 70 and 80 and State 49 and 89 are the main forest land routes. Much of the Plumas National Forest is in Feather River country; Tahoe National Forest extends south and east to the Nevada border. For a detailed map of roads, trails, campsites, and lakes, write to either Plumas National Forest, P.O. Box 1500, Quincy, CA 95971, or Tahoe National Forest, Highway 49, Nevada City, CA 95959.

Feather Falls—a picturesque leap

The Feather Falls Scenic Area is a 14,890-acre preserve of forested canyons, soaring granite domes, and plunging waterfalls in a remote section of Plumas National Forest just north and slightly east of Lake Oroville. Set aside by the U.S. Forest Service to preserve the special qualities of this segment of the Feather River drainage, the scenic area includes Feather Falls and Bald Rock Canyon.

Feather Falls, a 640-foot, plumelike cascade of the Fall River, lends its name to the scenic area. In the spring and early summer, you can see the falls by boating to the end of the Middle Fork arm of Lake Oroville and then climbing a hazardous ½-mile trail. For an eagle's-eye overlook, follow a 3½-mile trail from a road turning off at Feather Falls Village.

Along the Bald Rock Dome canyon rim, you'll catch some scenic views, but the canyon floor is primitive and inaccessible. Though the Milsap Bar Road crosses the Middle Fork at the upper end of the canyon, not even a foot trail descends to its inner depths.

To reach the Milsap Bar Bridge from Lake Oroville, follow the Oroville-Quincy Highway north for about 16 miles (along Berry Creek) to the Brush Creek Ranger Station. Then head east on the Milsap Bar Road about 7 miles to the river crossing.

Drop your line into Bucks Lake

Formed in 1929 when Bucks Creek was dammed, Bucks Lake is nestled in the Feather River country at a mile-high elevation. To reach the lake, follow the Feather River Highway (State 70) to Quincy and then turn west on the paved, 17-mile road to the lake. The lake can also be approached from Oroville on the Oroville-Quincy and Spanish Ranch roads.

Boating (rentals available), swimming, water-skiing, and fishing are prime attractions at the south shore resort area. Here, too, you'll find U.S. Forest Service and private campgrounds. For wilderness camping, cross the lake to the roadless north shore, where you'll find a number of excellent camping and fishing spots.

Hikers and equestrians can reach ten other lakes and numerous streams scattered through the back country. Good fishing destinations are Bear Creek, Grizzly Creek, and the Middle Fork of the Feather, reached on foot, by horseback, or by jeep.

At nearby Lower Bucks Lake, fishing is good for rainbows and browns. Undeveloped campsites are on the north side of this lake, too. Access is over a dirt road from Bucks Lake's south shore.

Plumas-Eureka State Park

On the slopes of Eureka Peak, surrounded by Plumas forest land, is the nearly 5,000-acre Plumas-Eureka

---

APPLES, WINE & TREES

Fresh-picked apples, apple pies, cakes, strudels, and cider tempt visitors to Apple Hill, that fabulously fertile stretch of land from Camino to Placerville off U.S. Highway 50. October is harvest month, but other attractions extend the season into December.

Though the emphasis is still on apples, many ranches have added other products for sale: pear juice, buckwheat honey, vinegar, pumpkins, gourds, and decorative Indian corn.

Several farms invite you to come to Apple Hill in December, cut your own Christmas tree, and enjoy apple goodies at the same time. Visitors find displays of handcrafted holiday season decorations.

Boeger Winery, reopened on Apple Hill, has a history of more than 100 years. The first wines were produced in the old winery building (now the tasting room) in 1872. If you look at the ceiling, you'll see the original chutes that dropped the grape juice into barrels. The old distillery up the hill still stands.

Four turnoffs from U.S. 50 at Camino provide access to Apple Hill; once you're off the freeway, roads are well marked. You can pick up brochures containing detailed maps at any stand or barn along the way. Pack a lunch to enjoy with your apples and wine at one of the many picnic grounds.

EMERALD BAY'S CLASSIC BEAUTY enchants lone painter and young couple (above) at Lake Tahoe. Eagle Point boldly juts into water; beyond is Nevada shore.

LONE SKIER GLIDES DOWN one of Heavenly Valley's well-groomed slopes (right). Tahoe ski resorts offer exciting runs for all—hot dog to beginner.

CARS ZOOM ALONG GLITTERING strip of flashy hotels and casinos (below). Big name nightclub acts and the games people play keep Tahoe jumping all through the night.

State Park. Park headquarters is at Johnsville (a partially state-owned town), 6 miles west from the intersection of State 70 and 89 near Blairsden. Hiking trails (many of them leftover roads from mining days) take you up Eureka Peak, Mount Elwell, and Mount Washington to the south. Picnic facilities are available, and there is a campground on Upper Jamison Creek. Trout fishing is excellent at Eureka and Madora lakes and in the numerous mountain streams.

The old mining town of Johnsville and the Plumas-Eureka stamp mill within the park recall gold mining days. The museum and hard-rock mining exhibit at park headquarters will interest California history buffs. Open from 8 A.M. to 4:30 P.M., the park charges a day-use fee for the campground.

After October 1 the campground closes, but the park is open all year. Heavy snowfall encourages skiing—even the miners of the 1850s raced down slopes. Eureka Bowl is open during the winter. Facilities include a rope tow, poma lifts, and an equipment rental concession.

LAKE TAHOE

Between the two main emigrant routes of California's early settlers (now U.S. Highway 50 and Interstate 80) lies Lake Tahoe. Surrounded by the heavily timbered Sierra Nevada, beautiful, unbelievably blue Lake Tahoe blossomed as a resort area in the 1870s when Lucky Baldwin built a large lodge and took guests out on the lake in his 168-foot steamer. Fifty years later skiing was introduced here, and roads to the lake were kept open in winter.

In the late 1950s and early 1960s the big boom began. Ski resorts and casinos dotted the basin, turning Tahoe into an all-year attraction.

Boating, swimming (the water is cold), water-skiing, hiking, and biking are the main summer activities; skiing is the prime winter attraction. Since Lake Tahoe never freezes, you can fish the year around.

Many people prefer to visit the lake in the spring or fall before the seasonal crowds arrive. Snow can fall from October to June. If you visit Tahoe during the winter, you should carry tire chains and check weather conditions that can make mountain driving hazardous. Snow conditions may force closing of the passes for short intervals.

Tahoe offers a variety of accommodations. You have a choice of resorts, motels, campgrounds (mostly summer only), or private cabins. For information on south shore accommodations and recreational facilities, write to South Lake Tahoe Chamber of Commerce, Box 15090, South Lake Tahoe, CA 95702. For north shore information, write to the Greater North Lake Tahoe Chamber of Commerce, Box 884, Tahoe City, CA 95730. Reservations are advisable the year around at the lake because of heavy visitor use.

Part of Lake Tahoe is in Nevada, and on the Nevada side are gambling establishments that operate around the clock. Principal gaming areas are at Stateline at the south shore and Crystal Bay at the north shore.

Circling the lake

Lake Tahoe is 22 miles long and 8 to 12 miles wide. You can drive around the lake on a 71-mile shoreline road offering excellent views of the lake, its many coves, and the sheer mountain sides that plummet into the water. Occasionally winter snows may close a section of State 89 between Tahoe City and Tahoe Valley.

The lively south shore

Lake Tahoe's south shore is more heavily populated than the north shore. Resorts, motels, and private cabins are plentiful, there are a number of public beaches, and Nevada's Stateline offers gambling and nightclub entertainment in such high-rise hotels as Caesar's, Harrah's, Harvey's, and Sahara Tahoe. South Lake Tahoe, sprawling against the California-Nevada border, is the major city in the area.

Visitors to the area can get a quick introduction to its colorful historic past by browsing about the Lake Tahoe Historical Society's quaint Log Cabin Museum, behind the South Lake Tahoe fire station.

To reach the south shore, take State 50 from Sacramento or State 88 and 89 from Stockton. Several intrastate airlines offer scheduled flights to Tahoe's south shore; many interstate air carriers fly into nearby Reno. Buses make daily runs into Tahoe from California and Nevada.

Emerald Bay, at the southwestern tip of the lake, is Tahoe's famed scenic attraction. The bay is entirely within Bliss and Emerald Bay state parks, and its waters surround Tahoe's only island—Fannette. The road around Emerald Bay is high above the water, and the view is unparalleled anywhere else on the lake.

Unseen from the road, at the southern tip of the bay, is a 38-room mansion called "Vikingsholm," once a summer residence. A striking example of Scandinavian architecture, Vikingsholm was patterned after an 800 A.D. Norse fortress. During summer the house is open to visitors daily. Park your car at Inspiration Point and then hike about a mile to the house. Daily excursion boats from South Lake Tahoe cross the lake, entering the bay.

At the head of the bay is a parking area for a short hike up to Eagle Falls. Picnic facilities are nearby, and camping units are located in both parks.

Sugar Pine Point State Park, up the road, is set in a dense grove of the trees for which it was named. Similar to other mountain parks in the vicinity, it is somewhat more protected from the heavy winter snows. Open all year, the park offers winter camping, cross-country skiing, and snowshoeing, in addition to its summer activities. The Ehrman mansion, acquired by the state with the property, is now an interpretive center and museum.

South of Emerald Bay you'll find several Forest Service beaches. The El Dorado National Forest Visitors Center, on State 89 north of Camp Richardson, offers slide presentations and group campfires at the Lake of the Sky Amphitheater; lecture programs at Angora Ridge fire lookout station; boat tours of Echo Lake; and short walks through surrounding meadows. Wilderness permits are available at the center.

A stream profile chamber allows you and the fish to exchange glances along an artifically created bypass of Taylor Creek, a natural trout and salmon spawning stream (October is peak season) flowing from Fallen Leaf Lake to Lake Tahoe. The visitors center is open from 9 A.M. to 6 P.M. daily mid-June to mid-September.

The South Lake Tahoe City Beach, on Lakeshore Boulevard, offers water-skiing and swimming. Picnic fires and overnight camping are prohibited on the beach, but approximately 150 campsites are within walking distance at the South Lake Tahoe El Dorado Recreational Area.

Nevada Beach Recreational Area, on the eastern side of the lake, is a popular picnic area for day-use visitors as well as a tent and trailer campground. Uphill from the beach, the U.S. Forest Service recently acquired 236 acres of meadows and pine forest that may be used to enlarge the campground.

Pocket resorts such as Zephyr Cove offer a campground, restaurant, swimming beach, and rental boats. Excursion boats dock here, including a paddle boat and sailboat.

What the north shore offers

The Crystal Bay area is a center of activity for the north shore. Here, motels, lodges, condominiums, cabins, and gambling casinos crowd State Highway 28 on either side. Once you cross into California, the casinos disappear, but the towns of Brockway, Kings Beach, and Tahoe Vista are fused to form a solid resort area.

A pine-forested area between Carnelian Bay and Tahoe City is relatively undeveloped. Tahoe City, closest town to Squaw Valley, Alpine Meadows, and other ski areas on the lake's west shore, offers shops, restaurants, and motels as well as winter and summer entertainment. You'll find a golf course, public beach, state recreation area, and a professional comedy theater company.

Tahoe State Recreation Area's beach and campground are nearly always crowded during peak summer season. The largest public beach at this end of the lake is sandy, 7-acre Kings Beach State Recreational Area.

Above the lake, the new North Tahoe Regional Park in Tahoe Vista encompasses 108 sprawling acres of pines. There are hiking trails through the forest, a ½-mile nature trail, tennis courts, picnic area, and a demanding parcourse.

Nevada's Incline Village complex, east of Crystal Bay on State 28, has a good family ski area. In summer you'll find golf (two 18-hole courses), tennis courts, riding trails, and bowling. Location scenes for TV's "Bonanza" series were filmed at the Ponderosa Ranch nearby.

Lake Tahoe Nevada State Park, south of Incline, makes up part of the northeastern shore, boasting rocky points (good for fishing), sandy beaches, launching facilities, and picnic grounds.

Summer fun on the lake

Lake Tahoe is a mecca for boaters and water-skiers. There's plenty of room for everyone, and the coves and harbors along the lake's shore are appealing. Many places around the lake rent boats. If you have your own boat, you'll find plenty of launching ramps, but during the busy summer season, you may have trouble finding a mooring. If a summer thunderstorm appears imminent, do not venture too far from shore; the lake can become very rough.

Swimmers unaffected by icy cold water will find plenty of public beaches. At the south end of the lake are three Forest Service beaches (Pope, Baldwin, and Kiva). You can also swim at D. L. Bliss and Emerald Bay state parks, Sugar Pine Point State Park, and South Lake Tahoe Recreation Area. North shore offers public beaches at Tahoe City and Kings Beach. On the Nevada side, try Sand Harbor Beach State Recreation Area and Nevada Beach Campground. Many boat harbors also have beaches.

Fishing is good for rainbow, Mackinaw, silver, brown, eastern brook, and cutthroat trout. Local anglers report the waters from the mouth of Emerald Bay south toward Baldwin Beach are excellent for Kokanee salmon, introduced into the lake in 1940. California and Nevada fishing licenses are valid anywhere on the lake, but you must depart from and return to the state that issues the license. In the many lakes and streams close to Tahoe, you can trout fish from May to October.

Bikers may choose from more than 12 miles of safe, paved biking trails with great lake views. The longest paved trail runs 5.2 miles from Tahoe City to Homewood. Near Camp Richardson is a delightful 3.5-mile trail meandering through forest and streams close to three national forest beaches. For a free biking brochure on Lake Tahoe trails, write to Caltrans, Box 911, Marysville, CA 95901. You'll find a number of bike rental centers at both the north and south ends of the lake.

Hiking and riding trails around Tahoe are excellent. The Forest Service publishes hikers' maps. Inquire locally for other trips. You'll be able to rent horses at several spots around the lake.

Skiing Tahoe—something for everyone

The Lake Tahoe Basin is one of the most compactly developed ski regions in the world. Downhill skiers can enjoy a variety of terrain in a cluster of fine ski areas. For the Nordic enthusiast, Tahoe Basin boasts over 30 ski-touring centers, some of which are located at the major downhill areas. Most offer rentals, instructions, and group tours. For maps and ski information, write to the South Lake Tahoe and Greater North Lake Tahoe chambers of commerce.

South shore's major ski area is Heavenly Valley. The tram operates all year, offering grand summer views of the lake.

North shore ski areas range from four in Nevada to a cluster of resorts north and west on the California side of the lake. Other nearby major ski areas include Echo Summit, Sierra Ski Ranch, and Kirkwood Meadows.

Squaw Valley, site of the 1960 Winter Olympics, is 8 miles south of Truckee. You turn off on a 2-mile side road from State 89. Squaw has facilities to challenge experts, nurture beginners, and satisfy everyone in between. You'll find restaurants and spectator centers from which you can watch the activity on the slopes.

For information on accommodations and skiing, write Squaw Valley USA, Box 2407, Olympic Valley, CA 95730.

Branching out from the lake

Two popular destinations lie at either end of Lake Tahoe. Donner Lake, off Interstate 80, is surrounded by summer cabins. Desolation Wilderness, west of State 50, is popular with summer backpackers.

Donner Lake

Just 2 miles west of Truckee along Interstate 80, Donner Memorial State Park is a popular recreation area alongside Donner Lake. The park stands as a memorial to the members of the ill-fated Donner Party who camped here during the winter of 1846-47. Almost half of the 89 persons in the party perished in the severe Sierra's winter cold and heavy snows. A monument stands in the park on the site of the Breen family shack. Its stone base is 22 feet high—the depth of snow during that fateful winter.

The Emigrant Trail Museum in the park displays Indian and Donner Party relics. On display near the museum is a steam trailer that once hauled cut lumber on the eastern slope of the Sierra. Most of the park trails begin at the museum.

Desolation Wilderness

Just over the ridge along Lake Tahoe's southwest shore lies Desolation Wilderness, a favorite of Sierra high country devotees. "Desolation" describes the area's wild and lonely terrain, its huge boulders and glacier-polished slopes nearly devoid of trees. Elevations range from 6,500 to 10,000 feet, with Pyramid Peak dominating the four high summits on the southern end of the wilderness. The area also offers exceptional alpine beauty. Streams trace forests of fir, pine, juniper, and hemlock, and over 70 named lakes provide tranquil oases for fishing. In the spring, delicate wildflowers brighten Sierra meadows.

With so much to offer, Desolation Wilderness is—despite its name—ironically crowded, especially during the peak summer months. In recent years the area has become so popular that a campground reservation and wilderness permit system is in effect from mid-June to Labor Day. Campground reservations can be made through Ticketron up to 90 days and no less than 7 days in advance. Wilderness permits, necessary for both day and overnight use, are available at the area's district ranger offices and at the visitors center at Camp Richardson.

Within these 63,469 acres, you can hike about 50 miles of trails from five major trailheads. The much-used Tahoe-Yosemite trail connects many lakes. Backpack trips are extremely popular, or, you can try a stock trip, using animals to carry supplies.

For more information on the wilderness and backpacking trips, write to District Ranger, U.S. Forest Service, P.O. Box 8465, South Lake Tahoe, CA 95705, or call (916) 544-6420. For a wilderness permit, visit the Pacific Ranger Station at Fresh Pond, or call (916) 644-2348.

Northern Wonderland

Majestic mountains, pristine lakes, verdant valleys, and rushing streams embody California's Northern Wonderland. Fish the Klamath River, hike the Cascades and Trinity Alps high country, explore volcanic remnants in a national park, or houseboat on Shasta and Trinity lakes. And for the rugged mountaineer there remains the challenge of Mount Shasta's 14,161 feet. Whatever you choose to do, you'll find this "undiscovered" part of California a treasury of scenic wonders.

Splashing streams, towering snow-covered peaks, snug valleys encircled by forested slopes, miles of deep blue waters, and some of nature's most unusual attractions make up the Northern Wonderland, an area stretching from the Coast Range east to Nevada and from the upper Sacramento Valley to the Oregon border.

Outdoor recreation is unlimited. You can fish the Klamath, water-ski on Whiskeytown Lake, houseboat on Shasta and Trinity lakes, hike magnificent wilderness trails, sail at Eagle Lake, or camp along clear mountain streams. At Lava Beds National Monument and Lassen Volcanic National Park, you can see unusual land formations caused by volcanic action. Snow activities in winter center around Lassen Park. Try skiing, snowshoeing, or cross-country treks.

Interstate Highway 5 is the main north-south route through the northern mountains, and State Highway 299, the main east-west route. The highways join at Redding, hub of this outdoor playland, 234 miles north of San Francisco and 173 miles north of Sacramento. U.S. Highway 395 provides easy access to the northeastern part of the state.

For maps, brochures, and detailed information on this area, write to Shasta-Cascade Wonderland Association, P.O. Box 1988, Redding, CA 96001, or stop by their offices at South Market and Parkview streets in Redding.

Bring a tent or trailer, backpack, and sleeping bag for delightful camping in the mountain country solitude. Accommodations are available throughout most of this region; it's advisable to plan ahead.

A water world

Boating is popular in the northland. Most of the activity centers at the lakes closest to Redding—Shasta, Whiskeytown, and Trinity. You can rent power boats, sailboats, or houseboats (Shasta and Trinity) and get water-skiing instruction at Shasta. Islands, inlets, and sandy beaches make picnicking popular. Campgrounds and marinas are plentiful and boat access is good.

Other good boating lakes lie north and east of Redding. Most are noted for fishing; several have good campgrounds and marinas; all are easily reached on good roads.

It's an angler's paradise. Mountain lakes and streams offer good catches all year. This is salmon and steelhead country; Chinook can weigh up to 55 pounds. Limits vary according to area. In some trophy waters, the limit is two trout. Anyone wishing to fish these waters should read the fishing regulations and restrictions on limits, size of hooks, type of lure, and stream closures.

Established in 1965 as part of the Federal Bureau of Reclamation's Central Valley Project, the Whiskeytown-Shasta-Trinity National Recreation Area con-

YOUNG ANGLER TRIES HIS LUCK in crystal clear Hot Springs Creek near Drakesbad at Lassen Volcanic National Park.

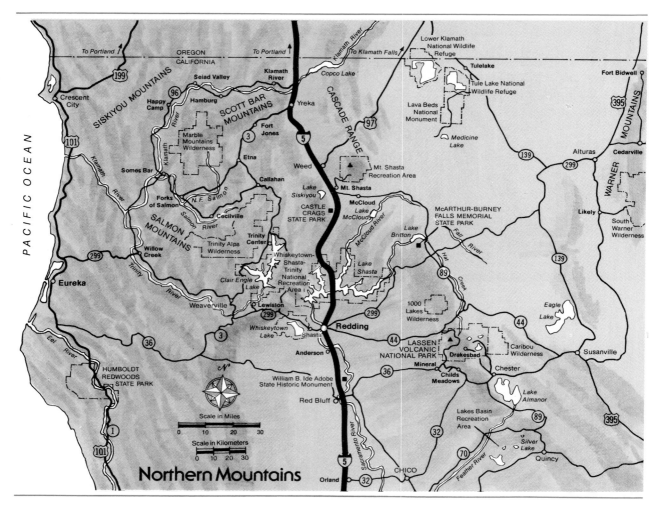

Northern Mountains

sists of three units—Whiskeytown Lake, Shasta Lake, and Clair Engle (Trinity)-Lewiston lakes. All are popular summer destinations with boaters, campers, waterskiers, and picnickers. For detailed information on the recreation area, write to Shasta-Trinity National Forest, 1615 Continental Street, Redding, CA 96001, or to Shasta-Cascade Wonderland Association.

Whiskeytown Lake—try trout trolling

Eight miles west of Redding on State 299 is the Whiskeytown Reservoir, created when the Whiskeytown Dam was constructed to divert water from the Trinity River into the Central Valley. The lake is good for trout and Kokanee fishing from either boat or shore. Best time to fish is fall or early spring. Water-skiing, scuba diving, swimming, and boating are popular because of the 36-mile shoreline with its large and small coves. Whiskeytown offers some of the top sailing waters in the northern mountains.

Two marinas—Oak Bottom and Brandy Creek—provide all services; boats launch from Whiskey Creek picnic area north of the highway. Other picnic and camping areas (some close to the beach) are designated. No fires are allowed on the beaches.

Some of Northern California's most beautiful scenery surrounds Whiskeytown Lake. A number of hiking and riding trails cross streams, climbing high enough to afford sweeping views of the lake's blue waters dotted with wooded islands.

The National Park Service maintains a visitor center just off State 299 on the east side of the lake. On the shore of the lake is the Kennedy Memorial, which commemorates President Kennedy's dedication of the dam and lake in 1963.

Below the dam, Clear Creek (once a major gold and silver-producing stream) winds through steep gorges and rocky hills. About 5 miles of the creek's waters are open to trout fishing.

The choices at Shasta Lake

Nine miles north of Redding is Shasta, California's second highest dam, serving as the great barrier between the mountains and the valley. Behind it splays Shasta Lake, the largest unit of the three-lake national recreation area. Everything about Shasta Lake is on a grand scale. This great, four-fingered reservoir, the largest manmade lake in California, covers 30,000 acres and has 370 miles of shoreline. Shasta's many arms reach back into the canyons of the Sacramento, McCloud, and Pit rivers, and Squaw Creek.

Shasta Lake is wide and unusually serene. Resorts on the lake (most clustered near Interstate 5) offer swimming, fishing, water sports, and boating (by the hour or day). Craft range from canoes to cabin cruisers. Houseboats offer the convenience of a small housekeeping cabin with the advantage of providing movable scenery. Boat and hiking tours and interpretive programs are offered during the summer season.

If you have your own boat, you'll find ramps at resorts and at several campsites along Shasta's shores. The Forest Service maintains a number of campgrounds around the lake. A few can be reached by boat only, and you may have to get your water from a spring or the lake itself. Several private campgrounds and trailer parks dot the lake area.

Shasta Lake is particularly inviting in spring when the redbuds bloom and in early autumn when the oaks change color. Summer is the heavy-use season: be sure to make houseboat, resort, or private campground reservations well in advance.

Lake fishing takes place the year around for 17 varieties of game fish, including German brown, rainbow, and Kamloops trout, black bass, Kokanee, and crappie. Since fish move frequently from one section to another, there's no "best place" for angling. Trout feed near the surface except during the summer, when they're found about 50 to 150 feet below. For crappie and bass, try angling around rocky points or where streams enter the lake. Limit is five fish.

Shasta Dam, the key structure in the Central Valley Project, is 602 feet high and two-thirds of a mile long at its crest. It's open daily and tours are now guided; a model and film explain how the dam works. You'll get a good view of Mount Shasta looming in the distance.

Shasta Caverns, a deep, complex series of limestone caves overlooking the McCloud River arm of Shasta Lake, are fun to explore; just getting there is an adventure. You travel first by boat and then by bus up a steep, 800-foot rise to the cavern entrance—a deceptively normal-looking "door" in the mountainside that leads to geological formations possibly a million years old.

Multicolored fluted columns, 60-foot-high stone draperies in symmetrical folds, and crystalline stalactite and stalagmite formations are featured on the 2-hour tour (including the cross-water trip). Knowledgeable guides take you through well-lighted tunnels and up stairs (over 10 at one point). Take a sweater, since temperature averages 58°F/14°C. The caverns are open daily the year around. From May 1 to September 30, tours start at 8 A.M.; service is reduced to three daily trips (10 A.M., noon, and 2 P.M.) from October 1 through April 30, weather permitting. Admission charges are moderate.

To reach the caverns, take the O'Brien-Shasta Caverns offramp from Interstate 5 about 16 miles north of Redding. Follow the signs for about 2 miles to the visitor center. If you're boating, you can dock at the caverns landing on the east side of the McCloud arm.

WHAT IS A STEELHEAD?

Why do you find anglers wading waist deep in bone-chilling waters or huddled in drifting dories with numbed fingers, fumbling to refasten snagged rig or bait? They're out to catch the elusive steelhead coming in from the sea to begin their remarkable winter journey back to their birthplace. This is a fish with one purpose—to make its way up the river to spawn.

The steelhead, which many consider the most spirited fish in the West, is nothing more than a seagoing rainbow trout. Like any other wild rainbow, the steelhead begins life in the clear running water of a mountain stream. Completely indistinguishable from its stay-at-home neighbor, it shares the coloring and scientific name *(Salmo gairdnerii)*.

But after a couple of years, the young steelhead yields to some primeval urge to migrate. Drifting downstream on the first leg of a long trek to the Pacific Ocean, it pauses at the river mouth just long enough to undergo a remarkable transformation: the blue green of its back turns steely blue, the spots disappear from body and fins, and its lateral red line fades to silver. The rainbow has become a salt-water steelhead.

Little is known about how the steelhead spends its life at sea for the next couple of years, but a larger, stronger, and wiser fish returns from the ocean depths and, once again changing its markings back to those of a rainbow, is off on its difficult trek back to the ancestral spawning ground.

Arriving at last (unless interfered with by some wily angler), the steelhead spawns. Unlike the Pacific salmon that spawn only to die, though, the steelhead may spawn and return to sea. Steelhead rarely live longer than 8 years, but some manage as many as five complete spawning migrations during their life span. This is a remarkable fish.

Only along the coast of the Pacific Northwest do factors of topography and climate permit a public fishery for large migrations of these anadromous trout through the winter season.

HOUSEBOATERS AND WATER-SKIERS CRUISE Shasta Lake on clear summer day. Lake's serene turquoise waters are perfect playground for all aquatic sports.

Clair Engle (Trinity)-Lewiston lakes

Though Clair Engle Lake is the official name on most maps, residents of Trinity County still call this 16,500-acre impoundage Trinity Lake. By either name, it's the focal point of the Trinity National Recreation Area, a sparsely populated expanse of lake and forest. It offers excellent fishing for trout and smallmouth trophy bass, large and small campgrounds (some with sandy swimming beaches), marinas and launching ramps, swimming and sailing, water-skiing, and houseboat rentals (Cedar Stock Resort, Estrellita, Fairview Marina, and Trinity Center). All facilities are on the west side of the lake in the shadow of the rugged Trinity Alps.

A visitor center is located on the highway near the Tannery Gulch arm of the lake, and another visitor center is 2 miles above Trinity Dam on Buckeye Road. Tours, self-guided trails, and amphitheater programs are available during the summer. For additional information write to the District Ranger, U.S. Forest Service, Weaverville, CA 96093, or to Shasta-Cascade Wonderland Association.

Lewiston Reservoir, downstream from Trinity Dam, is at an elevation of about 1,900 feet. Seven miles long, very narrow, and resembling a slow-moving river more than a lake, Lewiston offers good trout fishing. Trailer parks, campgrounds, boat rentals, and public boat-launching ramps sit on the west side of the lake. For noncampers, the Trinity country offers a selection of nearby resorts and overnight accommodations in Weaverville, Lewiston, and Douglas City.

To reach Trinity Lake, drive 49 miles west from Redding to Weaverville on State 299; then follow State Highway 3 about 10 miles. Turn off at Buckeye Creek Road to reach the northern end of Lewiston Reservoir, or approach the south end from State 299 at the Lewiston turnoff; it's about 6 miles.

A lake loop

Boaters, campers, and anglers all have their "favorite" lake. Here, singled out from the multitude of lakes in the north country, are some of the most popular, as well as a couple of the lesser known. Lodging is nearby.

Lake Siskiyou, a 430-acre impoundment of the Sacramento River in Box Canyon, was constructed solely for recreation purposes. Shoreline facilities include picnic and camp sites, boat rentals, a ramp and wharf, and a spacious, sandy beach. Besides swimming and boating, the lake offers year-round trout fishing. To reach the lake, take the Central Mount Shasta off-ramp from Interstate 5 just west of the city of Mount Shasta.

Lake McCloud is a little off the beaten track, but this is part of its charm. Tarantula Gulch provides boating access for year-round trout fishing or just cruising in crystal clear, blue water. From Interstate 5, take State

Highway 89 east to the town of McCloud (9 miles) and follow a signed road heading south from town for about 12 miles. Watch for lumber trucks in summer; the road could be closed in winter. On the way you'll pass a public, 9-hole golf course; it offers no sand traps but challenging water hazards.

The quaint, gas-lighted town of McCloud nestled at the foot of majestic Mount Shasta was first built as a lumber town. Don't miss the local emporium containing everything from hardware to jewelry.

Medicine Lake, about 500 years old, lies in what was once a volcanic crater. Burnt Lava Flow, to the south, has some of the most awesome lava formations in northern California. A high mountain lake, Medicine opens around July 1. Nights are chilly even in midsummer. Cold, clear, and deep, the lake is a popular fishing and boating area and even gets some hardy water-skiers. The Forest Service maintains a boat dock, ramp, and picnic area. The enclosed swimming area has a beautiful, sandy beach. From the south you can reach Medicine Lake by following State 89 east from McCloud to Bartle and turning north on a good (but not well-marked) road for 32 miles. From the north, take the marked road from Lava Beds National Monument or take State Highway 139 west from Perez.

Eagle Lake, in Lassen County, is one of California's largest natural lakes—and also one of its cleanest and least crowded. Here are plenty of spacious, tree-sheltered campgrounds and 27,000 acres of clear, blue water for excellent sailing. The lake also serves as a feeding ground for a rare breeding colony of osprey. Fishing is good for the large Eagle trophy trout, a natural hybrid that is the only game fish adapted to the unusually alkaline water. The limit is three, and catches up to 7 pounds are not uncommon.

Gallatin Beach, at the southern end of the lake, is a recreation center with store, marina, boat rentals, ramp, sandy beach, and shady picnic area.

From Interstate 5 take the Lassen Volcanic National Park turnoff from either Redding (State Highway 44) or Red Bluff (State Highway 36). The highways skirt the park on either side and join west of Susanville, closest town to the lake. The main beach and campground are reached on Eagle Lake Road. State 139 runs along the eastern shore.

Lake Almanor—52 square miles of azure water mirroring snow-capped Mount Lassen and rimmed with evergreen forest—is in Plumas County, 80 miles east of Red Bluff on State 36. Almanor, created by a dam on the Feather River, is also easily accessible from U.S. 395 and State Highway 70. Summer lake surface temperatures of 75°F/24°C make it ideal for swimming, water-skiing, and boating. Many resorts around the lake offer rentals, docking, and launching areas. A free public boat ramp is located west of the dam.

Fishing is excellent for trophy rainbow and brown trout, Kokanee, bass, catfish, and perch. Gould Swamp is a "hot spot" in spring, and summer night fishing near the shore is productive. During spring and fall, trolling for trout and Kokanee pays off. In addition to Almanor, there are about 50 lakes in the area and 500 miles of streams.

Additional recreational activities include a 9-hole golf course at Lake Almanor Country Club, holiday sailboat races, hunting, and rock collecting. Several nearby family ski areas (Stover Mountain, Lassen Park, Coopervale, and Eagle's Peak) operate during the winter. Slopes around the lake offer good tobogganing, sledding, and other snow fun.

Lakes Basin Recreational Area, almost on the border of Sierra and Plumas counties, is roughly halfway between Lassen Park and Lake Tahoe. A collection of small lakes conveniently located close to the road makes this a good family fishing and hiking area. A 23-site campground serves as a convenient base camp. Grassy Lake, the closest, is often overfished; nearby Big Bear and Little Bear lakes hold rainbow; in Cub and Silver lakes, look for brook trout; and at Long Lake, the largest, you can rent boats. Distances between lakes are short; you can hike, fish, and return to your car in the same day. There's trailside camping at Silver Lake; from there, it's an easy walk to less-fished lakes.

From State 89, turn off at Graeagle and follow Gold Lake Road south. From Lakes Basin you can continue south to Sierra City and State Highway 49.

Rivers for all anglers

Among the many rivers of the northern part of the state, a few stand out because of size, beauty, and accessibility, but primarily because of the fishing. Here you'll encounter the salmon and the steelhead (seagoing rainbow; see page 109), a challenge for any angler.

To see salmon spawn in a controlled environment, visit the Coleman National Fish Culture Station, the world's largest salmon hatchery, 6 miles off Interstate 5 at Anderson south of Red Bluff (or visit the new spawning channel at Red Bluff). Spawning salmon provide a spectacular show during the fall and winter run. You can also get a good look at salmon in Redding's Caldwell Park, where manmade falls on the Sacramento River are lighted during spring and summer nights. Falls are dismantled in winter.

But it's in the rivers that you catch fish, and below we have listed the major streams. For angling information, check with the Shasta-Cascade Wonderland Association in Redding.

The Klamath, though not a long river, is an impressive stream within cliffed canyons. It offers some of the state's best steelhead fishing. The Klamath River winds through the mountains from Oregon and heads west to the California coast. Most of its course is paralleled by State Highway 96.

Along the highway, river communities offer lodges and resorts. Several Forest Service campgrounds spread out beside the river's banks. Try Happy Camp, Seiad Valley, Klamath River, Hornbrook, and Yreka for accommodations.

The most sought-after fish in the Klamath is the steelhead; next in popularity are the Chinook and silver salmon. Fishing is best from late summer to early spring for anadromous fish (fish going from the sea up rivers to spawn), mainly steelhead. Above Copco Lake the Klamath is a trophy fishing water.

The Trinity River also offers good steelhead fishing, particularly during fall and winter. Fishing for salmon is at its best in late spring and early fall. Much of the Trinity follows State 299; accommodations are available at small towns along the highway. Campgrounds are scattered along the river.

The Salmon River, in the mountains west of Scott Valley, has its main salmon run in late July, August, and September. Steelhead start moving in just behind the salmon. Check angling regulations; there are special closures on this river. Seemingly unknown Forest Service campgrounds are found in some of the most beautiful mountainous terrain. Resorts offer guide service, and small towns in the Scott Valley have limited accommodations.

The Sacramento River starts in the Trinity Divide country and ends up all the way down in the Sacramento Valley. This is California's major navigable recreational river. You'll see bountiful wildlife, including some endangered bird species.

Anadromous fishing (below the dams) is excellent; several good salmon runs start around the latter part of August. This is when the big ones (up to 55 pounds) are caught. Spring runs begin the latter part of January and continue through March. Steelhead fishing is at its finest from mid-September into November.

Excellent trout streams abound in this great northern outdoorland. Anglers can usually wet their lines with good results. The season begins on the Sunday nearest May 1 and ends November 15. Here are a few favorite streams listed by county:
• *Lassen:* Willow Creek and the Susan River.
• *Modoc:* South Fork of the Pit River, East Creek, Mill Creek, Parsnip Creek, Pine Creek.
• *Plumas:* Middle Fork of Feather River, Nelson Creek, Yellow Creek upstream to Cottonwood.
• *Shasta:* Fall River (some trophy waters), Spring Creek, Hat Creek from Lake Britton upstream, upper Sacramento River including Castle Creek.
• *Siskiyou:* Scott River, McCloud River, Sacramento River, Indian Creek, Canyon Creek.
• *Tehama:* Deer Creek, Mill Creek, Battle Creek, Beegum Creek, South Fork of Cottonwood Creek.
• *Trinity:* Blue Tent Creek, Coffee Creek, Canyon Creek, Stuart Fork Creek.

A wilderness experience

Few roads lead into the heart of the northern mountains. Three large mountain ranges—Klamath-Scott (including the Trinity, Salmon, and Marble mountains), Cascades, and Warner mountains—contain beckoning wilderness areas accessible only to packers and campers. You can sample the fringes by car. Resorts offer lodging, meals, and guides into the interior. Remember, you will need a permit to enter any wilderness area.

Only a handful of towns in the region offer tourist lodging. But take heart: these mountains can be more inviting than the towering Sierra range to the southeast. They are less crowded, generally less rugged, and more compact. Rivers and mountain streams offer excellent fishing, rafting, canoeing, and kayaking; the national forests invite camping and packing.

Snow melts around the lakes about mid-June, but sometimes not until the end of June. July through September is best for the trails.

Packers and hikers use these points: Happy Camp, Seiad Valley, and Hamburg on the Klamath; Somesbar at the confluence of the Klamath and Salmon; Forks of Salmon and Sawyers Bar on the Salmon River; and Etna, Greenview, Fort Jones, and Scott Bar along the Scott River.

Trinity Alps—hidden high country

The unexpectedly high and rugged Trinity Alps are camouflaged by lower mountains; you scarcely notice them from Interstate 5. An easy approach on cross-mountain State 299 has never brought them heavy traffic.

The Trinity Alps have some striking resemblances to the Sierra. Massive granite peaks soar from an alpine highland. Dozens of lakes pocketed in glacial basins feed the outlet creeks and rivers. Over 50 alpine lakes can be found east of Trinity Lake and west of Interstate 5, at about 6,000 feet. But the Trinity Alps are much more compact than the Sierra (trails to the high mountains are shorter) and, being closer to coastal moisture, Trinity has proportionally more and fuller streams, greener and thicker underbrush.

Trinity splits the difference between the dry heat of the upper Sacramento Valley and the damp coolness of the Humboldt coast. It has two zones—a low, warm canyon country and a high, cool mountain wilderness.

The Trinity Alps are a small Mother Lode. Three main roads form a circle around the Alps and link old gold towns. The principal road, State 299, parallels the Trinity Trail, famous as an Indian path, pioneer trail, and Gold Rush wagon road. The second, State Highway 3, was once part of the main route—the old California-Oregon Wagon Road—north from Shasta to Callahan and Yreka. The third, a dirt road, taps the Salmon River settlement and the north and west slopes.

Marble Mountains Wilderness

A loop road encircles the Marble Mountains, winding up the Scott River from Hamburg to Fort Jones and Etna, and down the North Fork of the Salmon River to Sawyers Bar, Forks of Salmon, and Somesbar.

With over 200,000 acres, the Marble Mountains are walking mountains, easier to get around in than the Trinity Alps to the south. You have to fight brush along the streams, and the trails are precipitous in places but, for the most part, scenic and easy to follow.

Almost in the exact center of the wilderness area are the Sky High Lakes, a hub from which main and spur trails go in all directions. Most of the trails wind through forests of fir, mountain hemlock, western white pine, black oak, and rare weeping spruce.

The Salmon-Scott Mountains, bordering the Marbles on the south, offer many fine lakes to fish and explore.

The wild Cascades

Extending all the way from British Columbia through Washington and Oregon, the Cascade Range ends at Lassen Volcanic National Park. Mount Shasta and Lassen Peak are the two outstanding mountains in Northern California.

Around Lassen are two wilderness areas popular with backpackers and fishers because of the large number of small lakes.

Thousand Lakes Wilderness, about 12 miles north of Lassen Park, has four major trails. Since all trails lead uphill, backpacks can get uncommonly heavy. But the pleasure of camping beneath lodgepole pines and the number of lakes in this valley compensate for the rigors of the hike.

Three-mile Cyprus Camp Trail, beginning at Cyprus Campground at the northwest end of the wilderness, is the easiest trail, climbing about 1,000 feet to Lake Eiler, the largest lake. At least six of the lakes provide consistently good rainbow trout action. Another campground (Bunchgrass) is south of the wilderness. You can drive to the wilderness on several unimproved roads from State 89; check with the ranger at Hat Creek.

Caribou Peak Wilderness, with easy access from Silver Lake in Lassen County, is a popular but still isolated wild area. Just east of Lassen Park, Caribou contains a series of lakes along gradually sloping trails. Fishing for brook and rainbow is good.

Like Thousand Lakes, Caribou Peak is at its best from the latter part of June through the summer months. Several campgrounds are located close to Silver Lake.

Wandering in the Warners

If the Warner Mountains were near a large city, they would be famed for their scenery and aswarm with visitors. But because they are in Modoc County, in the northeastern part of the state, and reached by little-traveled highways, they still offer the adventure of discovery.

The topography may bring to mind parts of the Rockies—where unmodified rock strata slant steadily up to a summit ridge and break away abruptly on the other side. The long western slopes are carpeted in a random patchwork of pine, aspen, fir, juniper, sage, and grasses.

You won't find any resorts or lodges in the Warners. You can take one-day outings into the high country from Alturas, but if you want to remain in the mountains, you must camp out. Packers operate from Alturas.

The only paved road across the Warners is the Cedar Pass route, which descends into Surprise Valley, a ranching area. If you take this road to Cedarville (on State 299), you can return to U.S. 395 through Fandango Pass on a maintained gravel road. Cedarville's most historic building is the Bonner Trading Post, a log cabin built in 1865 as a trading post for early immigrants and settlers. At the valley's northern tip is Fort Bidwell, an army outpost from 1866 to 1892 and school for Paiute Indians from 1892 to 1930.

The highest part of the Warner Mountains is preserved as a 70,000-acre wilderness where no motor vehicles are permitted and the only signs of civilization are grazing sheep and cattle. Traversing the wilderness is the 24-mile Summit Trail, hugging the top of the range with views of Mount Shasta and Lassen Peak to the west and, to the east, Nevada in the distance and Surprise Valley 4,000 feet below. The trail skirts the three highest peaks—Squaw, Warner, and Eagle. All are climbable.

It takes 2 or 3 days to hike the entire trail; side trails lead to secondary roadheads that can shorten your trip. Side trails also lead to some fine trout fishing, especially in Pine, Mill, and East creeks and South Emerson Lake. Blue Lake (actually in Lassen County) is reached more easily on the road that goes from Likely toward Jess Valley, one of the prettiest spots you'll encounter.

From the south the Summit Trail starts at the Patterson ranger station, 42 miles by car from Alturas; it ends at Pepperdines Camp, 20 miles east of Alturas.

Nature's wonders

In California's far north you can discover some of nature's finest handiwork. Awe-inspiring Shasta's icy slopes still tempt the intrepid climber. Mount Lassen's snow-capped peak looms over a valley of bubbling sulphur pools, vestiges of volcanic activity of the not-too-distant past. Craters, chimneys, and cones of Lava Beds National Monument in the state's northeastern corner were the scene of California's only major Indian war. Not far away is the resting place for waterfowl traveling the Pacific Flyway.

It's a land of contrasts. You can climb the cluster of domes and spires that make up Castle Crags; hike down to Burney Falls, a scenic waterfall (familiar to many because it adorned a beer can); or take a lantern and clamber through Subway Cave, a lava formation set incongruously adjacent to Hat Creek just north of Lassen Volcanic National Park.

Mighty Mount Shasta

Lore and legend surround majestic Mount Shasta. This immense mountain, rising to 14,161 feet, dominates the landscape for more than 100 miles. Volcanic in origin, it is composed of two cones: Shasta itself, and Shastina, a small cone that rises from the western flank. Five glaciers mantle the eastern and northeastern flanks above the 10,000-foot level.

Mount Shasta City, on the west side of Strawberry Valley and right at the base of the mountain, was settled in the 1850s. When the Shasta route of the Southern Pacific Railroad reached the settlement in 1886, a townsite was laid out along the railroad. In 1924 the town took the name of the mountain that towers above it. Mount Shasta is considered sacred by many people; over a dozen sects flourish in the tiny town.

Perpetual glaciers, white water in deep canyons, jewel-like lakes, dense forests and open valleys, and wildflowers in spring call climbers to the mountain. Even though the angle of climb is rarely greater than 35 degrees, the ascent is taxing.

August is considered the best month to climb. Snow and ice are minimal then and weather conditions most stable. Special Forest Service brochures show recommended routes of ascent. Climbers are asked to check in and out at Mount Shasta City Police Department. Hiking equipment can be rented, and maps are available.

Lassen Volcanic National Park

Until May 30, 1914, Lassen's claim to fame was as a landmark for pioneer Peter Lassen, who guided emigrant parties over the mountains and into the Sacramento Valley. Then began the year-long eruptions of smoke, stones, steam, gases, and ashes that culminated in the spectacular events of May 19, 1915. On that day a red-glowing column of lava rose in the crater and spilled over the sides, melting the snow on the mountain's northeast flank and sending 20-ton boulders and devastating floods of warm mud 18 miles down into the valleys of Lost and Hat creeks.

Three days later, Lassen literally blew its top. A column of vapor and ashes rose 30,000 feet into the sky. A terrific blast of steam and hot gases ripped out the side of the mountain and rushed northeast, killing all vegetation in its path for miles. As far away as Reno, streets were buried under several inches of ash. Declining eruptions continued into 1917. On a visit to Lassen today, you will see striking examples of past volcanic activity, as well as evidence of present action.

One of the West's least discovered national parks, Lassen today has a sense of solitude and space. Over 150 miles of trails connect a rare combination of natural phenomena: glacial lakes, permanent snowpacks, boiling fumaroles, crashing waterfalls, and lush meadows.

Though much of the Lassen country is accessible only by trail, no point in the park's 163 square miles is more than a day's hike from the road. Permits are required to get into Lassen's back country. A brochure available at the park entrance shows the self-guiding nature trails and key points of interest.

Lassen Peak road, linked at both ends to State 89, traverses the western part of the park between West Sulphur Creek and Manzanita Lake. It crosses a shoulder of the volcano at 8,512 feet. Winding around three sides of Lassen Peak, the road affords stunning views of the volcano, examples of its destructive action, and vistas of woods and meadows, streams and lakes. After the first snowstorm, the road is closed until late spring, except for the section leading to the park ski area.

A good trail takes you to the top of Lassen Peak. The hike is not difficult; it takes about 2 hours to climb from the highway—an ascent of 2,000 feet. From the highest point you will see not only the clear-cut evidences of the 1914–17 activity but also the distant Sierra Nevada in the vicinity of Tahoe, the Coast Range ascending northward to the Trinity Alps, and the icy cone of Mount Shasta.

Sulphur Works Thermal Area, near the park's south boundary, is the most accessible of the hydrothermal regions. North of here you pass Broke-off Mountain, Mount Diller, Mount Connard, and Pilot Pinnacle—peripheral remnants of the much higher Mount Tehama, a huge strato-volcano that collapsed perhaps 10,000 to 11,000 years ago.

Well-marked interpretive trails wind among the park's hissing steam vents and bubbling mudpots. A steaming stream borders the road's edge.

Biggest and showiest of the thermal areas is Bumpass Hell. You'll first notice a vague smell of sulphur as you descend into a natural bowl eaten out of a hard lava rock by hot acids. The barren landscape includes violently roaring hot springs, boiling muddy pools, crystallized "solfataras," gurgling mud volcanoes, "morning glory" pools, deep turquoise waters over layers of fool's gold, and a mineralized "River Styx."

The eastern side of Lassen, from the town of Chester on State 36, is served by two main roads. On one road you drive 16 miles to Drakesbad, an old but comfortable summer spa. At Drakesbad is a 2-mile sign-guided trail around Boiling Springs Lake.

A second road from Chester leads to Juniper and Horseshoe Lakes. Horseshoe makes a good base camp for hikes to Snag and Jakey lakes.

Accommodations in the area include guest ranches, small lodges, and campgrounds. Drakesbad Guest Ranch, at the southern end of the park, accommodates over 50 in the main building and surrounding cabins. Guided saddle and pack trips can be arranged.

The facilities and campground at Manzanita Lake, in the northwest section of the park, have been re-opened after a 5-year closure, and there are a few small to medium-size campgrounds in or near the park. You'll find four campgrounds (Summit Lakes, Sulphur Works, Lost Creek, and Crags) located along the Lassen park road. Other campgrounds are at Warner Valley and Juniper and Butte Lakes.

For more lodging and camping information, write to the Superintendent, Lassen Volcanic National Park, Mineral, CA 96063.

Lassen in winter becomes a snow-covered, uncrowded, 106,000-acre playground. Winter activities are focused at the southwest park entrance (the main road through the park is closed). Entering the park at 6,700 feet, you'll find quiet, forested land where you can ski downhill or cross country, or take a ranger-led snowshoe walk. Ski tows and touring centers are open Wednesday through Sunday. Food, ski rentals, and lessons are offered. Overnight lodging is available at Mineral, Chester, and Mill Creek. For more detailed winter recreation information write to the national park headquarters in Mineral.

California's lonely corner

Centuries ago, flaming volcanoes in northeastern California spread rivers of liquid rock over the land below. Upon cooling, they formed one of California's most fascinating landscapes. It's a terrain made rugged by yawning chasms, cinder cones, and craters scattered

*HISSING HOT SULPHUR SPRINGS,
gurgling pools, and boiling mud
volcanoes envelop visitors (below) to
Bumpass Hell in Lassen Volcanic
National Park.*

*MIGHTY MOUNT SHASTA'S
snow-covered slopes provide awesome
backdrop to simple country church in
McCloud (right). Visible for miles,
Shasta (14,131 feet) attracts intrepid
climbers to its icy peaks.*

*RIDERS REST while horses
graze at Patterson Lake
(right) in South Warner
Wildlife Area. Camping is
the only way to explore this
lonely northeastern
California corner.*

over the surface. The official name is Lava Beds National Monument.

Adjoining the monument on the north are Tule Lake and Lower Klamath national wildlife refuges. At these havens for millions of migratory birds, some 200 species have been sighted during flight season.

Lava Beds National Monument is an area of volcanic caves and plains in northeastern California. "Nobody will ever want these rocks. Give me a home here," declared Modoc Indian Chief Captain Jack. Not so: the area received monument status in 1872.

Just off State 139, almost to the Oregon border, these 72 square miles contain 1,500-year-old lava flows, high cinder buttes, pictographs and petroglyphs, and what may be the world's most outstanding exhibit of lava tubes. Lanterns are provided for self-guided explorations. The largest concentration of caverns is along Cave Loop Road near the monument's headquarters.

If you park off the road and search with binoculars, you may see some California bighorn sheep in a large enclosure along Gillem's Bluff. In the southern section of the park is a campground near monument headquarters. Look for other lodging, food, and gasoline in nearby Tulelake.

Tule Lake and Lower Klamath wildlife refuges, north of Lava Beds, make the Klamath Basin in northern California a "stop off" for the largest concentration of waterfowl on the North American continent.

Lodging is available at Tulelake, Newell, and Dorris; a private campground and trailer parks are nearby. Get maps and regulations at the Tule Lake National Wildlife Refuge headquarters at the north end of the refuge.

Two great state parks

Castle Crags and Burney Falls are two gems that shouldn't be missed. Camp settings are particularly attractive.

Castle Crags State Park, a 3,447-acre reserve straddling Interstate 5 and the Sacramento River, rises in a cluster of gray-white granite domes and spires from an evergreen forest 48 miles north of Redding.

Long, warm summers and easy access make this park a popular place to camp or picnic from about the first of April to the end of October. Most popular activities are swimming and fishing in the river, hiking in the park or into the backcountry, and climbing in the Crags.

Though no hookups are provided, many campsites are large enough to accommodate trailers. Rest rooms, hot showers, and baths are nearby.

Burney Falls, one of the most beautiful natural phenomena in California, is the chief attraction in the McArthur Memorial Park, near the intersection of State 299 and 89. Burney Creek, welling up out of a subterranean source, divides into two fairly equal flows of water and goes streaming over a 129-foot cliff into an emerald pool. On sunlit mornings a little rainbow accompanies the mist blowing down the canyon.

The 565-acre park (open the year around) includes nearly 2 miles of frontage along Burney Creek, together with a bit of shoreline on Lake Britton, a 9-mile-long, manmade lake popular with swimmers, fishers, boaters, and water-skiers. Scattered throughout the forest are campsites (no trailer hookups); a grocery store and snack bar open from mid-April to mid-October.

BIGFOOT—MAN OR MYTH?

Leaving all the rest of California's scenic splendors behind, many people head for vacations spots among the relatively unspoiled wooded areas along the Trinity and Klamath river valleys near the state's northern border. Here, civilization encroaches slowly; much of the land is protected as a national forest and as a mecca for fishing, hunting, camping, or just getting away from it all. Yet there is one disconcerting, mysterious note in this idyllic scene—the occasional unexplainable footprints of Bigfoot.

Reported sightings of Bigfoot—supposedly a creature 7 to 14 feet high and weighing from 300 to 800 pounds—have spanned a century. The creature is said to be totally covered with hair except for his face, palms, and soles. Facial features are said to be more humanoid than those of apes or gorillas, with flat nose and broad nostrils, short

ears, and dark, leathery skin. Photographs show that Bigfoot walks upright with an erect stance and a stride ranging from 4 to 10 feet long.

Nevertheless, the giant footprints are the most tangible evidence of this "monster" (perhaps a relative of the Abominable Snowman of the Himalayas). You can buy footprint castings in Willow Creek and Weaverville and on the Hoopa Valley Indian Reservation.

Over Labor Day, Willow Creek, gateway to Bigfoot country, has an annual festival—Bigfoot Daze—during which spectators are invited to compare their foot sizes with those of Bigfoot. Happy Camp and Weaverville also host Bigfoot celebrations on that weekend. Skeptics and believers are about evenly divided as to the creature's actual existence, but at least it's cause for a celebration.

HISTORIC SAMPLER

Turn back the clock in the north country by sampling remnants of yester-year. A drive through now-quiet villages still shows evidence of the raucous 19th century when gold fever reigned. Visit the home of California's only president; photograph the roofless, grass-filled buildings of the one-time "Queen City" of the northern mines; tour a temple of Chinese worship; or wander around some of the gingerbread houses of early pioneers.

The Ide Adobe

Along the west bank of the Sacramento River, near Red Bluff, stands the William B. Ide Adobe State Historic Monument, a travelers' oasis. Picnic on verdant grounds overlooking the river, have a refreshing drink of cool water, or just stretch your legs by wandering through the shady 4-acre park, a landmark to the short-lived Bear Flag Party and California's president. The adobe ranch house is now a museum; a restored carriage house, smokehouse, and corral suggest ranch life in the 1850s. The park is open daily from 8 A.M. to 5 P.M.; admission is free. From Interstate Highway 5, take State Highway 36 through Red Bluff; turn right at Adobe Road. Mooring facilities for boaters are near the old ferry site.

Red Bluff Victorians

Of a later vintage are the grand Victorian homes of Red Bluff. The Kelly-Griggs House Museum (311 Washington Street) is a classic. Nearly 100 years old, it's open to the public Thursday through Sunday from 2 to 5 P.M. At the museum you can buy a Victorian "windshield tour" of central Red Bluff, including the cottage of Mrs. John Brown, widow of the celebrated abolitionist of Harper's Ferry.

Gold Country

Northern California's gold rush was never as well chronicled as mining in the Sierra Nevada. Yet many millions in gold were extracted by miners who thronged north in the 1850s. The La Grange Mine, started in 1851, was for years the largest operating hydraulic mine in the world. Two sample drives plunge you into Gold Country; one follows State Highway 299 within an hour's drive west of Redding; the other meanders through scenic Scott Valley at the foot of the Marble and Trinity mountains.

The Trinity Trail. Shasta, 6 miles west of Redding, is a mere ghost of its former lusty self. Today, shells and façades of "the longest row of brick buildings in California" speak for its prosperous past. Visit the Shasta County Courthouse (now a museum) to learn about Shasta's rise and fall.

Two tiny towns to poke around in are French Gulch and Lewiston. Both have historic hotels, picturesque churches, and one-room school-houses. Signs direct you to State 299 turnoffs.

Weaverville seems enchanted with its past. A hundred years have brought little change in its frontier-Victorian aspect except for the honey locusts grown tall shading the trim lawns, flowers, and picket fences. At the J. J. "Jake" Jackson Memorial Museum, open daily from May through November, you'll learn Trinity history amid nostalgic surroundings. Next door, across a pleasant park furnished with mining equipment, is the exotic Joss House, evoking memories of the important role of Chinese gold miners in California's history. Now it's a state historic park; rangers conduct guided temple tours daily.

Into Scott Valley. From Weaverville, State Highway 3 roams along the edge of Trinity Lake, through the mountains, and into peaceful Scott Valley. At Trinity Center the Scott Museum (open most of the year) gives you an idea of how it was to live during the days of the gold boom.

At the southern edge of agricultural Scott Valley, Callahan was a trading center for miners and ranchers. No traffic crowds the block-long main street. Several century-old buildings line the boardwalks. Plan to spend some time if you enter the Callahan Emporium, "Biggest Little Store in the World." Some of its wide variety of merchandise has been there for years.

Etna appears to be almost a metropolis if you see it after you visit Callahan. You'll enjoy many fine old buildings. A museum is usually open summer afternoons.

Fort Jones, up the road, was the site of an army outpost on the old stage road. You'll find an exceptionally fine Indian museum. Up the McAdam Creek Road are the remains of a couple of bullet-riddled cabins of Deadwood, where Lotta Crabtree danced and Joaquin Miller cooked.

Other towns offering turn-of-the-century nostalgia are Susanville and Alturas, now boasting museums filled with gold rush memorabilia. In the Yreka town courthouse, you'll find a fine display of nugget and placer gold.

The flat Central Valley provides strong contrast to its surroundings—the Sierra Nevada Mountains on the east, the Coast Range on the west. To the south rise the Tehachapis, and to the north the foothills of the southern Cascades and the northern Coast Range meet.

The Central Valley extends 465 miles from north to south and is 30 to 60 miles wide. The big valley actually includes two valleys—the Sacramento, through which the Sacramento River flows, and the San Joaquin, named for the river that runs part way through it.

Once called the Badlands, the Central Valley was changed by irrigation into the most fertile farm land in the world. Orchards, vineyards, and such staple crops as onions, sweet potatoes, and grain are the area's economic base. These lands are grazing grounds for dairy cattle and livestock. Two inland ports—at Sacramento and Stockton—provide the landlocked valley access to the sea.

Interstate Highway 5, on the valley's western side, is fast becoming the most traveled route between Southern and Northern California. A swift but lonely, monotonous road, it bypasses the towns that grew up along State Highway 99, which runs right through the valley. Feeder roads connect the two highways along their routes, leading through small agricultural communities.

Though the San Joaquin Valley extends south below Bakersfield, the section identified with Northern California ends at Fresno. For a description of the southern part of the valley, see the *Sunset* book *Travel Guide to Southern California.*

The Delta—a vast inland sea—offers miles of good boating and fishing. It's the Central Valley's greatest recreational asset.

The Sacramento valley – from gold to grain

The Sacramento Valley grew up during the Gold Rush days when river steamers and sailing schooners on the Sacramento and Feather rivers connected such communities as Marysville and Red Bluff to Sacramento. After gold panned out, agriculture developed. Grain ranches were built close to the Sacramento River, and grain soon became the valley's chief product

These large grain fields were later subdivided. Smaller, irrigated ranches became orchards, citrus groves, vineyards; alfalfa, vegetables, and some newcomers—cotton, rice, and sugar beets—were also planted. These crops remain the heart of the valley's agriculture.

The city of Sacramento, once a lusty boom town with its roots deep in the Gold Rush, soon emerged as an agricultural center and merchandising outlet for the rich valley. Some of its past still peeks out amidst the tremendous growth of its present.

SACRAMENTO'S GOLDEN-DOMED CAPITOL, completed in 1874, is outstanding landmark in downtown area.

Flatlands sprawl nearly 500 miles through the Sacramento and San Joaquin valleys; together they form the great Central Valley. Irrigation changed these once-barren "badlands" into acres of fruit orchards, golden grain fields, and rich pasturelands, turning the big valley into the nation's richest farming area. At the confluence of the Sacramento and American rivers lies Sacramento, the state capital. Here you'll find a modern metropolis studded with remnants of its rich gold rush past. And on the nearby Delta, an intricate network of lazy waterways, you'll discover exceptional fishing, water-skiing, and boating.

The Central Valley

California's capital city

Most of the major routes through central California pass through or around Sacramento, the state capital. To the east, Interstate Highway 80 and U.S. Highway 50 lead into the Sierra, to Lake Tahoe, and on to Nevada. For southern travel, State 99 and Interstate 5 are the main arteries. To the north, these highways, uniting at Red Bluff, lead into the northern mountains. The main route to the San Francisco Bay area is Interstate 80.

At the confluence of the American and Sacramento rivers, the city (whose summer temperatures soar into the 90s) offers skin diving, water-skiing, swimming, and all types of boating. You'll find public boat launches at Miller Park, Discovery Park, and Elkhorn Bridge, 10 miles north. For specific visitor information, write to the Sacramento Convention and Visitors Bureau, 1100 14th Street, Sacramento, CA 95814, or stop by the Morse Building in Old Sacramento State Historic Park.

The domed capitol building (9th Street between L and N streets), surrounded by its groomed park, has an impressive approach—across the Sacramento River on ornate Tower Bridge and east up well-landscaped Capitol Mall. Though the main building was closed in 1976 for restoration and renovation, the rest of the building, including the newer East Wing annex, is open to tours and is well worth a visit. The main building, to be completed in 1981 after a multimillion dollar facelift, will be restored to its original 1874 grace and beauty.

Public tours (weekdays at 10:30 A.M. and 1:30 and 2:30 P.M.) start inside the east entrance. A series of 58 exhibits—one for each California county—displays the state's commercial, scenic, and recreational assets. You can also view the Senate and Assembly in action from their chamber quarters. When a measure comes up for a vote, the legislator pushes a button that flashes colors on a board—red for "no," green for "yes."

Capitol Park, an oasis on hot valley days, has 40 acres of more than 40,000 trees, shrubs, and plants. You'll see plants and trees from all over the world, including a collection of trees brought from Civil War battlefields. Among 2,200 plantings, more than 800 varieties of camellias bloom; peak season is February and March. The park includes a trout pond, several monuments, and lots of squirrels. At the State Police Office on the ground floor of the capitol, you can pick up a booklet suggesting three walking tours.

Sutter's Fort (2701 L Street) is the reconstructed site of the settlement founded by Captain John A. Sutter. Sacramento's story began with the splash of his anchor in the American River in 1839. Sutter had navigated a little fleet up the Sacramento River from San Francisco en route to the land grant he obtained from the Mexican government. On a small knoll not far from the anchorage, he built a fort to protect his 76-square-mile land grant, established an embarcadero, and started farming the area he called New Helvetia. Here in 1844 he entertained the United States exploring party led by John C. Fremont and his guide, Kit Carson. During the Bear Flag Revolt of 1846, General Vallejo was detained here.

The town of Sacramento sprang up around the fort after James Marshall discovered gold at nearby Coloma in 1848. After gold was discovered, Sutter lost his land to newcomers and later went east. Between 1891 and 1893 the state of California restored the fort, following sketches and plans from Sutter's day. Now the fort stands in the center of the city, housing a collection of historical mementos. Exhibits include carpenter, cooper, and blacksmith shops, a prison, and living quarters. Headsets allow visitors to tour at their own speed. The fort is open daily (except holidays) from 10 A.M. to 5 P.M.; admission, including headsets, is nominal.

The State Library (open Monday through Friday from 8 A.M. to 5 P.M.), housed in a handsome granite building adjoining the capitol, is worth a visit, especially for history buffs. The general reading room, adorned with a Maynard Dixon mural depicting California's growth, maintains an excellent file of present and past California newspapers.

The California State Archives (1020 O Street) also displays historic California documents and exhibits, including California's original constitutions of 1849 and 1879. Open Monday through Friday from 7:45 A.M. to 5 P.M., the archives are closed on major holidays.

The Governor's Mansion (16th and H streets) stands empty today. Built in 1877, it was acquired by the state in 1903 for Governor George Pardee. Home to 13 governors, the 15-room Victorian-Gothic structure, now a state historic landmark, is open for public tours daily from 10 A.M. to 5 P.M. (except Thanksgiving, Christmas, and New Year's Day). There's a slight admission charge for adults.

The State Indian Museum adjacent to Sutter's Fort, interprets the Indian way of life in California through the use of frequently changing exhibits ranging from archeology to mythology. The museum houses a variety of Native American artifacts, including a fine basket collection. Hours are the same as for Sutter's Fort. Admission is free.

The E. B. Crocker Art Gallery (216 O Street), a stately Victorian mansion built by Judge Crocker in 1873 for his private art collection, is the oldest art museum in the West. The building's elegant interior—sweeping staircases, parquetry floors, repoussé ceilings, and grand ballroom—makes a perfect setting for the collection of paintings, drawings, decorative arts, and sculpture. Of particular interest are the Oriental and contemporary American art collections. A new wing increases exhibition space by nearly half. The gallery is open to the public Tuesday from 2 to 10 P.M. and Wednesday through Sunday from 10 A.M. to 5 P.M.

The Chinese Cultural Center (between 4th and 5th and I and J streets) features buildings of Oriental design, a mall with a Chinese garden, residences, stores, offices, and restaurants—a developing Chinatown set around the Confucius Temple at 4th and I streets.

The Sacramento Community/Convention Center (between J and L and 13th and 14th streets) frames the east end of the K-Street Mall. The handsome center consists of three main facilities: an exhibit building, an activity building, and the center theater—now the new stage for the performing arts. Located within walking distance from the capitol and capitol park, the center is also near Memorial Auditorium, scene of sporting events and concerts.

For just 10 cents, you can ride the K-Street tram 14 blocks along the K-Street Mall from the center to Old Sacramento and a rendezvous with the 19th century.

Old Sacramento historic area

Old Sacramento (on the eastern bank of the Sacramento River between Capitol Mall and I Street, west of Interstate 5) is now a national historic landmark. Restored brick and frame buildings, gas lamps, plank sidewalks, and turn-of-the-century museums take you back to Sacramento's golden age between the 1850s and 1870s. Happily, Old Sacramento is not a fossil, but a living, self-sustaining district with unusual restaurants, "watering holes," gift stores, antique shops, and business offices that mirror the city of a century and a quarter ago.

The re-creation began in the late 1960s when Old Sacramento, then a scar of deterioration and neglect, received a makeover from concerned and imaginative individuals. Now, nearly completed, the area boasts over 100 restored and renovated buildings, 41 of which are original structures.

Begin your tour at the John F. Morse Building on 2nd and K streets. Originally built in 1865 for Dr. Morse, Sacramento's first physician and editor of the *Sacramento Union*, it now houses the Old Sacramento Visitor Center. Here you can pick up an illustrated guide to the 28-acre area, with information on shops, restaurants, events, and historic landmarks.

B. F. Hastings Building (2nd and J streets), completed in 1852, is the site of the first western terminus of the Pony Express and the first Sacramento office of Wells Fargo. The California Supreme Court convened here from 1855 to 1869. Inside you'll find museums commemorating these famous tenants as well as an early telegraph display. The museum is open daily from 10 A.M. to 5 P.M.; admission is free.

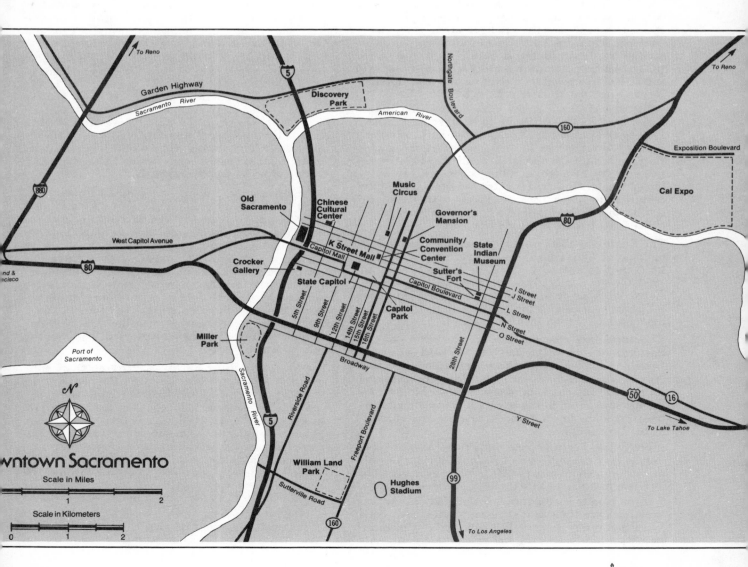

Across the street is the handsome statue of horse and rider memorializing the Pony Express, whose intrepid men rushed mail over 2,000 miles in just 10 days. Begun in 1860, the system lasted only 18 months, until the first telegraph message was received in 1861.

Old Sacramento Schoolhouse (Front and L Streets) evokes the atmosphere found in schools of the 1800s, with antiques and reproductions of the period. Bells call special classes to order between 9:30 A.M. and 4:30 P.M. Monday through Saturday, noon to 4:30 P.M. on Sunday; visitors are welcome.

Big Four Building, originally located in the path of Interstate 5, is now at I Street between Front and 2nd streets. One-time headquarters for the Central Pacific Railroad, the building now stands in tribute to the railroad's "big four"—Stanford, Huntington, Hopkins, and Crocker.

The California State Railroad Museum (Front Street between I and J streets) authentically re-creates an 1876 Central Pacific passenger station. Inside, train whistles blast, bells clang, dogs bark, and conductors yell "all aboard!" All these sounds serve as background for your recorded tour through the museum. You pick up a tour "wand" (actually a radio receiver) as you enter the depot. It explains the various exhibits and describes early railroad days. Rolling stock displays include three 1870 locomotives, two 19th century passenger coaches, and a 1908 Northwestern Pacific engine. The museum is open every day from 10 A.M. to 5 P.M.

The second phase of the railroad museum is the Building of Railroad History, to be completed in late 1980 by the California Department of Parks and Recreation. Covering over 100,000 square feet, this three-story, multimillion dollar facility will offer 40 interpretive exhibits, 21 pieces of rolling stock, and two wide-screen theaters that will backtrack visitors to the 19th century railroad era. Located adjacent to the passenger station, the museum will be a must for all train buffs, and a shiny tribute to the old iron horse.

The Eagle Theatre (Front and J streets) was the first building in California to be constructed as a theater. Its doors first opened in 1849. Destroyed by flood in 1850, the wood and canvas structure has now been restored. Weekend evenings you can enjoy live plays and rollicking musicals of the Gold Rush era. Tours are conducted daily from 10 A.M. to 4 P.M.

Dixieland jazz resounds through the streets of Old Sacramento each Memorial Day weekend when the Dixieland Jubilee begins. Sacramento's jubilee is rated tops by Dixieland buffs for its musical excellence and its growing international scope. In the past, over 75 groups have joined in the celebration, including bands from England, Japan, Canada, and Scotland, as well as the United States.

Festivities begin at noon on Friday and continue around the clock until early Monday afternoon. Crowds are not a problem since jazz rings out in as many as 25 different locations at once throughout Old Sacramento.

If you plan to go, buy tickets before May 15. Accommodations are tight so it's a good idea to make hotel and motel reservations well in advance. For more information on the festival and accommodations, write to the Sacramento Convention and Visitors Bureau, 1100 14th Street, Sacramento, CA 95814.

Family fun

With a variety of outdoor activities to choose from, family outings are popular. Biking, hiking, boating, and picnicking are all within minutes from downtown Sacramento.

William Land Park on Freeport Boulevard (State Highway 160 and Sutterville Road) in the southern part of the city is so vast it seldom seems crowded. It has pools, gardens, a 9-hole golf course, ball diamonds, picnic grounds, and a grove of Japanese flowering cherry trees among its 236 landscaped acres. Children's favorites include the large zoo, with fine reptile and feline collections, Fairytale Town (with child-size reproductions of fairy tale themes), kiddie rides in the amusement area, and pony rides nearby.

Gibson Ranch County Park, just north of Sacramento, is a child's delight. Youngsters can see domestic animals, peacocks, and pheasants or watch milking demonstrations. An 8-acre lake stocked with fish (children under 16 need no fishing license) makes a natural habitat for ducks, mudhens, geese, and muskrats.

One of the ranch buildings houses a historical museum displaying western objects. You can watch horses being shod in a blacksmith shop. Stables rent horses and ponies, offer hayrides, and provide riding lessons. On the 245 acres, you'll find many hiking trails and picnic spots. To reach the park, follow Watt Avenue north to Elverta Road. Turn left onto Elverta and follow this road to the entrance. Gibson Ranch is open daily from 7 A.M. to dusk. There's no admission charge for your children to meet the animals.

The Sacramento Science Center and Junior Museum (3615 Auburn Boulevard at Watt Avenue), now in its new facility in northern Sacramento, contains many interesting displays of California natural history and has an excellent collection of live animals native to the area. Children will especially enjoy the weekend and holiday program, "Playtime with the Animals," when critters can be taken from their cages to be petted and touched. They'll also find it hard to resist the unusual library that lends not books but animals. For a slight admission fee, you can visit the center Monday through Saturday from 9:30 A.M. to 5 P.M., Sunday from noon to 5.

The American River Parkway, an irregular, 23-mile-long strip of green, stretches along the banks of the American River from Nimbus Dam to the stream's junction with the Sacramento River. Along the parkway are several county parks: C. M. Goethe County Park offers hiking and riding trails; Discovery Park, at the confluence of the rivers, provides boat launching facilities; and Ancil Hoffman County Park has an 18-hole golf course. Picnicking sites are plentiful. Fishing the American River yields catches of shad, steelhead, or salmon. Group float trips are popular with kayakers and rafters.

Winding its way along the river bank is the American River Bicycle Trail, which eventually will run the en-

"IT'S GOLD!" James Marshall exclaims to a pleased Captain Sutter in Gold Discovery Room, one of 38 exhibits at Sacramento's Sutter's Fort.

tire 30-plus miles from Discovery Park to Folsom Lake. For now, more than 20 paved miles are open, with picnic tables, restrooms, and other facilities along the way.

Nuts are the theme for two family fun destinations. At the California Almond Growers Exchange (18th and C streets), you can tour and taste in the world's largest almond "factory," open weekdays from 8 A.M. to 5:30 P.M., Saturday from 10 to 4. Plant tours start at 10 A.M., 1 and 2 P.M., weekdays only. Admission is free.

Thirty miles west of Sacramento is the Nut Tree, a restaurant *cum* amusement park, complete with train and airport—a popular fly-in destination for pilots. It all started with a single black walnut tree planted in 1860 to shade passers-by on the Emigrant Trail.

Folsom is fun. Shops on gas-lighted Sutter Street intrigue visitors. The structures are a mixture of old and new, set in western surroundings. Tourists flock to the Flea Fair in April and Peddler's Fair in October. In addition, famous Folsom Prison has a craft shop you may visit. Free area tourist guides are available in the old Southern Pacific Depot. Folsom is 15 miles northeast of Sacramento, off U.S. 50.

North of Sacramento

The major highways running north of Sacramento are Interstate 5 and State 99. Both leave from Sacramento, with Interstate 5 taking a more westerly course. In Red Bluff the highways converge, and Interstate 5 continues into Oregon. The Sacramento River runs between the two highways; the Feather parallels State 99.

The quiet towns and countryside along the banks of the Sacramento River seem to have changed little since the early 1900s. To discover the surrounding area, you'll have to stray slightly from Interstate 5.

Spring is a good time to drive State Highway 45—a two-lane, lightly traveled back road that follows the Sacramento's meanderings. Then the tall cottonwoods along the river have leafed out, fruit orchards are in bloom, crops have been planted, and summer's heat hasn't yet descended on the valley.

To reach State 45 if you're coming from San Francisco on Interstate 80, turn north at Davis on State Highway 113 and drive 22 miles to Knight's Landing. From Sacramento, take Interstate 5 to Woodland (home of some turn-of-the-century architectural gems) and then head north on State 113.

In Knight's Landing—a small river community somewhat reminiscent of towns along Mark Twain's Mississippi—turn left on Fourth Street, a narrow levee road running along the south bank of the river. Fourth Street soon joins State 45, which angles northwest across open farmland. Notice the rice "checks"—flooded areas of land surrounded by low levees.

Past Sycamore, turn east on State Highway 20, across a narrow swing bridge, to visit Meridian. Poke around the quiet, shaded streets. Near the river there's a small grocery store with ancient floors that creak, a lazy paddle fan above the door, and a selection of ice cream bars for a hot day. After you cross back over the river, Colusa is 5 miles north. State 45 continues as far as Hamilton City (between Chico and Orland). The only cable ferry left on the Sacramento River operates at Princeton, north of Colusa on State 45.

Colusa National Wildlife Refuge, 3 miles southwest of Colusa on State 20, is one of four Sacramento Valley refuges providing a winter home for millions of migratory wildfowl. You can pick up guide-yourself tour booklets at refuge headquarters. The area is open from dawn to dusk.

Gray Lodge Wildlife Area, just west of Gridley and 65 miles north of Sacramento near State 99, is one of the best places to watch the massive late autumn and winter migrations of ducks and geese from the Yukon, Saskatchewan, and British Columbia breeding grounds. Aquatic plants and cereal crops are grown on the 6,800-acre state reserve to entice wildfowl away from feasting in surrounding private fields. One portion of the reserve is a wildlife sanctuary; on a larger section, hunting is permitted during the season. You must obtain a pass before driving through on hunting days.

More than 200 species of birds frequent the reserve. The wildlife area is open daily during daylight hours. At the area headquarters is a small museum with bird specimens.

Up the Sacramento River

Upstream from Sacramento as far as Colusa, the Sacramento is a river of commerce, though the commercial traffic it bears today (mostly tugs and oil barges) is insignificant compared to that of the past. Remnants of yesteryear are visible along the river: occasionally you'll see half-rotting wharves through the cottonwoods and willows that mark the sites of forgotten towns. The tall piers where steamers tied up have been replaced by long floats for pleasure boating and fishing.

Swimming and water-skiing are possible anywhere along the Sacramento—the farther you are from Shasta Dam, the warmer the water. Colusa is a popular water-skiing center, with public floats and a jumping ramp.

The Colusa-Sacramento River State Recreation Area, a delightful, 67-acre oasis on the west shore, has a launching ramp, picnic sites, sandy beach, and unimproved campsites. In summer, a 140-foot floating dock makes boat tie-up easy.

Most of the towns and fishing resorts along the river have launching facilities for trailered boats. Motorless boats are suitable only for downstream trips. Rowing or paddling against the strong current is always difficult—at some points, impossible. Below Colusa, tie up where barges won't swing close to shore and strike your boat or bounce it around in their wakes.

Fishing for salmon begins in June. The fall run, perhaps the most important, starts in late September and overlaps the steelhead migration that comes in October and November. Though most fishing is done from boats in the main current, bank fishing is perfectly practical.

Woodson Bridge State Recreation Area, bisected by the Sacramento River, is just 3 miles west of State 99 at Vina or 6 miles east of Interstate 5 at Corning. The park is an almost unspoiled example of riverbottom lands. Part of it is covered with oaks; a flood plain section is densely wooded with willows, cottonwoods, and sycamores. In the park you can swim, boat, hike, and camp. Fishing is excellent. Adjoining Tehama

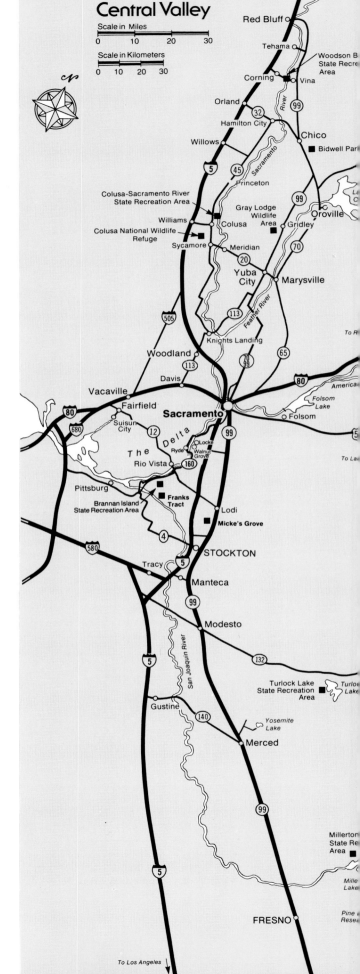

County Park has a small picnic area, playground, and concessions.

In Chico, you'll find the most impressive and unexpected park in the whole valley. The green excitement starts downtown with the campus of the California State University at Chico and the grounds of the colonial mansion of town founder John Bidwell. Then Bidwell Park winds up Chico Creek, 10 miles into the foothills. Swimming, golf, and picnicking are popular.

The delightful Delta

One of the most startling experiences for new visitors in the Delta region is to look across an island field of softly swaying grain and see the profile of a freighter moving silently along the levee top. Yet this is one of the Delta's most characteristic sights. Here, too, pleasure craft throw sudsy wakes across narrow sloughs and find hidden anchorages under bowing trees, where shipboard anglers throw out lines to hook lurking fish.

What is the Delta? The Sacramento-San Joaquin Delta is an irregularly bounded area of almost 740,000 acres that extends from Sacramento south a little beyond Tracy and from Pittsburg east to Stockton. About 50,000 of its acres are water, strung out in more than 700 miles of meandering channels bearing such astonishing names as Hog, Little Potato, Lost Whiskey, Little Conception, and Lookout Slough.

Once a great inland everglade densely forested with stands of valley oak and bull pine, the area was devoured by the furnaces of old river boats. Denuded expanses of mud that remained were later transformed into levee-rimmed islands (many still called tracts) that produced fortunes in asparagus and fruits for Delta farmers.

The first "resorts" in this area were farmhouses that just happened to have a boat or two for rent. After reports of excellent fishing began to spread, small, makeshift fishing camps sprang up along levee roads. Recreational fishing and boating became big business, and resort marinas replaced small fishing camps.

As you drive between Sacramento and Manteca on State 99, you're never more than 10 or 15 miles east of the Delta region, but you hardly know it's there. Until now, major highways have circumvented it entirely; however, Interstate 5 now crosses the heart of the Delta.

If you take the John A. Nejedly Bridge across the San Joaquin River to the scenic Delta Highway (State 160), you travel 45 miles along the meandering Sacramento River, skirting levees, drawbridges, and tiny Delta towns. It's a more scenic route to Sacramento from the Bay Area.

Cruise the Delta's rivers in anything from a simple fishing skiff to a deluxe houseboat. You don't have to be a boat owner to enjoy cruising on the Delta—more than a hundred marinas, resorts, harbors, and fishing camps rent boats. You'll find the rivers' waters also offer fine swimming, water-skiing, and fishing.

"Floating motels" range from small, nonpowered barges ($10 to $12 a day) to luxurious, well-appointed floating homes (with electricity, running water, complete kitchens, and, in some cases, bathrooms) that sleep six or more people. Rental for one of these large, better-appointed houseboats runs about $50 to $75 a day or $300 to $600 a week. Rates vary according to the number of persons aboard and the season.

The remainder of the Delta rental fleet is an assortment of cruisers, ski boats, sailboats, and miscellaneous small craft.

There's not much chance of getting seriously lost in the Delta, but it is easy to become temporarily confused. A good map, marine chart, or guide book is essential for the newcomer. The basic guide to navigation in the Delta region is Chart 5527SC (San Joaquin River). For the chart, write to the Distribution Division (C44), National Ocean Survey, Riverdale, MD 20840. Chart 5528SC is a navigation guide to the Sacramento River from Andrus Island to Sacramento, including the northern reaches of the Delta. These charts indicate channel depths, bridge and overhead cable clearances, channel markers, and various hazards to navigation.

Though commercial traffic is found throughout the Delta, there are only two main deep-water channels. Pleasure craft are required to yield right of way to ships navigating these confined channels. For free pamphlets on California boating regulations and water safety, write to Commanding Officer (B), 12th Coast Guard District Office, 630 Sansome Street, San Francisco, CA 94126.

Swimming and water-skiing along the Delta's waterways are popular, despite the rather sluggish nature of the water. Considerate water-skiers avoid quiet anchorages where people are fishing.

Fishing is an all-year activity in the Delta, but spring is a peak season for one of the Delta's most sought-after game fish—the striped bass. Salmon and steelhead pass through the Delta on their fall migration up the Sacramento River, but the Delta itself seldom presents the ideal water conditions for trout fishing.

Most of the resort operators in the Delta have been there a long time and can guide you to the best fishing holes.

Sightseeing along the Delta can reap rewards. You can buy fresh produce at the roadside stands and pack a picnic to Brannan Island State Recreation Area (5 miles north of the Nejedly Bridge). Poke around small riverfront communities like Walnut Grove, Freeport, Locke, and Ryde. Here discover small cafés, asleep during the week, but roaring on a Saturday night.

Locke, a ramshackle Chinese community that may someday become a historic park (the state is making a study), is worth a visit. It's on River Road just north of Walnut Grove on the east side of the river. Its quaint two-story buildings rise only one story above the levee.

South of Walnut Grove, the small town of Ryde (population 60, elevation 1), is one of the few Delta towns offering overnight accommodations. Once a notorious hotel and speakeasy during Prohibition, the town's only hotel now re-creates the 1920s atmosphere while offering food, accommodations, and entertainment.

Accommodations in the Delta are not plentiful, but you'll find modern motels lying along the edge of the

OPULENT RIVER MANSION (above) in fertile Central Valley is surrounded by pear orchards. German banker Louis Meyers built 58-room architectural extravaganza in 1917.

SLEEK SPEEDBOAT ZIPS symmetrical slalomers (right) around Delta waterway. Central Valley's popular aquatic arena is favorite spot for houseboating, water-skiing, fishing, swimming.

Delta, and some hotels in the towns along the Sacramento River. A few of the resort marinas offer housekeeping cabins or small campgrounds. Brannan Island State Recreation Area (the only developed public campground in the Delta) has a 100-unit campground with room for trailers. Franks Tract Recreation Area, reached only by boat, is mostly underwater. There is a boat-in campground, but walk-around facilities are limited to a small dock, two picnic tables, and toilets.

Most of the larger resorts operate snack bars, and you'll find a few isolated cafés. The seasoned Delta sailor, though, brings provisions because stores are far apart and difficult to find.

The San Joaquin Valley

South of Sacramento the Central Valley follows the course of the San Joaquin River, which flows northward to meet the Sacramento. Agricultural development came later in this part of the valley. State 99 and Interstate 5 are the main routes south of Sacramento; Stockton and Fresno are among the largest valley cities.

The Lodi and Fresno areas are famed for their sweet appetizer and dessert wines. Long, warm summers give grapes their maximum sugar content. About a half-dozen wineries and tasting rooms are open to visitors in the Lodi area, home of the table wine pressed from the Tokay grape. Fresno, hub of the other wine district, also has wineries welcoming visitors. For a listing of wineries open for touring, write the Wine Institute, 165 Post Street, San Francisco, CA 94108, or consult the *Sunset* book *Guide to California's Wine Country.*

Stockton: A port city

Stockton was a booming mining town in the 1850s; today, it's an important port city delivering agricultural and manufactured goods to the San Francisco Bay Area by way of a 76-mile channel. Docks on the west edge of downtown Stockton serve around 700 cargo vessels a year. The campus of the University of the Pacific, at Pacific Avenue and Stadium Drive, has ivy-covered Gothic buildings surrounded by expansive lawns and tall shade trees.

Victory Park, at North Pershing Avenue and Acacia Street, offers picnic tables under lofty trees, as well as playground equipment, a duck pond, open spaces, and a museum. In the Pioneer Museum and Haggin Galleries, you'll find an art collection strong in 19th century French and American paintings and usually a traveling or local art show. Several rooms depict Indian and pioneer life in the valley. Admission is free; hours are 1:30 to 5 P.M. Tuesday through Sunday.

Pixie Woods, in Louis Park 2 miles west of Stockton, is a children's fantasyland playground with dragons to climb on and a giraffe to slide down. Hours from mid-June to mid-September are 11 A.M. to 6 P.M. Wednesday through Friday, noon to 7 P.M. Saturday and Sunday; closed Monday and Tuesday. The park closes earlier the rest of the year.

Fresno's fresh face

Downtown Fresno radiates a parklike atmosphere. In the central business district—Fulton Street from Inyo to Tuolumne streets—you can stroll through a mall embellished with trees, flowers, fountains, and sculpture.

A pioneer nurseryman planted verdant Roeding Park with hundreds of trees, including lots of bark-shedding eucalyptus. A 157-acre oasis, it's great for a picnic; children can enjoy a zoo, amusement area, and boat rides.

Seven miles west of Fresno, at 7160 West Eucalyptus Avenue, is the Edwardian mansion and estate of wealthy land developer M. Theo Kearney; it's open to afternoon tours Thursday through Sunday.

Stops along the way

Often it's much easier, especially with children, to pack a picnic lunch on a long, hot trip. Even a stop to stretch your legs will be more pleasant if you know where to go. Here is a list of parks or stops to enrich your trip:

Lodi Lake, once a swamp overflow from the Mokelumne River, is now a big, tree-lined recreation spot offering boating, swimming, and picnicking on the north side of Lodi.

Micke's Grove, 5 miles south of Lodi and a mile west of State 99 by way of Armstrong Road, is now a San Joaquin county park containing one of the few remaining large stands of native valley oaks. It has a small garden zoo where flowers separate animals' cages.

Caswell Memorial State Park, 16 miles south of Stockton and about 5 miles west of State 99, provides a cool place to picnic in a 258-acre park, 90 acres of which remain a primitive area.

Miller Ranch has an impressive collection of antique vehicles (farm machinery, horse-drawn vehicles, bicycles, tractors, and automobiles). The privately owned ranch, 10 miles east of Modesto at 9425 Yosemite Boulevard, also has antique household items, a general store, blacksmith shop, and old-time barbershop.

Turlock Lake State Recreation Area campsites are along the Tuolumne River; picnicking is on the lake. River fishing is good; you can also swim there during low-water season. On the lake side are swimming beaches, a water-ski beach, a boat harbor, and launching ramps. The park is 23 miles east of Modesto on State Highway 132.

Three state parks around Merced offer picnicking, swimming, and fishing alongside rivers. The first two have campsites: McConnel Park (a few miles east of State 99 on the south shore of the Merced River); George J. Hatfield Park (5 miles east of Newman on the San Joaquin River); and Fremont Ford Park (between Merced and Gustine on State Highway 140).

Seven miles northeast of Merced, just up into the hills, 400-acre Yosemite Lake is popular for boating, swimming, and shoreline picnicking

Millerton Lake, 22 miles north of Fresno, has campgrounds at the north shore (7 miles north of Friant) and boat and motor rentals on the south bay.

Index

Alcatraz, 20, 23
Alexander Valley, 85
Allied Arts Guild, 44
Almanor, Lake, 111
American River Parkway, 122
Ames Research Center, 44
Angel Island, 37
Angels Camp, 9, 95
Año Nuevo, 9, 48
Apple Hill, 101
Arcata, 72, 74
Asilomar State Beach, 54
Auburn, 97
Audubon Canyon Ranch, 64
Audubon Wildlife Sanctuary, 36
Austin Creek State Recreation Area, 85
Avenue of the Giants, 62, 72

BART, 15, 38
Bay Area, 34–49
Bay Meadows Race Track, 44
Bear Valley, 65, 93, 96
Berkeley, 40, 43
Berryessa, Lake, 81
Big Basin Redwoods State Park, 46
Big Sur, 50, 51, 57, 59
Bodega Bay, 66
Bolinas, 64
Boonville, 9, 69, 71
Bothe-Napa Valley State Park, 80
Bucks Lake, 101
Burbank Memorial Gardens, 84
Burney Falls, 116
Burns, Julia Pfeiffer, State Park, 59

Calaveras Big Trees, 96
California Historical Society, 32
California State Railroad Museum, 122
Calistoga, 80
Candlestick Park, 44
Cannery, The, 23
Cannery Row, 52, 55
Capitola, 49
Caribou Peak Wilderness, 113
Carmel, 9, 54, 57, 58
Carmel Valley, 57
Carquinez Straits, 43
Cascade Range, 113
Castle Crags State Park, 116
Castle Rock State Park, 46
Caswell Memorial State Park, 127
Chico, 125
Clear Lake, 81
Cloverdale, 69, 71
Coe, Henry W., State Park, 61
Coloma, 97
Colusa, 124
    State Recreation Area, 124
    Wildlife Refuge, 124
Cowell, Henry, Redwoods State Park, 46
Cow Palace, 44
Crescent City, 74, 77

Del Norte Coast Redwoods State Park, 76
Delta, 125–127
Desolation Wilderness, 105
Dillon Beach, 65
Donner Lake, 105
Doran Beach County Park, 66
Drakes Bay, 65
Drytown, 9, 94, 96, 97
Duncan's Landing, 66
Duxbury Reef, 64

Eagle Lake, 111
East Bay Regional Parks, 43
Emerald Bay, 103
Emigrant Wilderness, 92
Empire Mine State Historic Park, 97
Eureka, 73–75

Feather Falls, 101
Feather River, 98, 101
Ferndale, 74
Festivals, 9

Filoli Estate, 46
Fisherman's Wharf, 21, 22
Folsom, 123
Fort Bragg, 72
Fort Humboldt State Historic Park, 73
Fort Ross, 66–68
49-Mile Drive, 12, 16
Fresno, 127

Geysers, 80
Ghirardelli Square, 23, 27
Gilroy, 61
Goat Rock Beach, 66
Gold Country, 93–102, 117
Golden Gate Bridge, 3, 10, 11, 13
Golden Gate National Recreation Area, 3, 20, 24, 26, 38
Golden Gate Park, 25–26, 28–29
Golfing, Monterey Peninsula, 53
Gray Lodge Wildlife Area, 124
Grizzly Creek Redwoods State Park, 73
Gualala, 68
Guerneville, 85

Healdsburg, 82, 85
Hearst Castle, 59
Hollister, 60
Howarth Memorial Park, 84
Humboldt Bay, 74
Humboldt Redwoods State Park, 73

Ide, William B., Adobe, 117
Incline Village, 104
Indian Grinding Rock State Historic Park, 96
Inns
    Gold Country, 100
    North Coast, 77
Inverness, 65

Jack's Peak Regional Park, 52–53
Jenner, 66, 68

Kezar Stadium, 26
Klamath, 76
Klamath River, 111
Knight's Landing, 123
Knowland Park, 40
Kruse Rhododendron State Reserve, 69

Lassen Volcanic National Park, 5, 106, 107, 114, 115
Lava Beds National Monument, 116
Lawrence Hall of Science, 41
Lewiston Reservoir, 110
Lick Observatory, 45
Lighthouses
    Point Arena, 71
    Point Bonita, 37
    Point Piños, 53
    Point Sur, 59
Limantour Beach, 65
Little River, 77
Locke, 125
Lodi Lake, 127
London, Jack, 40
    Square, 40
    State Historic Park, 82
Los Gatos, 46
Lower Klamath Wildlife Refuge, 116

McCloud, 110–111, 115
McClures Beach, 65
MacKerricher State Park, 71
Malakoff Diggins, 97, 99
Manchester State Beach, 71
Marble Mountain Wilderness, 112
Marin County
    beaches, 62, 64
    Civic Center, 36
    parks, 36
Marin Headlands, 37, 39
Marine World/Africa USA, 49
Marriott's Great America, 47, 49
Medicine Lake, 111
Melodrama, Gold Country, 9, 94
Mendocino, 5, 9, 71–72
Merced, 88, 127
Micke's Grove, 127
Miller Ranch, 127
Millerton Lake, 127
Mill Valley, 36

Minarets Wilderness, 92
Missions
    Carmel, 54, 57, 58
    Dolores, 31
    San Antonio de Padua, 60
    San Francisco Solano, 81, 83
    San Juan Bautista, 61
    San Raphael Archangel, 36
    Santa Clara de Asis, 45
    Soledad, 60
Modesto, 127
Molera, Andrew, State Park, 59
Monterey, 51–53
    Peninsula, 5, 50–61
    State Historic Park, 56
Mount Diablo, 43
Mount Shasta, 5, 113–114, 115
Mount Tamalpais, 37
Muir, John, State Historic Site, 43
Muir Trail, 90, 92
Muir Woods, 38
Murphys, 95–96

Napa Valley, 5, 78, 81
North Coast, 62–77

Oakland, 38, 40
Oroville, 98
Oroville, Lake, 98, 101

Pacific Grove, 53–54
Pebble Beach, 55
Petaluma, 84
Pfeiffer-Big Sur State Park, 59
Pinnacles National Monument, 5, 59
Pixie Woods, 127
Placerville, 97
Plumas-Eureka State Park, 101, 103
Point Lobos State Reserve, 57
Point Reyes National Seashore, 5, 64–65
Port Costa, 43
Prairie Creek Redwoods State Park, 76
Pulgas Water Temple, 46

Quincy, 101

Red Bluff, 111, 117
Redding, 106
Redwood Highway, 72–73
Redwood National Park, 5, 72, 74, 76–77
Renaissance Pleasure Faire, 36, 39
Richardson Grove State Park, 73, 75
Roaring Camp and Big Trees Railroad, 46
Russian Gulch State Park, 71
Russian Hill, 29
Russian River, 84–85
Ryde, 125

Sacramento, 5, 118–122
Sacramento River, 112, 124
St. Helena, 80
Salinas, 60–61
Salmon River, 112
Salt Point State Park, 68
San Andreas, 96
San Francisco, 5, 9, 10–33
    Aquatic Park, 20, 23
    bridges, 10, 13
    Broadway, 21
    cable car, 14, 15
    Cannery, 23
    Chinatown, 18, 21, 22
    Civic Center, 16
    Cliff House, 20
    Coit Tower, 19, 28–29
    dining, 33
    Embarcadero Center, 17–18
    financial district, 17
    Fisherman's Wharf, 21–23, 27
    49-Mile Drive, 12, 16
    Ghirardelli Square, 23, 27
    Golden Gate Park, 25–26
    hills, 28, 29, 31
    Jackson Square, 18
    Japanese Tea Garden, 26, 30
    Japantown, 24–25
    Marina, 16, 24
    museums, 25–26, 32–33
    North Beach, 21
    performing arts, 32

San Francisco (cont'd.)
    Pier 39, 24
    public transportation, 15
    sightseeing tours, 15, 23
    streets, 14, 31–32
    Union Square, 16, 17
    waterfront, 21–24
    zoo, 28
San Francisco Bay National Wildlife Refuge, 43
San Francisco International Airport, 44
San Joaquin Valley, 127
San Jose, 44–45
San Mateo Coast State Beaches, 46–48
San Rafael, 36
San Simeon, 5, 59
Santa Cruz, 48–49
Santa Cruz Mountains, 46
Santa Rosa, 82, 84
Saratoga, 46
Sausalito, 34, 35–36
Scott Valley, 117
Sea Ranch, 68
17-Mile Drive, 54, 55
Shasta
    Caverns, 109
    Lake, 108–109
Silverado Museum, 80
Siskiyou, Lake, 110
Skunk Train, 72
Smith, Jedediah, Redwoods State Park, 77
Smithe Redwoods State Reserve, 73
Sonoma, 81–82
    Coast, 66–68
Sonora, 95
Squaw Valley, 105
Standish-Hickey State Recreation Area, 73
Stanford University, 9, 44, 47
Steinbeck, John, 60
Stevenson, Robert Louis, State Park, 81
Stewart's Point, 68
Stillwater Cove County Park, 68
Stinson Beach, 64
Stockton, 127
Sugarloaf Ridge State Park, 82
Sugar Pine Point State Park, 103
Sunset, publishing headquarters, 44
Sutter's Fort, 120, 123

Tahoe, Lake, 102, 103–105
Tall Trees Grove, 76
Thousand Lakes Wilderness, 113
Tiburon, 35, 36
Tomales Bay State Park, 65
Trinidad, 74, 75
Trinity
    Alps, 112
    Lake, 110
    National Recreation Area, 110
    River, 112
Tule Lake National Wildlife Refuge, 116
Tuolumne Meadows, 90, 91
Turlock Lake State Recreation Area, 127

Ukiah, 85
University of California
    Berkeley, 40–41, 42
    Santa Cruz, 48

Valley of the Moon, 81–82
Van Damme State Park, 71
Victory Park, 127
Vikingsholm, 103

Warner Mountains, 113
Weaverville, 110
Westside County Park, 66
Whiskeytown Lake, 108
Winchester Mystery House, 45
Wineries, 61, 78–85
Woodson Bridge State Recreation Area, 124
Wrights Beach, 66

Yosemite National Park, 5, 6, 86–92
Yountville, 80

Zephyr Cove, 104